Advance Praise

Using the Dholera 'Smart City' as a microcosm, Rakib Akhtar's superb book provides an up-close look at the confluence of neoliberalism and Hindu nationalism in contemporary India. This book is a must-read for students of politics and development in India, and all those interested in the political economy of ethnonationalist regimes.

Michael Levein, Johns Hopkins University

Rooted in Dholera this book sharply brings out the intimate self-sustaining relationship between Hindutva and neoliberalism. By showing us how the 'actually existing state' functions, we come to understand afresh, as an interlocutor from Dholera notes, the illusory power of development. An important new addition to the literature on the state and urbanisation in India.

Nayanika Mathur, University of Oxford

India is a key reference point for scholars seeking to understand the frictions and contrasts between Global North and Global South state, industry and civil society practices. Akhtar's book represents a major contribution, identifying contradictions in the enactment of smart city policy as a key manifestation of Hindu nationalist neoliberal development strategies in India.

Nicholas Phelps, The University of Melbourne

Smart city projects present alluring images of technological futures that overcome the resource limitations of our current ways of living. This book focuses on this form of development as it has played out in India, taking a pragmatic view on both promise and the politics of smart cities. The research and analysis show how contemporary capitalism and religious nationalism have been drawn together to create unique forms of urban promise: a record of a historic moment and a compelling analysis of how infrastructure can be used to shape the realm of the political.

Edward Simpson, Lancaster University

Neoliberalism and Hindutva in the Making of an Indian Smart City

This book studies the intersection of neoliberalism and right-wing Hindu nationalism through smart city projects which are often advertised as solutions for sustainable development. Globally, the rise of right-wing nationalism has progressively shaped urbanization projects, also furthering political agendas. The book demonstrates how state institutions both are influenced by and contribute to the intricate linkages between these two ideologies at various levels of government. It shows how neoliberalism and Hindutva support each other, strengthening both ideologies within the state and society.

The book highlights the disagreements between the ideologies' foundational principles and their practical applications, showcasing the strategic manoeuvres that help these ideologies gain traction within political and governmental institutions. By investigating these dynamics, the book offers understandings into the intricacies of modern governance shaped by neoliberalism and nationalism.

Rakib Akhtar is Lecturer in Urban Planning at the University of Birmingham.

Neoliberalism and Hindutva in the Making of an Indian Smart City

Rakib Akhtar

CAMBRIDGE
UNIVERSITY PRESS

Shaftesbury Road, Cambridge CB2 8EA, United Kingdom

One Liberty Plaza, 20th Floor, New York, NY 10006, USA

477 Williamstown Road, Port Melbourne, VIC 3207, Australia

314–321, 3rd Floor, Plot 3, Splendor Forum, Jasola District Centre, New Delhi – 110025, India

103 Penang Road, #05–06/07, Visioncrest Commercial, Singapore 238467

Cambridge University Press is part of Cambridge University Press & Assessment, a department of the University of Cambridge.

We share the University's mission to contribute to society through the pursuit of education, learning and research at the highest international levels of excellence.

www.cambridge.org
Information on this title: www.cambridge.org/9781009605496

First published 2025

Printed in India by Avantika Printers Pvt. Ltd.

Cover image: A billboard announcing the arrival of a new era of smart cities through Dholera by author.

A catalogue record for this publication is available from the British Library

ISBN 978-1-009-60549-6 Hardback
ISBN 978-1-009-60546-5 Paperback

For EU product safety concerns, contact us at Calle de José Abascal, 56, 1°, 28003 Madrid, Spain, or email eugpsr@cambridge.org.

Contents

Tables and Figures

Tables

Figures

Acknowledgements

This book is part of my PhD project that I completed at the University of Oxford. Hence, there are many persons and institutions to thank, many more than I could list here. The financial and institutional support came from the Oxford Department of International Development. Somerville College's grants were of immense help. If there is one person who made this research possible, it must be Prof. Nikita Sud. From the day I wrote to her with a research proposal for a possible PhD, she stood behind me at every stage. She had the patience to read every word of my drafts and provide feedback in a manner equally insightful and inspiring. Her support and constructive criticism pushed me to think beyond the obvious with the 'so what' question lurking in the background, creating the foundation of the research. For someone with a disadvantaged background such as mine, it would not have been possible without her. The research gave me a great friend in Sudheesh who had the patience to bear me in the same house, read my drafts and provide considered and thoughtful feedback while giving me a clear map on how to improve those.

From the fieldwork in Gujarat, there is a never-ending list of people without whose help the project would be unthinkable. Sagar Rabari, the farmer leader with his endless energy to work for a better society, opened the field to me. In Dholera, the learned Pradyumansinh, a man of great wisdom, helped through long interviews along with access to every document regarding the project. In Ahmedabad, Prof. Navdeep Mathur was always there for support, taking me out for lunch despite his busy schedule. Leader of Opposition Paresh Dhanani, Jignesh Mevani and Lalji Desai all spent time helping with my research along with the assurance of my safety. I am forced to hide a number of names to ensure anonymity due to the sensitive nature of the research who helped me gain access to politicians, high-level bureaucrats or private consultants.

My dear parents (Maa and Abba), despite their financial constraints, never stopped dreaming of the best education for their two sons. Maa's hardship to raise us took an emotional as well as physical toll on her. Abba's 'never back down' approach when it came to education despite earning a paltry sum as a laboratory technician went a long way for me to undertake a DPhil, the result of which is the book. However, I believe they too would have stopped dreaming if there was no state-subsidised/free higher education. I will always support free education (and a socialist state too) for the opportunities that can change the lives of the underprivileged while giving equal chances to everyone. Both my parents wanted their children to become 'doctors'. I ended up in an engineering college to study architecture whereas the elder son went on to study mathematics and computing. Getting a DPhil was the only way I could be a 'doctor'—even if I could not prescribe medicines, the way they would have liked! My elder brother happens to be my closest friend who supported my emotional and financial misadventures without ever raising a question. Knowing that he was always behind me, I continued with those misadventures. My sister-in-law is more like a sister, always supporting the family and me. The two kids, Saaim and Myna, completed the family.

Another way I have tried addressing my failure to become a doctor was by convincing Dr Samira (who can prescribe medicines) to become part of the family. She has been a constant support and source of motivation, exemplary in her great level of patience since I met her in the first year of the PhD. Her actions are impossible to reciprocate. Pradyumansinh, one of my main interviewees during fieldwork, would often make fun of me, pointing out three events which seemed near impossible: (*a*) construction of the Dholera smart city, (*b*) completion of my DPhil, and (*c*) my marriage. Whereas I still never want (*a*) to be realised unless it helps local farmers, I tied the latter two together, and Samira agreed to go off to a wedding venue the moment I completed the project!

Abbreviations

AES	actually existing state
ABVP	Akhil Bharatiya Vidhyarthi Parishad
BBS	Bhal Bachao Samiti
BJP	Bharatiya Janata Party
BJS	Bharatiya Jana Sangh
CEO	Chief Executive Officer
DDIS	Dholera Developers and Investors Summit
DICDL	Dholera Industrial City Development Limited
DMIC	Delhi Mumbai Industrial Corridor
DP—TPS	Development Plan—Town Planning Schemes
DSIRDA	Dholera Special Investment Region Development Authority
DSP	Deputy Superintendent of Police
EIA	Environmental Impact Assessment
GDIPL	Greater Dholera Infracon Private Limited
GDP	gross domestic product
GIDB	Gujarat Infrastructure Development Board
GIDC	Gujarat Industrial Development Corporation
GIFT	Gujarat International Finance Tec-City
GTPUDA	Gujarat Town Planning and Urban Development Act
HVM	Hotel Vision Modi
IAS	Indian Administrative Service
ICT	information and communications technology
IMF	International Monetary Fund
INC	Indian National Congress Party
INR	Indian Rupee
KHAM	Kshatriya–Harijan–Adivasi–Muslim
L&T	Larsen & Toubro
MNC	multinational corporation

MoU	memorandum of understanding
OBC	Other Backward Classes
PPP	public–private partnership
RSS	Rashtriya Swayamsevak Sangh
SC	Scheduled Castes
SP	Superintendent of Police
ST	Scheduled Tribes
SEZ	special economic zone
SIR	Special Investment Region
SPV	special purpose vehicle
USE	Universal Success Enterprise
VGGS	Vibrant Gujarat Global Summit
VHP	Vishwa Hindu Parishad

1

Smart Cities
The Urban Panacea

As developing countries continued to witness urbanisation at a rate never seen before in the history of humankind, the year 2008 delivered a key moment, when the global population in urban areas surpassed that of their rural counterparts for the first time in human history. Such a scale of urbanisation resulting in intensive use of resources is often linked with environmental challenges including climate change that can make human life unsustainable on planet Earth. This has put the need for long-term sustainable development at the heart of any such urbanisation. The case is acutely severe in the Global South as countries such as India, China and Nigeria will be responsible for 35 per cent of the increase in urban population worldwide from 2018 to 2050 (UNPD, 2018). Thus, with such a large majority of the population living in the cities, it is crucial to solve the contradictions of developing these areas in a sustainable manner. This has resulted in a range of initiatives and scholarly discussions around technology's possible role in resolving climate change and sustainability issues.

Proponents argue that urbanisation should be seen less as a challenge and more as an opportunity to deliver economic growth and infrastructural upgrades while also addressing associated environmental concerns. Here, technology, and more specifically information and communications technology (ICT), is often proffered as a panacea to deliver sustainable urban development, addressing the challenges while maximising the opportunities. When ICT is applied at the scale of cities and towns, what we have are smart cities:[1] 'places where information technology is combined with infrastructure, architecture, everyday objects and our own bodies to address social, economic and environmental problems' (Townsend, 2013: 15). ICT's growing dominance is evident in the global smart city industry's valuation at USD 549.1 billion in 2023, a total that is expected to reach more than a trillion dollars by 2028 (Statista, 2024).

India, the most populated country as of 2024, has arguably been the epicentre of such rapid urbanisation and infrastructural transformations, including smart cities. In 2015, for example, the prime minister of India, Narendra Modi, launched the National Smart Cities Mission,[2] a multibillion-dollar project to upgrade 100 existing Indian cities to smart cities. To explore the intersection of urbanisation and technology, this book studies one such project called Dholera Smart City, a project that is also the microcosm of India's urbanisation and development journey. It is situated in the western Indian province of Gujarat (Figure 1.1) and is supposed to include 920 square kilometres, twice the size of present-day Mumbai (Sampat, 2016). Launched and continuously promoted by Modi since his days as Gujarat's chief minister for more than a decade (2001–2014), Dholera has been a platform to reimagine the state and ideas of development. The project has witnessed protests by local farmers who stand to lose their farmlands to it. This book provides a detailed picture of how smart cities of the future are likely to be planned, delivered or governed against the backdrop of the socio-environmental collapse that has become a real threat to the entire planet.

Importantly, countries adopting such a model of economic growth have often chosen to practice liberal economic policies, referred to as neoliberalism,[3] the set of laissez-faire socio-economic policies practised since the 1980s across the globe (Harvey, 1989). Here, the market is projected as crucial to the management and delivery of such urban transformations to deliver growth with a limited role for the state to play (Brenner et al., 2002). Cities are to act as growth engines of the economy by incentivising investment by private sectors in the urban sphere. On the other hand, as technology is proffered as the solution to economic growth and environmental concerns, many political leaders with authoritarian and/or populist tendencies have used such policies of urbanisation and infrastructure building through 'seductive language and technologically utopian imaginings of the future' (Bunnell, 2015: 1). In the process, these leaders often combine liberal economic policies with illiberal political and cultural or religious agendas. Over the last few decades, countries as diverse as the United States of America, India, Brazil, the Philippines and Turkey, along with parts of Europe, have witnessed this coming together of neoliberalism and right-wing nationalism (Bello, 2019).

Essentially, these projects have become vehicles for the leaders to reimagine the concept of state and delivery of development. As the book will show, state and development become key platforms for the propagation of the two ideologies of neoliberalism and right-wing cultural or religious nationalism.

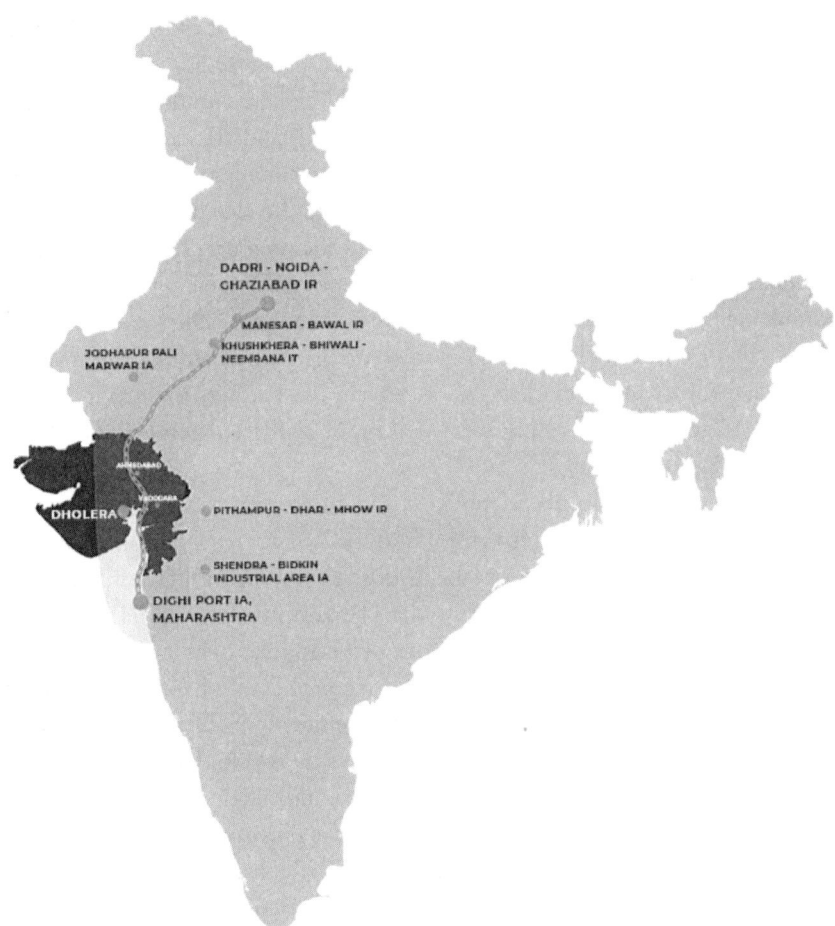

Figure 1.1 Map of India with the location of Dholera and the Delhi–Mumbai Industrial Corridor (DMIC)

Source: DIPP (2018).

Note: The corridor connecting Delhi to Mumbai is marked light grey. Gujarat is highlighted in dark grey within which Dholera is located. Other important nodes along the corridor are shown. IR stands for Industrial Region and IA for Industrial Area.

Thus, this book lies at the intersection of themes concerning development, neoliberalism, smart urbanism and right-wing nationalism, and is of topical significance to a host of countries across the globe. At a critical juncture when neoliberalism and right-wing nationalism are becoming further entrenched, this book demonstrates the intricate connections between these two ideologies, showing how they mutate and adapt in particular geographies.

India embraced market-oriented neoliberal policies in the early 1990s, a departure from the erstwhile state-led planning and development models towards a new private and market-oriented development (Jenkins, 1999). Gujarat has been amongst the leading provinces in the race to implement such policies.[4] Within such neoliberal endeavours of the province, Modi as the chief minister played a critical role through his unapologetic backing of a series of economically liberal policies. In that context, Modi saw Dholera smart city to be built in the hinterlands as the vehicle to 'use urbanisation as a business model' actively creating markets while turning its back to the challenges of existing Indian cities struggling with pollution, traffic congestion and slums (Datta, 2015: 9).

As India adopted neoliberal policies, the country also witnessed the rise of right-wing Hindu nationalism or Hindutva[5] in the everyday lives of the state and citizens, especially since the 1990s. Here too, Modi's tenure as the chief minister of Gujarat and now as the prime minister of India is crucial, as they are marked by the continued rise of Hindutva. Scholars have rightly argued that his liberal economic policies have gone hand in hand with political illiberalism (Sud, 2012). As the book will document, in Dholera smart city, a quintessentially neoliberal project, Hindutva networks have taken newer forms to drive forward its exclusionary cultural and religious ideologies while accruing material benefits from the project. In the process, what is witnessed is a coming together of actors and practices of neoliberalism and Hindutva. The book tells the story of how Indian urban development policies have become ideological, technocratic and avowedly Hindu nationalist in their scope under the Modi administration.

Most importantly, the book will illustrate how both neoliberalism and Hindutva exhibit a number of contradictory traits between their ideologies and their practices. This theorisation of contradictory traits, what is termed as 'disjuncture', is a key contribution of the book. While neoliberalism is taken to imply an ideological emphasis on market ethics, competition and commodification, the practices in Dholera manifest the lack of competition or an ideal type of neoliberalism as it mutates depending on the context. Thus, the book challenges the textbook understanding of neoliberal development by demonstrating how the state and its actors with myriad interests work in practice. Similarly, Hindutva in practice in Dholera exhibits a departure from its foundational ideologies to be successful. In all, the target remains the capture of the state and society for both neoliberalism and Hindutva. At the intersection of development, smart urbanism and right-wing nationalism, the book is of topical significance to understand how the very idea of the state is being transformed in Gujarat and India—beyond recognition—with implications that are global.

The book uses the state as an analytical lens to understand micro-practices of development in Dholera. Based on nine months of ethnography observing numerous actors across villages, corporations and the state, the dissertation explores how the everyday state functions in Dholera. The study finds that at various levels of government, the state constitutes and is simultaneously constituted by multiple intricate linkages between the actors and practices of neoliberalism and Hindutva. It shows how these linkages help to promote the cause of both ideologies, further entrenching them into institutions across state and society. In doing so, both neoliberalism and Hindutva use strategies that display disjuncture between their foundational ideologies and practices, which help them further their cause.

Dholera and Development: The Perpetual Association

Development neither reaches us nor leaves us. It's an illusion….

—A Dholera farmer

Within such stories of global change, a small place in the hinterlands, Dholera represents a peculiar history of development. The above quote by a local farmer epitomises the protracted history of development in Dholera. Dholera is one of the twenty-two villages located in a low-lying area off the Gulf of Khambhat (on the Arabian Sea) in Gujarat. These villages are being pooled together to build the first greenfield smart city of India called the Dholera smart city, also referred to as the Dholera Special Investment Region.[6] Although famous for producing the Bhalia wheat,[7] in recent years the provincial government of Gujarat has often termed the quality of land in the Dholera region as saline or infertile.[8] Through such narratives and the siting of an infrastructure project, Dholera's land has been rendered investible by enabling flows of commodities and capital to circulate between sites of investment and (global) markets (Li, 2014). The project has captured global attention due to its sheer size and continued promotion by Prime Minister Modi (Sampat, 2016). The delivery of the project, however, has witnessed the coming together of such market forces along with right-wing nationalist actors in this small place. Analysing Dholera's history, present and future, this book tells the story behind the planning and implementation of the project, demonstrating the hegemonic roles played by the philosophies of Hindutva and neoliberalism.

As the book will elaborate, equally interesting is Dholera's protracted development history which mirrors the journey of development of the Indian state.[9] Since India's independence from the British, this small place called Dholera has been promised a number of major 'development' projects in accordance with, or against, the wishes of its people. They include proposals to build dams, canals, a sea port, an industrial estate, the smart city—as discussed in the following chapters. None of these projects has materialised. James Ferguson (1994) mentions the story of a villager from Lesotho saying: 'It seems that politics nowadays is nicknamed development.' This was due to the failure to deliver development despite multiple projects, while social problems such as inequalities remained. Not very different was the view of the Dholera farmer. Despite newer versions of development, be it state-led or market-led, none of those has ever been implemented. Although Dholera's land continues to lie idle, the visions around it mutate and multiply, becoming bigger, global and smarter.

Dholera is also part of the largest infrastructure project of India to date, the Delhi–Mumbai Industrial Corridor (DMIC) along which industrial areas and investment regions are to be developed as smart cities along with a host of other infrastructure. As discussed earlier, such infrastructure and urbanisation projects have increasingly become key vehicles for economic growth in the last few decades. In addition to the global acceptance of neoliberalism as the main economic ideology that led to the adoption of such policies, a key factor has been the increasing urban population. At the current rate, 68 per cent of the global population will be urbanised by 2050 (UNPD, 2018). The major proportion of this is to come from the developing countries in Asia and Africa. For example, India, China and Nigeria will be responsible for 35 per cent of the increase in urban population worldwide from 2018 to 2050 (UNPD, 2018). This impetus behind urbanisation in the Global South led many proponents to argue that urbanisation should be seen as an opportunity and not as a challenge. Here, urbanisation itself becomes the growth engine of the economy as outlined previously. Hence, the solution is technology-led urbanisation, that is, smart cities to be delivered through neoliberal policies. Dholera is part of these imaginaries that technology can continue to deliver unlimited economic growth while tackling the side effects.

Urbanisation: A Confluence of Neoliberalism and Right-Wing Nationalism

While urbanisation is used as the engine for economic growth in the neoliberal era in distinct ways, its symbolic use is not new. Whereas the British built New Delhi as a symbol of the Raj to mark a break from India's previous rulers (the Mughals), the first prime minister of independent India, Jawaharlal Nehru, often called the architect of modern India through his developmental state model with a socialist ethos, similarly opted to build new planned cities. While laying down the foundations of Chandigarh, India's first planned city in the modern era, Nehru argued: 'Let this be a new town symbolic of the freedom of India, unfettered by the traditions of the past ... an expression of the nation's faith in the future' (Kalia, 2004, 2006). Nehru hired Le Corbusier, the Swiss-French architect while local Indian planners were behind the newly planned city of Gandhinagar, the provincial capital of Gujarat built on a similar ethos (Kalia, 2004). In recent years, governments have hired planners, and consultants seeking to use the 'blank slate' that potential sites such as Dholera provide to make a radical break from previous ideas of the state. As Modi launched the flagship 100 smart cities project, he said (Tolan, 2014):

> Cities in the past were built on riverbanks. They are now built along highways. But in the future, they will be built based on the availability of optical fiber networks and next-generation infrastructure.

Modi's comment that cities in the future will depend on 'next generation infrastructure' is an attempt to mark a departure from the previous ways of city planning where modern technology and market forces are key. Hence, the case of Dholera is significant as Modi continues to champion the project, possibly to mark a break from previous Nehruvian ideas of state socialism and bring in a sense of newness. The idea of delivering development through an infrastructure project such as Dholera comes at the back of significant changes witnessed over the last few decades following the hegemony of market forces. The task of analysing the practices of neoliberalism is significant in the current period. It is doubtful if there is any place in the world that remains untouched by market forces. The question of whether neoliberal policies are good or bad goes unchallenged by political parties from both the right and left. Ultimately, the triumph of the market seems imminent, being at the centre of various processes discussed under the rubric of economic liberalisation, globalisation, development and even democracy.

However, as the market has become the norm, issues of inequality between rich and poor, rural and urban, labour and capital have resulted in myriad reactions across societies. One of the common reactions to this has been the rise of authoritarian populist leaders often in the form of the 'strong man'.[10] Among such leaders, be it Modi, Donald Trump, Recep Tayyip Erdoğan or Rodrigo Duterte, often there is a push to increase natural resource extraction and similarly environmentally destructive practices. These leaders have often moved towards authoritarian tendencies, utilising state powers to increase surplus for a few, while moving away from any idea of welfare for the majority of the citizens (Scoones et al., 2018). We are witness to a distinct moment in history of the rise of right-wing nationalism hand in glove with neoliberal capitalism even if with variations. Of course, the intensity and scale vary across countries or even within a country. However, their global relevance is beyond doubt and that is where the study of Dholera in this book becomes important.

Scholars have elucidated how leaders with similar authoritarian or right-wing nationalist tendencies use seductive language and technologically utopian imaginings of the future (Bunnell, 2015) in these projects that are essentially embedded in neoliberal policies to bring in a semblance of progress even if at the cost of dispossession of large populations. The construction span of these infrastructure projects is usually rather long, during which such leaders may have sold their imageries at various platforms or won many elections using the project's grandeur as a measure of the leader's own success or ability to do something 'big'. Thus, what matters most for Dholera is how it is the biggest or the first smart city or how it is double the size of Delhi or six times the size of Shanghai.[11] Whether its promise has been delivered or not remains less important. At the same time, when such projects have faced protests by farmers, the 'charismatic' leaders have turned to authoritarianism or have gone back to other populist welfare measures to mitigate some of the losses of farmers or protestors, as this book will document. Overall, what we get is a combination of neoliberalism and right-wing nationalism, trends that are widespread across countries in Asia, Europe, North and South America (Scoones et al., 2018).

The extension of neoliberalism and right-wing nationalism to newer geographies across the world has driven countries and societies at an alarming pace towards heightened levels of inequality across income, race or religion. Whereas the confluence of the two ideologies continues to expand across India, Gujarat witnessed it at least a decade earlier, culminating in the rise of Modi. With respect to India, there have been theoretical (Chacko, 2018a, 2018b; Gopalakrishnan, 2006) or macro-level accounts of the commonalities between neoliberalism and right-wing Hindu nationalism by various scholars (Breman, 2020; Corbridge and Harriss, 2000; Desai, 2006; Sud, 2012). Kohli (1990) argued that Hindutva has been used as an electoral strategy by the pro-business elite to connect with the large Hindu majority of the country. Varshney (1999) analysed it through identity politics that helped implement the economic reforms in the 1990s. Corbridge and Harriss (2000) argued it to be the outcome of an 'elite revolt', coming especially from the middle classes and upper castes[12] against an earlier model of state-directed economic development and social justice. While many of these explanations can be witnessed simultaneously in Gujarat, what is usually missing are micro-level studies that can give a richer account of the coming together of these ideologies in a particular place that this book provides.

The combination of economic liberalisation and right-wing nationalism may at first glance appear somewhat unexpected because the former is based on a liberal view of the economy while the latter is based on an illiberal, exclusionary view of state and society. Neoliberalism is a 'free trade faith' being essentially a transnational project reflecting the interests of finance capital (Bourdieu, 1998). On the other hand, Hindutva's foundational ideology vociferously opposes such global integration, instead invoking vague arrangements of economic nationalism. However, in practice, both have seen very little such contradiction as noticed by scholars across the world (Brenner et al., 2002). Despite apparent tension between the two ideologies, the disjuncture[13] between what they profess and what they practice enables the two ideologies to come together and align their interests. This is addressed through an analysis of the empirical observations and related literature in the book, leading to the arguments discussed across the remaining chapters.

Studying the State

Within this framework of neoliberalism and right-wing nationalism, the state remains at the centre of all developmental endeavours. Hence, the book examines these ideologies by using the state as an analytical lens while neoliberalism and Hindutva provide the context. It disentangles how the state has come to be constituted due to profound changes brought about by policies of neoliberalism and an extension of Hindu nationalism into these geographies. State refers to the set of institutions of political and executive control, 'a palpable nexus of practice and institutional structure centred on government' (Abrams, 1988: 58; Harriss-White, 2003: 72; Mitchell, 1998). In other words, the state 'refers to the state apparatus—a set of political, administrative and coercive institutions and organisations, more or less well coordinated by an executive authority: the government' (Mooij, 1996, cited in Sud, 2007: 604). However, studying the everyday functioning of the state at the ground level in Dholera or in Gandhinagar, the book explores other dimensions that complicate such an understanding of the state as a concept. The state in practice here is referred to as the 'actually existing state' (AES), a multi-faceted, internally differentiated, pluralised entity rather than a homogenous one (Sinha, 2011). This proposed concept of the AES is explored further in the next chapters using four proposals. Through this, a more nuanced, situated understanding of how state policies emerge, how they take root in a particular place and their impact on the entity of the state is outlined.

To study the state in such a project, this book follows anthropologists of the state. Scholars have stressed the importance of 'studying the interactions between local functionaries and ordinary people' as the starting point for an ethnography of the state (Gupta and Sharma, 2006: 17). As Gupta and Ferguson (2002: 981) have pointed out regarding such interactions, '... it is here that it becomes possible to speak of states ... as "Imagined"—that is, as constructed entities that are conceptualised and made socially effective through particular imaginative and symbolic devices that require study....' In trying to understand this, the book is interested in the everyday state and society's role in Dholera smart city, the practices and representations of the state, and people's experiences in the dynamics that are the outcomes of the project. How do everyday state practices in a project of urbanisation in a rural area affect state–society relations? What constitutes the AES in Dholera? Studying the everyday state highlights how it is a divergence from the idea that the state is a fixed or coherent unit while guiding us towards its multifacetedness (Gupta and Sharma, 2006: 10). Everyday practices of the state and the resulting representations bare the process, illuminating how the state or the idea of the state is 'created, negotiated, and contested' (Gupta and Sharma, 2006: 10).

But how does one connect a small place such as Dholera with the transformations taking place across the globe? Burawoy (1998, 2000) argued that the local cannot be studied as mere local places but only as places of interconnectedness. In this, the researcher moves 'from specific small observations in their ethnographic field towards outside to wider problems and larger structures within which the subject is contained or constrained in their practices' (Burawoy, 2000: 5; Appadurai, 1997; Gupta and Ferguson, 1997). This also addresses the debate around the generalisability from a single case study. Any ethnographic field (or case[s]) is not simply a site contained within itself but is 'a meeting point' with the wider world (Burawoy, 2000: 5; Appadurai, 1997; Gupta and Ferguson, 1997). Field 'is not just a parochial local place, but a place that has its connected links and networks with the outer world and its interests' (Gupta and Ferguson, 1997: 39).

This book connects the production of Dholera smart city along with the transformations it has brought to the locals in the area to the larger forces that drive ideas of development in a particular place. These forces emerge from the state, neoliberalism or right-wing nationalism. The theoretical underpinnings of the state subsumed the globally and locally prevalent phenomena, neoliberalism and Hindutva, both of which profusely affected the site. Importantly, as the book illustrates, the global (neoliberalism) could be found in the local and the local (Hindutva) could be found on a global scale. The concepts in this research emerged because of continuous exchange between what was observed, inferred in the field and my own implicit and spontaneous reflexivity, along with the analytical engagement with a range of theories. The fieldwork mainly focused on the villages and the cities of Ahmedabad and Gandhinagar involving participant observation and interviews with farmers, activists, villagers, brokers, civil society activists, real estate developers, local politicians, government bureaucrats and private consultants, among others. Government documents and reports, court case details, and similar related documents were obtained via formal as well as informal means and appraised.

The Book

The book uses the state as an analytical lens to understand micro-practices of development in Dholera. Based on nine months of fieldwork observing numerous actors across villages, corporations and the state, the book explores how the everyday state functions in Dholera and finds that at various levels of government, the state constitutes and is simultaneously constituted by multiple intricate linkages between the actors and practices of neoliberalism and Hindutva. It shows how these linkages help to promote the cause of both ideologies, further entrenching them into institutions across state and society. The following chapters take this discussion forward.

Chapter 2 lays out the conceptual framework of the book. Through an analysis of the role of the state at multiple levels in Dholera, the chapter disentangles how the state has come to be constituted due to profound changes brought about by policies of neoliberalism and an extension of Hindu nationalism into the countryside. By using the state as the analytical framework, the chapter puts forth a set of propositions to better understand Dholera. Each following chapter then elaborates on one or more of these propositions through the field data.

Chapter 3 maps the background story of the province, providing an overview of post-independent Gujarat's political economy through four key moments that are crucial to understand Dholera. Focusing on development, the chapter analyses the evolution and outcome of the famed 'Gujarat model of development' that has incorporated both Hindutva and neoliberalism, resulting in unequal development across regions, sectors of the economy and industries, as well as across axes of class, caste and religion. The unequal development that even a small place such as Dholera has witnessed over the years replicates the patterns of the political economy of the province. The chapter argues that unequal development is inherent in both the ideologies of neoliberalism and Hindutva and, hence, they further exacerbate societal inequalities across multiple spheres, let alone address these.

Chapter 4 empirically explores the central themes through a series of early neoliberal projects that arrived in Dholera, showing how Hindutva actors used them to spread in these villages. This provides the context of neoliberalism and Hindutva in the 'development' process in Dholera. It takes these observations forward and links them to the formal and shadow elements of the state, addressing the question of how the coming together of liberal economic policies and illiberal Hindutva is even possible.

Chapter 5 analyses the second proposition concerning the AES, namely, that a number of actors, referred to as middlemen, simultaneously constitute both the shadow and formal elements of the state. Middlemen often use their proximity to the state as well as Hindutva networks to make land deals happen or to corner the benefits provided by investment by private corporations. These practices delineate Hindutva's capture of development and its role in the everyday state and its outcome on citizens' access to the state. Through these practices, Hindutva is strengthened on the ground while the project of neoliberalism takes shape.

Chapter 6 looks at the blurred boundaries of the formal and shadow state, which smoothen business deals at multiple levels of the state by studying the functioning of the special purpose vehicle based in Gandhinagar and examines the impact of blurred boundaries between state and non-state, public and private, or formal and shadow elements at higher echelons of the state. The chapter illustrates that even there, the actors of the AES undertake a host of shadow practices to take forward the project of neoliberalism while also being guided by the ideologies of Hindutva. These shadow practices by formal state actors take place due to the demands on the state to be entrepreneurial, a key facet of neoliberalism.

Chapter 7 explains the contradictory case of how soon-to-be dispossessed farmers continue to vote for the ruling party that causes the dispossession. As actors of AES adopt various strategies that mark a departure from the foundational ideologies of neoliberalism and Hindutva, the chapter gives a vivid picture of how and why the two economic and cultural ideologies come together and help each other to take root in a particular place.

Chapter 8 summarises the findings and the main contributions of the book, commenting on the implications of the findings on understanding the state and its developmental endeavours in India and beyond. It also points out the importance of the empirical study of projects of urbanisation and industrialisation that have adopted newer genealogies, such as smart urbanism, for the development of theory.

Notes

1. The concept of smart cities refers to the simultaneous 'use of information and communication technology (ICT) to stimulate economic development', along with the 'extensive embedding of software enabled technologies into the fabric of cities to augment urban management' (Kitchin, 2015: 131). It emphasises that a smart city can be monitored, managed and regulated in real-time using ICT, infrastructure and ubiquitous computing to increase efficiency, productivity, sustainability (Townsend, 2013). Scholars such as Greenfield (2013), Kitchin (2014, 2015) and Townsend (2013) have covered the debates around the concept.
2. 100 Smart Cities or the National Smart Cities Mission is an urban renewal and retrofitting project launched by Prime Minister Narendra Modi in 2015. This was one of the pledges from his 2014 parliamentary election campaign. The status of the project is debatable. For details, refer to Das (2020) and Praharaj et al. (2018).
3. Neoliberalism, primarily, refers to the laissez-faire economic liberalism practised since the 1980s, which includes policies such as privatisation, free trade agreements between nations, state deregulation, the opening up of financial markets, encouragement of foreign direct investment and reductions in government spending in order to increase the role of the private sector in the economy (Harvey, 1989).

4   A host of provincial institutions targeting privatisation, financialisation, global investment or other liberal policies underline this. Some of those institutions include Gujarat Infrastructure Development Board (GIDB), Vibrant Gujarat Global Summit (VGGS), the provincial Special Economic Zones Act and the SIR Act, which are in addition to existing organisations such as Gujarat Industrial Development Corporation to make the province more efficient and investment friendly.

5. Hindutva is a distinct form of Hindu right-wing nationalism. Pioneered by V. D. Savarkar (1969 [1923]), the concept portrayed Hindus, for the first time, as the original people of India, 'with a distinct territorial, racial, and linguistic identity'. Hindutva translates into *Hinduness*. I expand on the definition in Chapter 2.

6. The current version of the project launched in 2009 as the Dholera Special Investment Region (SIR) to build an industrial city. However, as the proposed city was to 'have smart and sustainable infrastructure spanning transportation, water, power, wastewater, drainage and urban design' (AECOM, 2020), it has frequently been referred to as 'Dholera smart city'. I will refer to the project using both terms interchangeably throughout the book. As of now, within the 920 square kilometres, work has started in what is called the 'Activation Area', a 22.5 square kilometre zone proposed to be developed as an industrial park.

7. Bhalia wheat is cultivated in the 'Bhal' region of Gujarat. Bhal is a region within the province of Gujarat spread over areas within the districts of Ahmedabad, Bhavnagar and Surendranagar. The organic wheat is famous for its high carotene, low water absorption and/or high protein content and commands 40–50 per cent higher prices compared to the standard wheat in Gujarat (PTI, 2011). The wheat is cultivated under conserved moisture that the soil retains from monsoon rain without irrigated water or rain.

8. Bureaucrats and politicians involved in the planning and implementation of the Dholera smart city project often argue that the land in Dholera is saline, infertile or unproductive. Yet while the proximity to the Arabian Sea does render some of the land in the region saline, agriculture has thrived over the years.

9. 'State' here is a concept similar to 'government' referring to institutional aspects, including the bureaucracy, political executive or police machinery (Sud, 2007; Harriss-White, 2003). The 'state' is defined and explored in detail in later sections and in Chapter 2. Indian regions or sub-national units are also called 'states'. However, I prefer to use 'province' throughout the book to avoid confusion.

10. Narendra Modi, during his 2014 election campaign, would frequently boast of having a 56-inch chest to take down the enemies of India. Similar 'strong man' talk has come from the likes of former Brazilian President Jair Bolsonaro,

Turkish President Recep Tayyip Erdoğan, US President Donald Trump and former Philippines President Rodrigo Duterte.

11. Narendra Modi, in one of the 2014 parliamentary election campaign speeches in front of a business group, Indian Merchants' Chamber, claimed that Dholera city will be double in size of Delhi and six times the size of Shanghai. This is, of course, factually wrong (Newsd, 2020).

12. Caste in India refers to the four subdivisions of the traditional Hindu hierarchy: Brahmins (priests), Kshatriyas (warriors), Vaishyas (merchants) and Shudras (labourers). Dalits, treated as the 'untouchable' caste lie outside this hierarchy. While the first three groups are usually referred to as 'upper' or 'forward' castes, the Shudras form the 'middle' castes, or the Other Backward Classes (OBCs) and Dalits are the 'lower'/'backward' castes or the Scheduled Castes (SC). The indigenous tribes, variously referred to as tribal or Adivasis, also remain outside the hierarchy and are called the Scheduled Tribes (ST). However, there is a significant variation across provinces in India. A system of affirmative action, the 'Reservation system' provides representation for some of these historically and currently disadvantaged castes (largely middle and lower castes), especially in education, public employment and positions of political representation. Reservation is primarily given to three groups: SCs, STs and OBCs.

13. 'Disjuncture', the word, for this book, is used to refer to the gap between the ideal worlds and the social reality that are encountered in the process of establishing those, similar to Lewis and Mosse's (2006) use of it. Scholars have suggested that disjuncture might be a strategy rather than a by-product of a process (cited in Rossi, 2004: 559) which also is the case in the book. Although the term can be interpreted in different ways, I use it to refer to 'the fact of disjoining or condition of being disjoined; disjunction; separation' as the *Oxford English Dictionary* defines it. While scholars, including Appadurai (1990), have used the term in similar contexts, it has not been elaborated yet by scholars.

2
The 'Actually Existing State'

The problem with our protest is that we cannot find who to fight against or where to fight. The 'sarkar'[1] is nowhere ... You go to the collector's office with your application letter, s/he will say, 'I do not have the power...' I ... went to meet the [Town Planning] officer.... Useless. Then, I went to the SIR office in Gandhinagar. Nobody knew who would speak [to me]. If you go to Sharma,[2] he will say I am just implementing the orders ... Go and meet the MLA, he has no idea of SIR. Where should we go? Where is the sarkar then? Who is the sarkar? It is absent when we want to fight against it....

... Whereas when they want our land, [even] the *talati*[3] will snatch it away from me. Now see, the sarkar is everywhere and everyone is sarkar ... If you say now that you came to Dholera to buy land, you will find thousands of people telling you that they know how it works, they have people in offices ... Go and meet a BJP leader, he will tell you that he can complete the [land] deal in one or two days because it is their sarkar. Now because you want to buy, everyone knows the sarkar, everyone is part of it. [But] if I go to the BJP leaders and ask for help in the protests, he will not know anyone in the sarkar.

—A Dholera farmer

A retired government employee who leads the protesting farmers' platform named Bhal Bachao Samiti, Vijayrajsinh aptly articulated the role of the 'sarkar' in Dholera. He used 'sarkar' to refer to the state or the government. His struggle to find the sarkar to lodge his protests against land acquisition by the state sums up the importance of the 'state' in Dholera and, by extension, in such projects of urbanisation. It also signifies the hide-and-seek game the state plays with its citizens. From interviews with other stakeholders, especially farmers, two more themes emerge as they talk of the sarkar. First is the prevalence of the Dholera smart city or the Special Investment Region (SIR) project in the everyday lives of these citizens and how the character of the sarkar changed since the announcement of the project. This elucidates the conceptual basis of the book and the analysis in the following sections and chapters. Farmers often associate the sarkar with their imminent dispossession, linking privatisation with how the sarkar is handing over their land to corporations.

Second is the role of Hindutva actors and how they were enmeshed with the everyday state. As the farmers protesting against the project were largely opposed to the BJP, one may argue that they may have exaggerated views. However, both these ideas are buttressed upon observing the state from close quarters. As Vijayrajsinh struggles with the state's deceptive nature of being everywhere and still nowhere, the state and its relationship with society become the key analytical lens to understand Dholera. Of course, there is considerable scholarship across disciplines emerging from various geographies and cultures on the concept of the state. This has ensured that even the most fundamental questions, such as whether the state should be studied at all as an analytical category, have been raised. However, the state is still the most useful concept to base the analysis of the case of Dholera. Not only does the empirical data demonstrate how the state remains a category that society is compelled to grapple with (as with the farmers mentioned earlier), but also, theoretically, the fluidity of the concept opens up new possibilities for analysis. This dual face of the state has been explored by scholars working on the Indian state such as Chandra (2015), Gupta (2012), Herring (1999), Jenkins and Manor (2017) Levien (2013), Sinha (2005, 2019) and Sud (2009). This chapter will formulate the conceptual framework to understand Dholera through the deceptive leviathan, the state.

The state's relationship with society has particularly captured the attention of scholars. From seeing the state as a solitary unit unaffected by the dynamics of society, several scholars have argued against a false dichotomy of two bounded entities, 'state' and 'society', in opposition to one another (Nugent, 1994). Berenschot (2010) asserts that on the ground it is difficult, if not impossible, to distinguish between the state and society since they meet at a 'blurred boundary' (Gupta, 1995: 375) or at a 'spongiform interface' (Harriss-White, 1997: 17). As Vijayrajsinh, the Dholera farmer, pointed out, the same state may play hide and seek with its citizens, at once both concealed and visible in its interactions with society. The strikingly self-interested state in Dholera disappears when people are in need and reappears when the state is in need.

Fuller and Harriss (2001: 15) have rightly argued that in the case of India, sarkar—understood as both 'state' and 'government' in Hindi—appears on many levels and in very different shapes and forms. When it interacts with everyday citizens at its lowest echelons, the state is usually staffed by people with whom citizens may have some kind of social relationship. Here, the state is not always 'faceless' (Fuller and Harriss, 2001: 15) and could also be trespassed by actors who are not necessarily part of the state in the strictest sense. Studying the everyday functioning of the state, at the ground level in Dholera or in Gandhinagar, brings newer dimensions that complicate not just a unified understanding of the state but also urges us to take onboard the newer intermeshing of practices and actors that have now become part of the state. This state in practice in Dholera is the 'actually existing state', a multi-faceted, internally differentiated, pluralised entity rather than a homogenous one (Sinha, 2011). To understand what constitutes the state in Dholera and also answer the research questions raised in the previous chapter, the framework of the actually existing state (AES) has four key propositions:

1. First, the AES is characterised by both formal and shadow elements. Formal state officials accept tribute, patronage or clientage whereas non-state actors use the shadow of the state to earn their livelihoods. In the process, the activities of the formal state are shadowed from within or outside and by both state and non-state actors. This makes the state porous to the actors of society as well as businesses. The porosity of the state shapes and, at the same time, is shaped by the disjuncture in economic or cultural ideological projects. The book looks at the impact of the shadow and formal elements on citizens' access to the state. This is covered in Chapter 4 of the book.

2. Building on this, the second proposition is that a number of actors simultaneously constitute the shadow and formal elements of the AES. The state is shaped by the practices of these middlemen, who do not neatly belong to either of the two realms even if they distinctly represent state and/or non-state organisations. Through their ability to manipulate their proximity to the state, society or other non-state organisations, they affect the entity of the state and the delivery of its services. Chapter 5 of the book covers this proposition through empirical data.

3. The third proposition looks at the consequences of the two previous propositions. As the Dholera project attracts both support and resistance, the blurred boundaries of the formal and shadow state work together to diffuse protests against the project or to smoothen business deals. In the process, the two projects of economic and

cultural–religious ideologies (neoliberalism and Hindutva respectively) are used in various ways. Such interactions are present at multiple levels of the state. Chapter 6 of the book focuses on this dimension.

4. Fourth, the AES in everyday practices in Dholera constitutes and is, simultaneously, constituted by intricate linkages between these two economic and cultural ideologies at multiple levels of the state. The networks provided by these ideologies facilitate the AES's functioning as their material benefits determine the success, failure or longevity of the state. This is covered in Chapter 7 of the book.

The term 'actually existing state' (AES) is particularly influenced by Brenner and Theodore's (2002) concept of 'actually existing neoliberalism'. Both Harriss-White (2003) and Jessop (1990, 2015) have also used the terminology of the 'actually existing state' (both scholars do not use the term with abbreviations, AES). To Harriss-White (2003: 72), the AES is the local state that explains a great deal of overlap between the state and the economy present at administrative levels below the state capital. However, this book understands the AES as being present at various levels of the state; it is not limited to the informal sector or the local state (Harriss-White, 2003: 72). As this book will illustrate, the formal economy also taps into the informal economy, and the formal state taps into the shadow state in Dholera.[4] Similarly, AES actors are active at multiple levels of the state. Similar to Mamonova et al. (2020: 2), the term 'actually existing state' focuses on 'the historically and culturally conditioned and context-specific manifestations' of the state in Dholera to analyse the uneven and variegated realities of how the state helps neoliberalism and Hindutva entrench, guided by 'empirical manifestations of the phenomenon, not by its precise definition or conceptualisation' of the state (Mamonova et al., 2020: 2). Thus, instead of 'moving analytically from the general and the ideal to the concrete' that would have necessitated assuming the state as a more or less coherent concept that then 'takes hold of specific social realities', the approach here is from 'the perspective of practice, focusing on how it emerges out of variegated forms of socio-economic structures that are experienced from specific socially situated positions' (Mamonova et al., 2020: 2).

The State

To start with, Weber's concept of the modern state, 'a compulsory association with a territorial basis characterised by a system of administrative and legal order, which claims binding authority, not only over the members of the state, the citizens ... but also to a very large extent, over all action taking place in the area of its jurisdiction' has stayed central since its articulation (1964: 156). Over the decades, this concept has been critiqued for its utility and relevance; nevertheless, it remains significant for understanding the essence of the state. Later influential scholarship comes from Abrams (1988) who proposes two distinct objects of study while dealing with the state: the state-system and the state-idea. The state-system is a palpable nexus of practice and institutional structure centred in government and characterised as extensive, unified and dominant in any given context. Its sources, structure and variations can be examined in fairly straightforward empirical ways. Second, there is a state-idea, projected, purveyed and variously believed in different societies at different times whose modes, effects and variations are also susceptible to research. The state starts its 'life as an implicit construct; it is then reified acquiring an overt symbolic identity' which is then 'progressively divorced from practice as an illusory account of practice' (Abrams, 1988: 58). This book draws from Abrams's proposals regarding the state to explain how the state-system and state-idea work together in the everyday practices of actors in state and society.

In a similar vein, Mitchell (1991) argues that the state has remained difficult to define especially due to the nature of its boundary with society that appears elusive, porous and mobile. The edges of the state are uncertain as societal elements penetrate it on all sides, ensuring that the resulting boundary between state and society is difficult to determine (Mitchell, 1991). Mitchell (1991) points out that the elusiveness of this boundary should not lead to sharper definitions of either concept but lead us to explore more deeply the empirical clues to the state's actual nature. According to Mitchell, the state is not to be analysed as a structure but as a structural effect (Mitchell, 1991). These effects are products of practices that give the state the appearance of a structure. When we approach the state as an effect of its practices, it is easy to acknowledge the power of its political arrangements as well as explain its elusiveness. As Migdal (2001) similarly argues, the state should be defined on the basis of the image of the state and the practices of its actors. This means that through the analysis of its practices or the effects those practices create, it is easy to explain why the state simultaneously seems to stand apart from society and comes across as an internal arrangement. Further, the boundary of the state is merely the effect of such arrangements and does not mark a real edge (Mitchell, 1991). Hence, such an illusory boundary can be trespassed on by actors with any formal or non-formal associations with the state. These perspectives are important for the book as they explain the significant role played by state and non-state actors in Dholera in creating the idea of the state. It is through their practices that the AES comes into existence in the everyday life of the citizens. These actors, whether part of the formal state or mimicking its practices, create an effect of the state in the Indian case.

The Indian State

After independence from the British in 1947, similar to most post-colonial states, India opted for a state-led development-planning model under the first prime minister, Jawaharlal Nehru. Placing emphasis on the economies of scale associated with the manufacturing industry, Nehru tried to address the 'agrarian question' in the context of a grim picture of underemployment and low productivity in agriculture (Corbridge and Harriss, 2000). Democracy, socialism and secularism were the foundational principles of the post-independent Indian state. These principles came to be challenged over the subsequent decades, particularly from forces of neoliberalism and Hindutva, as discussed in the later sections of this chapter.

Some of the early influential scholarship on the Indian state focused on the organisation of the state through a coalition of dominant class interests (similar theses were developed by Bardhan, 1984; Rudolph and Rudolph, 1987; Vanaik, 1990; and Varshney, 1995). Chatterjee (1986, 1998) and Kaviraj (1984, 1988) put forward a richer analysis through the thesis of 'passive revolution' taking the dominant class coalition argument further. They point out that because Nehru and his small coterie of supporters were in a minority within the Congress, Nehru had to water down, if not completely abandon, progressive policies such as land redistribution. The state's elite involved in planning were relatively weak within society and were politically isolated. Hence, they were unable to exercise cultural leadership through society and came to rely heavily on 'state-bureaucratic agency' for bringing about social transformation (Chatterjee, 1998). Such bureaucrats who came in touch with society were not entirely 'faceless' (Fuller and Harriss, 2001: 15) and came with their own caste and kin relations along with adherences to ideologies.

The thesis of passive revolution is supported by anthropological perspectives of the Indian state that discuss the role of 'big men' who were in coalitions with state elites (Bailey, 1963; Kothari, 1970). They played key roles in the elections, in the functioning of the bureaucracy or in the everyday lives of citizens or subjects. They were often local notables—landed, wealthy, in positions of power in institutions of local government—exercising authority coming largely from the locally dominant castes. These 'big men' oiled by 'patronage—the exchange of offices, jobs and access to public resources for the mobilisation of electoral support'—formed the organisational base of the Congress-dominated political system (Weiner, 1967, cited in Corbridge and Harriss, 2000: 50). Bailey (1963: 111) argued that because of 'the fundamental fact of the economic and social cleavage, [the] politician cannot reach his electorate, the voters cannot communicate with the politicians and administrators, [and] the gap is bridged by the political broker and his network' (cited in Corbridge and Harriss, 2000: 50). This is supported further through works on specific themes such as patronage, in which these 'brokers' have found different names: middlemen, patrons, 'gatekeepers', *dalal*, and *pyarveekar* amongst various scholars (Manor, 2000; Oldenburg, 1987; Reddy and Haragopal, 1985; Sud, 2014a; Witsoe, 2012). Whereas their nature and profiles have changed over the decades, they play a key role and often become part of the state in Dholera.

Looking through the analyses of Abrams or Mitchell, these middlemen come to create the state effect through their practices despite not being formally part of the state system. Through the everyday practices of these actors (covered in Chapter 5), the idea of the state 'is reified' amongst subjects (Abrams, 1988: 58). Further, non-state actors pervade state spaces both physically as well as ideologically, creating the state effect while opening up the avenue of 'reimagining' the state (Chapter 4). Some of the images this book elucidates from the field underscore the reification described by Abrams (1988) or the 'state-effect' of Mitchell (1991), an outcome of the role of AES actors at multiple levels of the state. However, this reification ultimately creates an impression of the state when actors from the shadows of the state become formal state actors.

An impact of their practices is that the boundary between state and society appears blurred as they trespass on state spaces through their practices. This boundary is not only unclear but also fluid and negotiable according to social context. In that porosity and fluidity, the question is: how and where do we find the state to study? Where does the state begin or end? In an interesting study, Mathur (2015) argues that even state officials themselves are often confused and find the state illegible and unreadable. To look into how states are constituted, substantiated or constructed in the lives of citizens, one starting point is the study of the bureaucracy's everyday workings and interactions with society (Gupta and Sharma, 2006). This is particularly useful when studied at multiple levels as the Indian state has come to be constituted through everyday interactions of citizens in villages or towns often involving personal, kin or caste relations with state officials. While the state does operate within localised structures of power, it is also constituted by networks with outside actors such as higher-level bureaucracy, private consultants and international financial institutions, and, most importantly, global discourses such as neoliberalism.

Within this literature on the blurring of state–society boundaries in India, a major contribution comes from Barbara Harriss-White (1997, 2003) in her study of the intermediate classes in a town in the southern province of Tamil Nadu. She explains how they colonise the state to further their interests and expand the scope of what she calls the 'shadow state' which exists alongside and, in some ways, interlocking with the 'formal' state (Harriss-White, 2003). Here, the formal state refers to the set of institutions of political and executive control centred upon government while the shadow state represents the practices that are outside the formal counterparts. However, when one analyses the state and practices of its actors, the line between formal and shadow elements are blurred.

The term 'shadow state' has been used to refer to the state in countries such as Sierra Leone which were characterised by 'the emergence of rulers drawing authority from their ability to control markets and their material rewards' (Reno, 1995: 3), especially through the exploitation of precious resources.[5] Following Harriss-White (2003), whereas the informal economy of the shadow state in Sierra Leone was loosely connected to its formal counterpart, the economy that the shadow state in India (or in Dholera) generates cannot operate without the formal state. As documented throughout the book, the shadow state and the economic activities generated in Dholera due to the coming of the neoliberal project are then strongly tied to the actors and practices of Hindutva. This is one key aspect of the book that runs through Chapters 4, 5 and 6.

Importantly, official bureaucrats simultaneously play some roles in the shadow state while other actors make the shadow state a source of their self-employment, something we will witness throughout the book. These actors (covered especially in Chapters 5 and 7) play a key role in taking Dholera smart city forward or in negotiating the politics of delivering the project. This is shown through an elaboration of the overlap of the shadow state with the formal state that is so obvious that it 'spills into the lanes surrounding state offices and into the private domestic space of officials' residences', providing perhaps the most vivid images of blurred boundaries (Harriss-White, 2003). Where I depart from Harriss-White is in arguing that the AES is present at multiple levels of the state, going beyond just the small towns and villages about which she writes. Whereas the local shadow state and the informal economy that its practices generate are central to the functioning of the new Dholera, the network goes higher up, to the provincial or the federal level. Second, adding to the scholarship, the book demonstrates that these actors working in the shadow of the state in Dholera trespassed the state by virtue of their affiliation to ideologies like Hindutva. In doing so, the book explains how the blurred state–society boundary has enabled the entry of new actors of Hindutva and neoliberalism.

Neoliberalism

In the 1970s, states across the globe faced a series of existential crises, especially due to economic policies. During this period, neoclassical economists and international financial institutions strongly advocated policies of economic liberalisation, state retrenchment and a turn to competitive markets—measures that came to be called neoliberalism. Neoliberalism refers primarily to the laissez-faire economic liberalism practised since the 1980s, including policies such as privatisation, free trade agreements between nations, state deregulation, the opening up of financial markets, encouragement of foreign direct investment and reductions in government spending in order to increase the role of the private sector in the economy (Harvey, 1989, 2005). In short, neoliberalism entails the triadic combination of 'deregulation, privatisation, and withdrawal of the state from many areas of provision' (Harvey, 2005: 2–3; Wacquant, 2012).[6]

The extensive scholarship on neoliberalism has demonstrated its wide relevance across the world. An example of its significance, even at the scale of Dholera's villages, can be located by looking at the reduced number of village-level officials (called *talatis*, explained in note 2, Chapter 5) over the years, as the state has preferred outsourcing over new hiring. Previously, one such village official would look after a village each. Now, they are responsible for more than two villages in most cases. Outsourcing can be witnessed in the revenue department at sub-district levels too. The computer operators in the land record offices are employed by private companies, with paltry salaries ranging from INR[7] 6,000 to 10,000 per month. This in turn has led to these employees looking for other sources to earn money, making use of such an important office, leading to the creation of the AES.

With the proliferation of neoliberal policies across the globe, many scholars in the 1990s concluded that the state had diminished, becoming 'hollow' (Sassen, 1991). However, none of these prophecies has been found to be factually true as the state remained at the centre of most activities, providing at least the larger macroeconomic framework and the critical infrastructure for neoliberalism to become successful (Gupta and Sivaramakrishnan, 2011). Interestingly by the late 1990s, the same set of institutions, which previously argued for the retrenchment of the state, came to assert the key role of the state in pushing towards economic liberalisation and market economies (World Bank, 1997) that Stiglitz (2008: 41) termed as the 'post-Washington Consensus consensus'. Scholars have argued that in practice, states deviate from the doctrinal template of 'small government' only to promote a business-friendly climate for capitalistic endeavours, to safeguard financial institutions and to repress popular resistance to the neoliberal drive toward accumulation by dispossession (Harvey, 2005; Wacquant, 2012).

This inconsistency in neoliberalism is a fundamental theme in this book. In many contexts, the set of policies that have come to be associated with neoliberalism does not always mark a significant departure from the pre-neoliberal set-ups. There is path dependency and a crisis-driven tendency, which is why Aihwa Ong (2006) defines neoliberalism as a logic of governing, which travels and mutates with different actor networks and diverse contexts. In their influential scholarship, Brenner, Peck and Theodore (2010a, 2010b, 2011, 2013, 2018) argue that the idea of 'neoliberalism' as an immutable ideology, centred on an ideal end state should be discarded and instead the focus should be on the process of neoliberalisation, which involves the ceaseless evolution of 'opportunistic' ideologies. We come back to this discussion after situating the neoliberal case of India.

Against the backdrop of a massive fiscal deficit, foreign reserves sufficient to pay for barely two weeks' worth of imports and on the verge of defaulting on external balance of payment obligations, the newly appointed finance minister, Manmohan Singh, rolled out a slew of policies of economic liberalisation in 1991.[8] The result was a fundamental restructuring of the Indian economy. Over the next two decades, India's gross domestic product (GDP) grew between 5 and 10 per cent constantly while continuing to add to these reforms becoming a successful neoliberal story. As with the global trend, the state did not wither away following economic liberalisation in India. Its 'central role in social change, politics, and policymaking' remains an 'empirical reality' (Mooij, 1999: 44) while retaining a preeminent place in the popular imagination of the citizens (as underscored by the farmer at the start of the chapter). With the set of new economic policies since 1991, the Indian state 'is now represented as just one of the many agencies, organisations, or associations that dot the [political] landscape' (Chandhoke, 2003: 2958). However, the scale of the national government has witnessed a reorganisation of some of its powers with provincial and urban levels receiving considerable autonomy to formulate their own policies that also came with added fiscal responsibility.[9]

Provincial governments proposed spatial policies seeking domestic and international investments from private sectors with an idea of competition and free markets gaining prominence in these policies. Tax breaks, subsidised natural resources (such as land or water) and provision of physical infrastructure to investors were central to those policies which Harvey (2005) calls 'urban entrepreneurialism'. A host of policies were framed to regenerate existing urban spaces or to create new ones, resulting in considerable growth in urban and real estate sectors. Investment into these sectors led to a surge in demands for access to land, fostering a spike in land value. This ultimately placed land-based revenue, and control of land markets, at the centre of the political as well as economic agenda.

Gooptu (2011) argues that economic liberalisation brought in a distinctive feature in policies, targeting 'growth-oriented urban developmentalism'. The 'city captured the imagination of both the state and the private corporate sector as the most important engine of national growth and development and as the site of market expansion and investment … [The] urban economy has become an important driver of economic growth. It is also the bridge between the domestic economy and the global economy….' (Gooptu, 2011: 37). The special economic zones (SEZs) of the early 2000s represent the set of spatial neoliberal policies in India (Cross, 2010; Jenkins et al., 2014, 2015). SEZs often created tax-free zones for investment in manufacturing and service industries along with a portion of land to be developed for housing and other commercial purposes in both public–private partnership (PPP) as well as completely privately owned models. The policy of SIR launched in 2009 while Narendra Modi was Gujarat's chief minister, through which the Dholera project came into existence, is a similar example of provincial scale taking the lead to 'develop' previously urban fringes or rural areas. Taking a step further, Modi, upon becoming the prime minister of India in 2014, announced a project to build '100 Smart Cities' across the country. While Dholera received more focus and funding was allocated during Modi's prime ministership, it was not part of the 100 Smart Cities project.

Is Dholera smart city then a neoliberal project? Dholera, being the *terra nullius* where the state envisions building a smart city, is a project which would be a representative case of Scott's (1998: 115) 'high modernism'. Scott defined it as 'a rejection of the past as a model to improve upon and a desire to make a completely fresh start….' In similar ways, everything in Dholera is 'barren, unproductive or primitive', as a bureaucrat from Dholera SIR Development Authority (DSIRDA) pointed out. On numerous occasions during his speeches, Modi, the key proponent of Dholera smart city, displays faith in 'smart technology' to drive the growth of Dholera and, by extension, Gujarat and India, similar to the previous generations propagating that Scott theorised as high modernism.

However, this faith in science is tied to the market as the driving force of the economy in Dholera, making the case for it to be a representative case of neoliberalism. The policy of SIRs is essentially a scaled-up version of SEZs in Gujarat. SIRs are proposed to cover a minimum of 100 square kilometres. Dholera SIR intends to create 'improvements' of an otherwise 'underdeveloped' countryside by creating an environment for investment to fuel economic growth (as laid out in the SIR policy). These are often the standard features of a neoliberal project. Looking through Harvey's (2005) 'accumulation by dispossession' that he argues to be central to neoliberalism, the SIRs are targeting urbanisation with an inherent dispossession of thousands of local farmers. Dispossession is imminent as the SIR's success is based on the legal transfer of land for 'development' to private corporations along with other incentives such as tax breaks or physical infrastructure.

Overall, Dholera embodies most characteristics of neoliberalism: be it commodification of land, privatisation or financialisation. Ong (2006: 4–5) defined economic zones such as SEZs or SIRs as 'an extraordinary departure in policy that can be deployed to include as well as exclude' in order to create new socio-economic possibilities. An SEZ or SIR to Ong (2006: 19) is 'a country within a country' carved out from the territory of the nation for economic freedom and entrepreneurial activity without following the laws of the main territory. Dholera can be clubbed under this. A private entity, Dholera Industrial City Development Limited (DICDL), is to manage and govern the future city, jumping the usual municipal governance model of India. It also brings into the scenario the privatisation of governance to justify urban entrepreneurialism, a phenomenon that is seen elsewhere in India as Idiculla (2016) demonstrates for Bengaluru. With its set of policies, business incentives or governance model, Dholera displays similar notions.

What then is idiosyncratic in Dholera's neoliberalism or the Indian story of neoliberalism? It is the myriad ways in which neoliberal policies have been framed, passed or implemented or how the support or opposition towards them has been sustained, underlining the inconsistency in neoliberalism. The Dholera case shows how neoliberalism mutates itself. For example, breaking from the previous proposition of the private sector building its own infrastructure, the federal state continues to pump in money to the tune of INR 30 billion to build basic infrastructure (referred to as Trunk infrastructure) in the 'Activation Area'. This is in addition to state investment into building an expressway connecting Dholera to Ahmedabad or building a massive solar energy park to power Dholera. Marking a departure from ideas such as state withdrawal, the role of the state is key to instituting the neoliberal project of Dholera. However, this in itself was a mutation as a DSIRDA bureaucrat explained:

> [This was] not the case on day one. We expected the private sector to carry out everything. [But] with so much happening in those years, financial crash, farmer protests, we changed track. A lesson [was] learnt from the SEZs that faced massive hindrance as the private corporations felt powerless on many occasions against oppositions....

As he argued, the state is heavily involved in land acquisitions for the project, which are not left simply to market forces. Such disjuncture is key to neoliberalism entrenching further in a particular place as this book will demonstrate. Hence, rather than a specific set of policy templates, the book focuses on the political and social processes to provide a far more complex and richer explanation of the developments and dynamics of neoliberalism.

This disjuncture between its ideologies and practices shows that neoliberalism as a process is often quite contradictory. This approach is what Brenner and Theodore (2002) referred to as 'actually existing neoliberalism' or 'variegated neoliberalisation' (Brenner et al., 2010a), focusing on the differences between neoliberal ideologies and their practices. They consider neoliberalism not as an 'end-state' but as a process—and as a project embedded in the context, 'produced within national, regional, and local contexts defined by the legacies of inherited frameworks, policy regimes, regulatory practices, and political struggles' (Brenner et al., 2010a: 349). The process with its ultimate pursuit of market-driven development is fraught with negotiations and contradictions. What these contradictions, however, depict is a dogged capacity to exploit the crises which it generates in the course of its own adaptive reinvention (Brenner et al., 2010a). The process is non-linear and multi-dimensional marked by policy failures, leading to improvised adaptations through combative encounters with obstacles and counter-movements (Brenner et al., 2010a; Peck and Theodore, 2012). The path taken is often 'shaped by opportunistic moments, workarounds and on-the-hoof recalibrations' which barely come closer to the ideologies of neoliberal proponents (Peck and Theodore, 2012: 179). For example, as shown in Chapter 7, while one of the foundational policies of neoliberalism is the removal of farm subsidies when it faced protests by farmers in Dholera, the state went back to launch a set of subsidies to negotiate with the protestors.[10]

Another aspect of Indian neoliberalism has been what Jenkins (1999) shows as the practices of the 'dirty state' of India in which a host of state actors involved in 'shady' land deals are often found hand in glove with criminals. The state seems to have entered newer and previously unexplored territories. Its practices simultaneously display a similar disjuncture between the ideologies and practices of neoliberalism. Overall, looking through the lens of the state, neoliberalism in India has resulted in a further blurring of the boundary between the state and society, opening up newer nodes to which new actors of the (shadow) state could cling on to or find newer avenues to enter state spaces.

Hindutva and the Disjuncture in Its Ideologies and Practices

Although India is constitutionally secular, what one witnesses in Gujarat or Dholera is that the balanced relationship between the state and various communities does not always exist. This supports the literature put forth by scholars such as Spodek (2002) or Sud (2012), among others, that points to the 'un-secular' nature of the state. The rise of right-wing Hindu nationalism or Hindutva is a key reason for this. The story behind this rise is a multifaceted narrative and the existing scholarship covers a number of related debates.[11] These debates are beyond the scope of the book, which focuses instead on the workings of Hindutva within the Dholera site and their implications on our understanding of the state.

Right-wing Hindu nationalism draws its origins from movements within the Hindu religion such as Arya Samaj or Sanatana Dharma. V. D. Savarkar reframed these movements into a one-eyed form of mobilisation supporting the idea of 'Hindutva'—a distinct form of Hindu right-wing nationalism where, for the first time, Hindus were portrayed as the original people of India, with a distinct territorial, racial and linguistic identity. Hindutva loosely translates as Hindu-ness and is used often to refer to right-wing Hindu nationalism. Savarkar's writings such as 'Hindutva: Who Is a Hindu?' (1969 [1923]) provide the ideological foundations for the phenomenon. Savarkar linked Hindutva with an identification with India as simultaneously 'fatherland' and 'holy land'. 'Fatherland' alludes to the idea of a common nation and 'holy land' incorporates culture, the 'rites and rituals, ceremonies and sacraments' as well as an identification with the 'sacred geography' of the land itself (Reddy, 2011).

Hence, Muslims and Christians can partially possess the attributes of Hindutva, but they cannot be counted as Hindus because their respective holy lands are elsewhere, and he claims their love is divided and patriotism questionable. Hence, the basis of the ideology is an othering of these communities.[12]

Critical to the rise of Hindutva was the formation of different social and political organisations, chief among them is the Rashtriya Swayamsevak Sangh (RSS) whose aim was to discipline and train a Hindu nation (Jaffrelot, 2007). Another important organisation is the Vishwa Hindu Parishad (World Hindu Council, VHP hereon) that focuses both on working in tribal areas and on the Hindu diaspora abroad (Van der Veer, 1994). A political wing, previously Bharatiya Jana Sangh (BJS), which became Bharatiya Janata Party (BJP) in 1980, remained active since independence. This, along with similar other groups that represent students, youths, farmers, labour unions and women, came together to form the Sangh Parivar (Hindi: 'family of organisations') under the symbolic saffron flag (Basu et al., 1993; Damle and Anderson, 1987). Corbridge and Harriss (2000) point out that both before and after independence, alongside the Congress, the RSS has been the most significant and innovative organisation in India, keeping itself relevant and growing across the country and abroad for a century now.

Most accounts from Gujarat on the rise of Hindutva in the province study the recurring communal riots, particularly in urban regions such as Ahmedabad (Berenschot, 2010, 2011a; Ghassem-Fachandi 2012; Shani, 2007). Concerning the key focus of this book, the overlap of economic liberalisation and Hindutva in India, existing scholarship has largely analysed the macro-scale, usually the provincial scale (some of these include Chacko, 2018a, 2018b; Corbridge and Harriss, 2000; Desai, 2006, 2011a; Gopalakrishnan, 2006; Kohli, 1990, 2009; Sud, 2007, 2012; Vanaik, 2001). Although these studies illuminate the rise of both Hindutva and neoliberalism, the myriad ways through which they unfold on the ground are not always explained. The study of Dholera in this book attempts to provide a more contextual analysis by proposing an understanding of the phenomenon that has rendered it banal, present in everyday forms as nothing special, which itself is an outcome of the disjuncture in its practice and ideologies.

This 'disjuncture in Hindutva' is used in this book to illustrate how the ideology of Hindutva penetrates the state and moves together with the economic ideology of neoliberalism through mutations. The disjuncture between Hindutva ideologies and practices is a similar trait mentioned in the earlier discussion on neoliberalism. Scholars have referred to the phenomenon as 'neo-Hindutva' (Reddy, 2011, 2018), 'banalisation of Hindu nationalism' (Jaffrelot, 2015b) or 'banal Hindutva' (Jeffrey et al., 2017). These scholars have highlighted the practices that make the everyday forms of Hindutva 'normal' or 'nothing special'. At the same time, these practices help Hindutva to increasingly permeate different aspects of the state and society, developing and spreading far beyond the organisational network that is conventionally linked to the Sangh Parivar (Longkumer and Anderson, 2018). These practices lack a strict framework for categorisation as they do not always restrict themselves to the orthodox ideologies of Savarkar or fellow Hindutva proponents (Longkumer and Anderson, 2018).

This scholarship has elaborated on the 'dynamic and idiosyncratic' ways in which Hindutva has evolved over the recent decades to become 'increasingly mainstream and normalised' even if in an obfuscated manner (Longkumer and Anderson, 2018: 374). For example, through this, Longkumer (2020) examines how Hindutva actors have successfully made inroads into North-East India, a region traditionally seen as a recalcitrant periphery. According to Longkumer (2020), Hindutva is re-fashioning itself by reforming Savarkar's core ideologies in new ways. From a different perspective, Simpson (2004, 2013) and Bhattacharjee (2019) demonstrated the rise of Hindutva forces in the backdrop of the earthquake that devastated large parts of Kutch in Gujarat in 2001. They highlight how Hindutva can exploit the mundane economic, social or religious aspects of everyday life to take its project forward while simultaneously gaining material benefits. Simpson's (2004) analysis of the town planning mechanism in the post-earthquake scenario reflects how the everyday bureaucratic processes from a seemingly apolitical dimension can be used by Hindutva groups to further their ideologies, a theme this book covers.

Although Hindutva may be prone to internally generated issues of caste, or to processes where its support leads to the dispossession of the larger population (as in Dholera), akin to neoliberalism, the actors of Hindutva demonstrate a dogged capacity to exploit the same contradictions and crises 'in the course of its own adaptive reinvention' (Peck and Theodore, 2012: 178). In the actual world of practice, we cannot reduce Hindutva to a process of enacting a singular plan or grand design or a singular image of the Hindu state in the form of Savarkar's proposals. It instead displays a staggering dynamic that is marked by regular improvisations and/or manipulations when it faces obstacles.

What this has resulted in is the banal Hindutva, which has an economic, religious as well as cultural logic. Hindutva's distinctive configurations of economic or political programmes are shaped by the ways in which they collide with existing landscapes to produce distinctive forms. Hence, in the North-Eastern province of Nagaland with a Christian majority population, the argument is framed not around Hindutva but around an economic logic (Longkumer, 2020). In the neighbouring province of Assam, it latches on to the issue of illegal immigrants from Bangladesh (Saikia, 2020). Consequently, rather than examining a specific set of ideologies that came from Savarkar or similar ideologues of Hindutva, the focus of the book is to understand the strategies that affect everyday political and social processes, similar to neoliberalism. This would allow a multifaceted understanding of the avatars that Hindutva may take within different contexts. Nevertheless, this should not distract us from the fact that the achievement of the Hindu state that Savarkar projected remains the ultimate target.

To explain the relevance of Hindutva in the everyday state or society of Dholera, the book brings in observations which underscore its presence in different forms and expressions that help it to become entrenched further in society or corner benefits from the neoliberal project. In these practices, they may appear to position themselves with contradictory ideas. For example, in Dholera, many Hindutva supporters stand with the farmers' protests while also undertaking land brokering. They oppose the dispossession of farmers while also claiming that 'the Dholera smart city is the only way' through which the region can witness 'development'. In similar ways, the idea of disjuncture in Hindutva helps explain why the local head of the opposition Congress party uses his past Hindutva networks to broker land deals while arguing that Modi is the 'Hindu *hriday samrat* (king of Hindu hearts) who is capable of developing India' (covered in Chapter 7). This proposition on Hindutva's disjuncture between ideologies and practices also enriches our understanding of the state or the AES, which is trespassed by numerous actors with affiliations to Hindutva. Through the proposition of disjuncture in Hindutva, the everyday state practices in the villages that display a blurring of state and non-state identities amongst a range of actors will be explained. At the same time, such practices go upwards to the scale of the provincial capital where policymakers of the SIR find similarities between the philosophies of neoliberalism and Hindutva to justify support for privatisation or deregulation (covered in Chapter 6). Thus, through the proposition, the book explains the overlaps in the cultural or religious ideology of Hindutva with the economic ideology of neoliberalism at multiple scales of the state.

Notes

1. Among the many different meanings, the *Oxford English Dictionary* defines 'sarkar' (or 'sirkar') as the 'state' or the 'government'. Occasionally, it can be used to refer to a person in a position of authority by a subordinate. It is also a common surname in India. It has an Urdu/Persian origin. I use the term to refer to the state unless otherwise specified. Simpson (2006: 346) similarly noted common citizens in Gujarat usually use terms such as 'government' or 'sarkar' to refer to the 'state'.

2. Sharma (pseudonym) was the chief executive officer of the Dholera SIR Development Authority.

3. *Talati* is a village-level bureaucrat in Gujarat who work under the local government. They keep village records and implement various development plans and projects.

4. To clarify, the informal economy is not equated with the shadow state; these are two distinct even if overlapping entities.

5. In a different context, Geiger and Wolch (1986) introduced the term 'shadow state' to theorise structural changes in the US and UK nonprofit sectors during the 1970s and 1980s (Trudeau, 2008; Wolch, 1990).

6. For the history and relevance of neoliberalism, refer to Harvey (1989, 2005), Venugopal (2015), Wacquant (2009, 2012) and the scholarship of Brenner, Peck and Theodore (2010a, 2010b, 2011, 2013, 2018). Also, refer to Peck (2013), Saad Filho and Johnston (2004), and/or Venugopal (2015) on the usefulness of 'neoliberalism' and the tendency to make it a catch-all phrase to explain a host of practices.

7. 'INR' (₹), variously termed 'rupees' or 'Rs', refers to the currency of India. At the current exchange rate (as of September 2024), 1 GBP equals INR 110.

8. The scholarship on India's economic liberalisation covers most aspects on the context or the events leading to its initiation as well as its outcomes over the decades. Refer to Bardhan (2000), Bhagwati (1993), Corbridge and Harriss (2000), Jenkins (1999, 2006), Kaur (2007), Kohli (2006a and 2006b), Manor (1995), Mooij (2005), Nagaraj (1991), Nayar (2006), Panagariya (2008), Pedersen (2000), Rodrik and Subramanian (2004) and Varshney (1999). Also, scholars have pointed out that there was a sharp growth in GDP (5.5–6 per cent) around 1980 and the impact was not necessarily immediate.

9. Kennedy (2013), Kennedy and Zérah (2008), Mahadevia (2005) and Maringanti et al. (2015), among others, have commented on the rescaling of the state. Indian provinces received financial autonomy post-liberalisation, tied to the idea of making them fiscally responsible and generating their own funds. By the late 1990s, provinces could directly negotiate loans from transnational organisations such as the World Bank.

10. Ferguson (2015) also briefly explores the idea of neoliberal redistribution.

11. On Indian secularism since independence, refer to Corbridge and Harriss (2000) and Fuller and Harriss (2001) who provide detailed commentaries based on various scholarships. On Hindutva, refer to Basu (2000), Hansen (1999), Hansen and Jaffrelot (1998) and Jaffrelot (1996, 2005, 2007). Also, see Gooptu (1997) for an account of the rise of Hindu nationalism in the province of Uttar Pradesh during the British era discussing how the urban poor were attracted to a militant form of Hinduism.

12. Savarkar's many demagogic views include advocating rape of Muslim women as a political tool to subjugate the Muslim community (1971). Hindutva leaders', including Savarkar's, tacit support for the Nazis in Germany or Fascists in Italy is well documented (Casolari, 2000). Savarkar himself compared the German majority and Jewish minority in Germany to India's Hindu majority and Muslim minority, condemning how German Jews and Indian Muslims failed to assimilate (Gier, 2014).

3

The Gujarat Model of 'Unequal' Development

In August and September of 2017, as the monsoon left the province of Gujarat in India and the upcoming provincial election gathered steam, the slogan 'vikas gando thayo chhe' meaning 'development has gone crazy' became one of the most trending topics on social media. It was used to mock the poor state of development across the province. The ruling Bharatiya Janata Party (BJP) was taken by surprise because development was the territory in which they claimed to have delivered. Suddenly a campaign targeting them head-on, unexpected to say the least, was proving those claims to be hollow (Langa, 2017). It began spontaneously after a twenty-year-old engineering student posted some photographs of a dilapidated state-owned bus on Facebook (Langa, 2017) with a tagline: 'Stay Away! Vikas has gone crazy in Gujarat' (Langa, 2017). The post set off a conflagration of memes mocking the BJP's claim of development. People shared photographs as well as video clips of broken roads and bridges, rickety state-owned buses, garbage dumps on the streets, flooded roads, unfinished construction and records of swine flu-related casualties, all with the catchy tag line of 'vikas' (development). What helped was the fact that 'Vikas' is a common male name in Gujarati society. Hence, comments about 'Vikas' falling in love (HT Correspondent, 2017), getting lost, going mad or having his engagement cancelled because he had gone crazy, resonated (Akhtar, 2024). Adding to the humour and wit, the Hindu festival of Navaratri brought with it new songs on 'vikas gando thayo chhe'.

The moment was both natural and political. The monsoon downpour of July-August washed away the BJP's roads and highways as well as their claims of world-class infrastructure. The opposition Indian National Congress Party (Congress hereon) latched on to this with the impending provincial assembly elections in December 2017. It became a major embarrassment for the BJP as the party's top brass was forced to respond. However, it was a tough task to create a narrative against the more relatable social media campaign that solely focused on issues such as fuel price hikes, the recently introduced high Goods and Services Tax rates and growing unemployment. This was after the provincial government reeled under the massive agitations by Other Backward Classes (OBCs), Patidar[1] youths and followed by similar Dalit protests.[2] Never has the word 'vikas' exasperated BJP in Gujarat as much over the last two decades as it did then.

This prompted people to question the 'Gujarat model of development' that the BJP has managed to sell at many elections, including the federal elections of 2014. After all, the Gujarat model of development and slogans such as 'sabka saath, sabka vikas' (all together, development for all) were the major platforms of Narendra Modi's successful prime ministerial campaign in 2014. However, the reality of development in Gujarat has been very different. The remote areas of the province were also in bad shape, especially when it came to sectors such as health, education and other social areas. Rising unemployment has remained a major concern. For instance, one survey showed that more than 80 per cent of engineers in the province are jobless (Shekhar, 2017). It was around this time when the fieldwork for the book was undertaken.

To tell the background story of Gujarat, this chapter uses the lens of the Gujarat model of development and its unequal impact. Some key questions emerge. What exactly is the Gujarat model of development and why is it important? What is the role of the state and society within it? Why should the background of the province be told through the Gujarat model of development? Does it signify the past actions of the state or indicate a future course of action? Was the formal state driving it or shadow state or non-state actors? The chapter illustrates that this model needs to be addressed if the context of the neoliberal growth of Gujarat is to be understood. Importantly, for this book, the Dholera smart city project is very much part of the Gujarat model of development that intends to deliver development in a backward region of the province.

The model primarily refers to the slew of policies and measures when Modi was the chief minister of Gujarat between 2001 and 2014. The set of mainly neoliberal policies encouraged private participation, being business-friendly while breaking down laws, which safeguarded environment or labour rights. The period witnessed high GDP growth, although investment in the health and education sectors decreased. As can be expected, there have been contesting academic views of the Gujarat model of development. Neoclassical economists such as Jagdish Bhagwati, Arvind Panagariya or Bibek Debroy have projected Gujarat as a model for the country, while Amartya Sen and

Jean Drèze have criticised it for the poor progress on indicators of human development (Bhagwati and Panagariya, 2012a, 2012b; Debroy, 2012; Sen and Drèze, 2013). Critics also describe the model as one which signifies unequal development (Hirway et al., 2014; Mahadevia, 2005) being all about economic growth without social development (Hirway et al., 2014: 7; Jaffrelot, 2015a: 2017), involving crony capitalism and the ills resulting from an overlap of business and politics (Jaffrelot, 2019; Sud, 2012), and capital led growth laced with elements of Hindutva (Desai, 2011b, Jaffrelot, 2019; Sud, 2012). The model often flirts with practices of illiberal Hindutva while following economic models of liberalism.

It is important to acknowledge here that the marginalisation of economically and socially backward populations or the key role of non-state actors in state and society precedes economic liberalisation or Hindutva in Gujarat. As Sud (2012: 188) remarked, illiberal political conditions long precede market-oriented reform or the rise of Hindutva, for religious minorities, lower castes and other disadvantaged groups. Scholars have shown the social polarisation and paradoxical growth process with respect to economy and polity through their works on Gujarat's political economy in the 1970s, 1980s and 1990s.[3] However, the impact of the coming of neoliberalism and Hindutva is no less important. In fact, the state of affairs of Gujarat before the full-throttle commencement of the two ideologies makes it a more comprehensive study to understand how they exacerbate existing marginalisation along with creating new ones. Within this, Dholera is a microcosm of the political changes that have taken place in Gujarat over the years. Electorally, it is not necessarily a bell-weather constituency (the villages belong to the Dhandhuka constituency), but the election results tell a significant story of the province's politics, especially the shift from the Congress to BJP. The chapter provides the story with a focus on four key defining moments in the history of the province that are crucial to understanding Dholera.

Moment One: The Creation of Gujarat

Gujarat is divided into four geographical, socio-cultural sub-regions and this categorisation has had a historical influence on matters of every aspect of life: whether culture, economy, trade, or caste (Figure 3.1). These regions are: (*a*) mainland Gujarat extending from the southern tip of Aravali and Vindhya Satpura ranges to the beginning of the Western Ghats, (*b*) Saurashtra or Kathiawar, (*c*) Kutch and (*d*) the eastern Adivasi belt (Yagnik and Sheth, 2005: 9).

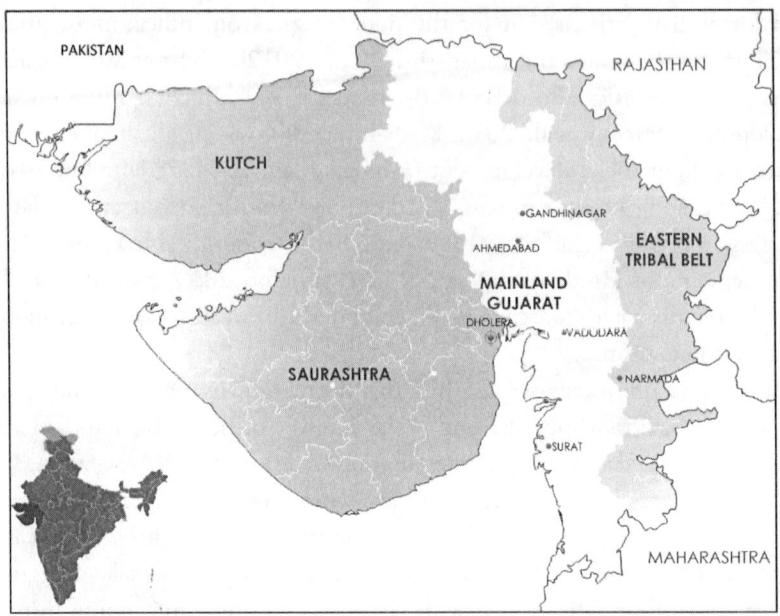

Figure 3.1 The regions of Gujarat

Source: Author.

Note: Map not to scale and does not represent authentic international boundaries.

The British ruled barely one-seventh of what is currently Gujarat, and the remaining area composed of a number of small and large princely kingdoms spread across the province. For example, the region of Saurashtra was divided into 222 princely kingdoms and estates (Yagnik and Sheth, 2005: 226).

However, to analyse the political economy of the province, a more useful lens is the categorisation in terms of the 'core' and the 'periphery' that was an outcome of the British-era infrastructure of roads and train routes (Patel, 1991). While mainland Gujarat forms the 'core', the rest of the three regions become the peripheries, illustrating the inequality of economic development witnessed by the province. The core consists of the fertile areas on the coast of central and southern Gujarat and plains along the Sabarmati and Mahi rivers (Hirway, 1995; Patel, 1991). The 'peripheries' included the less fertile regions of Saurashtra, Kutch and north and eastern Gujarat. The core is also referred to as the 'Golden Corridor' and would run through mainland Gujarat.[4] In 1947 as India attained independence from the British, current Gujarat became part of three different provinces. While British Gujarat along with other princely kingdoms such as Baroda went to Bombay province, Kathiawar's princely kingdoms were joined together to form the United States of Saurashtra. The third province, Kutch, was directly ruled by the federal government (Yagnik and Sheth, 2005). In 1956 through the States Reorganisation Act, Kutch and Saurashtra were absorbed into Bombay. Bombay province was split again in 1960 along linguistic lines creating the present-day provinces of Gujarat and Maharashtra.

Gujarat's coastline of 1,600 kilometres constitutes more than a quarter of India's total mainland coastline, leading to a long mercantile history that has left a great impact on societal composition (CCZMCSB, 2020). Trade has long been a forte for the economy (Yagnik and Sheth, 2005). As modernising agriculture was prioritised in India from the mid-1960s onwards, Gujarat was amongst the key beneficiary states of the federal government's policies of initiating a green revolution. Gujarat remains one of India's most industrialised and urbanised provinces. Successive provincial governments have promoted industrial development through various initiatives, favourable policies and special institutions[5]—all meant to support and diversify industrial development. The industrial and trade lobbies have been significantly influential and shaped many of the government strategies and policies. With the green revolution, a second important lobby of rich farmers emerged.[6] Groundnut is one of Gujarat's main cash crops, and groundnut oil producers (industrialists) formed a third important lobby (Hirway, 1995).

In the last census of 2011, Gujarat's population was 60 million spread over 196,000 square kilometres (Census India, 2011). The population comprises 88.6 per cent Hindus, 9.7 per cent Muslims and the remaining less than 2 per cent consisting of Jains, Christians and others. Caste remains a key marker when it comes to the Indian populace, especially among Hindus (Census India, 2011). Caste-wise, the composition of the population is: (a) upper castes: 26 per cent (Vanias/Baniya: 3 per cent, Brahmins: 4 per cent, Rajputs/Darbars: 5 per cent, Patidars: 13 per cent); (b) Other Backward Classes (OBCs): 40 per cent; (c) Scheduled Castes (SCs): 7 per cent; (d) Scheduled Tribes (STs) or Adivasis: 15 percent (Census India, 2011). To refer to the caste categories, the terms 'upper' and 'lower' castes are used in this book. The use of these terms has been contested by many scholars who instead prefer to use 'backward' or 'marginalised', etc. However, 'lower' (castes) is preferred here because of the structure of the caste system in Hindu society that has put these groups in a 'lower' category ultimately leading to their marginalised or backward economic and social status. Lower refers more towards the structure and less towards the outcome.

The twenty-two villages located within Dholera SIR (Figure 3.2) have a population of 39,000 with 60 per cent to 70 per cent Koli caste members and 10 per cent to 20 per cent Darbars (Senes Consultants, 2013). Koli is a peasant community, classified as OBC in Gujarat, belonging to the middle castes. On the other hand, Darbar is an upper-caste group amongst Rajputs who were the rulers of this area before and during the British era. While OBC communities have been playing an important political role in Gujarat in recent years (Modi himself is from OBC), in Dholera, Kolis are far less influential both politically and financially. They practise subsistence agriculture, owning middle-sized land holdings. Politically, despite being the majority in the Dhandhuka constituency to which the twenty-two villages belong, it was only in 2007 when a Koli or non-upper caste candidate won it for the first time (Election Commission of India, 2020). Interestingly, both Koli and Darbar groups are clubbed under what is called Kshatriya.[7] Ghanshyam Shah (1975) argues that as the Patidar community came to control the Congress party post-independence, the previous rulers and landlords, the Rajputs, were sidelined from the corridors of political power. The numerically inferior Rajputs engineered a mobilisation under the banner of Gujarat Kshatriya Samaj (Hindi: Gujarat Kshatriya Society) which worked to bring together the diverse Kshatriya communities such as Kolis under the same banner. The Gujarat Kshatriya Samaj argued that these communities shared a common history of taking up arms for society, which is why they have been called 'Kshatriyas'. For a start, it suited communities such as the Kolis as it increased their societal status while also becoming part of a significant alliance. However, as Dholera locals pointed out, everyday discrimination continued, including multiple accounts of physical violence.

The site of the Dholera smart city spread over twenty-two villages is interesting within the Saurashtra–Gujarat geography. While two of its villages, Otariya and Sandhida, were part of the Bhavnagar princely kingdom, and hence the Saurashtra province between 1947 and 1956, the rest of the villages were British-administered and fell under Dhandhuka block of Ahmedabad district. Later, in the reorganisation of 1960, the former two villages, along with a few others, were added to Ahmedabad. However, culturally as well as in the core–periphery categorisation, the villages remain closer to Saurashtra than the prosperous Ahmedabad. Darbars still find glory claiming fraternity with the rulers of the Bhavnagar princely kingdom. The pre-independence developmental work of the king of Bhavnagar, such as the building and annual

Figure 3.2   The twenty-two villages inside Dholera SIR. Dholera village is highlighted in grey.

Source: Author.

maintenance of the bund along the sea that saved the region from floods while storing freshwater from the rivers for agriculture, is often cited by local Darbars in contrast with the failures of the independent Indian state in delivering development. Furthermore, a key reason for the region remaining backwards is expressed by the movement of Saurashtra nationalism, in its grievances of being demoted from a province to become part of Gujarat, losing significant resource allocations (Spodek, 1972, 1976; Tambs-Lyche, 2004, 2012).

Dholera itself used to be a bustling port town[8] until the early 1900s. During the initial mechanisation of cotton processing, places such as Dhandhuka and Dholera were at the forefront. The British appointed a superintendent of cotton experiments, C. Daley, in Dhandhuka who was behind the first steam-operated saw gin in Ahmedabad in the 1850s (Mehta, 1982). As the experiments on mechanisation became successful, these were accompanied by efforts to improve transport and communication networks to facilitate cotton exports. A tramway was to be planned to connect the town and port of Dholera, and a tramway company was set up in 1850 in Dholera, with merchants of Ahmedabad buying most of its shares (Mehta, 1982). The locals, especially the Darbars, vividly recount the 'glorious past' as narrated by a local:

> … There was a port in this area, I guess 100 years back. I have been *sarpanch*[9] of the village for 10 years. Until 1910, Dholera wasn't a village, [it] was a municipality, and I have the records of tax and trade … in my office…. After that due to silting, the port was shut, the population at that time was around 40,000, now it's 4,000. We were bigger than Ahmedabad in the 1800s…. So, we have gone downwards….

Understanding the trajectory of development in Dholera in the post-independence era requires a discussion of what Rajni Kothari (1964) called the Congress 'system' that had a stronghold in Dholera, as with other parts of Gujarat. Since independence, the Congress party in Gujarat remained unchallenged for a decade and a half. Two key figures of Indian independence, Mahatma Gandhi and Vallabhbhai Patel, built a party oriented around the principles of pragmatism, discipline and social work (Ludden, 1996; Varshney, 2002). As discussed in the previous chapter, upper-caste leaders acted as patrons for the 'lower' caste masses. In Dholera, the patrons came largely from the Darbars who had owned large land holdings. By the 1950s, while continuing to win elections, chinks could be seen in the Congress armour with a major section opposed to the socio-economic programme or the socialist ideas of the post-independence federal government headed by Jawaharlal Nehru (Kohli, 1990). Business communities, politicians and bureaucrats came together and resisted Nehru's policies, and many dimensions of the state-owned economic regime were circumvented (Sinha, 2005). One of Nehru's flagship policies, land redistribution, was poorly implemented in Gujarat (Sud, 2012: 75–96). This was a case of Chatterjee or Kaviraj's concept of passive revolution that was discussed in the last chapter. It is interesting to note that land redistribution was successful in Saurashtra where the Patidars were beneficiaries and failed significantly in regions where Patidars tend to lose, underlining the influence of the community. Scholars on land redistribution in other provinces of India have similarly commented on the incomplete implementation of the process (Byres, 1991; Sinha and Pushpendra 2000).

The resistance to such Nehruvian policies resulted in the Swatantra Party coming within striking distances, especially in the 1967 provincial elections (G. Shah, 1976). The party comprised a loose association of Rajputs, (or Kshatriyas) and the Patidars (G. Shah, 1976). Dholera's Darbars and Kolis came under the Kshatriya banner and the Swatantra Party went on to win the Dhandhuka constituency in 1967, having come second in 1962 (Table 3.1). The Hindu right-wing ideologies were very much on the fringes during these periods. Gandhi's assassination by a former member of the Rashtriya Swayamsevak Sangh (RSS) in 1948 resulted in their temporary ban (G. Shah, 2002a). In the 1950s and 1960s, the right-wing Hindu political parties such as Bharatiya Jana Sangh (BJS) remained marginal. However, their ideologies found many takers within the broad church of the Congress Party.

Moment Two: The Division of the Congress

After the death of Vallabhbhai Patel in 1950, the next supreme leader in Gujarat Congress was Morarji Desai, who also favoured a conservative party. Indira Gandhi, daughter of Jawarhalal Nehru and then prime minister, clashed with some of the strong provincial satraps such as Desai, leading to the formation of Congress (Requisitionists) of Indira Gandhi and Congress (Organisation) of Desai (Congress [R] and Congress [O] hereon, respectively). The Gujarat Congress largely remained with Desai. The middle-class communities who were opposed to the Nehruvian idea of the state or Congress policies towards lower castes and Muslims transferred their resentment to Desai's Congress (O) (Yagnik and Sheth, 2005). While the Swatantra Party disappeared after the 1967 election, its core constituencies of rich Patidars and Kshatriyas remained a potent political force (G. Shah, 1976). However, the Gujarat Kshatriya Sabha lost its political appeal as the poor and non-Rajput Kshatriyas went behind Indira Gandhi's Congress (R), although the division was not strictly along class and caste lines (G. Shah, 1975). Hence, the erstwhile rulers, the Darbars, in Dholera were looking for non-Congress parties while the Kolis went back to support Indira's Congress. This was an important moment when young Darbar

Table 3.1   Assembly election results of Dhandhuka vis-à-vis Gujarat

Year	Dhandhuka Constituency		Overall Results (Governing party/ coalition in bold)
	Winner	Runner-up	
1962	INC	Swatantra Party	**INC** (113/154) Swatantra (26)
1967	Swatantra Party	INC	**INC** (93/168), Swatantra (66)
1972	INC	Bharatiya Jana Sangh (BJS)	**INC** (140/168)
1975	INC (O)	INC	[**INC (O)**: 56/182 + **BJS**:18 + **KMLP**: 12], INC:75
1980	INC	BJP	**INC**: 141/182, JP: 21, BJP: 9
1985	INC	Janata Party	**INC**: 149/182, JP: 14, BJP: 11
1990	BJP	INC	**JD**: 70 + **BJP**: 67, INC: 93 [Later **JD** + **INC** (1991–95)]
1995	BJP	INC	**BJP**: 121/182, INC: 45
1998	BJP	All India Rashtriya Janata Party (2nd), INC (3rd)	**BJP**: 117/182, INC: 53
2002	BJP	INC	**BJP**: 127/182, INC: 51
2007	IND (INC support)	BJP	**BJP**: 117/182, INC: 59
2012	BJP	INC	**BJP**: 120/182, INC: 57
2017	INC	BJP	**BJP**: 99/182, INC: 78

Source: Election Commission of India (2020).

Note: INC: Indian National Congress. 'O' stands for Organisation and 'R' for Requisitionists. INC (O) and INC (R) were the outcomes of the split in INC in 1969 explained in the following section.

locals from Dholera such as Bhupendrasinh Chudasama, active in the RSS and BJS, emerged as Hindutva groups began finding takers amongst the Darbars. This support for Hindutva groups is significant for the coming decades as they eventually took over the Congress system of patronage in the Dholera villages. Chudasama is currently a powerful BJP provincial minister holding a host of portfolios. A contemporary and friend of Modi, they spent a long time together with the RSS.

This split of the Congress party in 1969 was significant for the future of Gujarat's political economy. It was accompanied by the first major

Hindu–Muslim riot in Ahmedabad and some other towns that killed close to a thousand people, mostly Muslims.[10] The riot set a trend that was repeated over the next decades which ultimately brought Hindutva forces to power. With the spread of the riots into lower-caste and lower-class workers' areas of Ahmedabad, Patel (2002) identifies certain patterns that emerged which would then be repeated in the coming decades: politicisation of the riots, lukewarm attitude of the government, the involvement or connivance of the police, the role of the Gujarati vernacular press and the large-scale killing of Muslims and burning or looting of their properties, alongside the call for a boycott of Muslims.

Following the 1969 riots, Hindutva forces witnessed an increase in support reflected by the noticeable rise in the number of RSS offices across Gujarat (G. Shah, 2002a). Although the 1969 riots were a watershed moment, scholars also argue that tensions had been building for a while (Shani, 2007; Spodek, 2011). Before independence, the Muslim League had received considerable traction amongst the Gujarati Muslims and many scholars have alluded to this as a factor in the later growth of Hindutva ideologies (Shani, 2007; Spodek, 2011). The history of foreign aggressors in Gujarat supposedly plundering the province's cities and places of worship remained in public memory told and retold through various novels and poems.[11] Gujarat also faced the impact of Partition riots, when a large number of Hindu refugees fled to Gujarat from Sindh, now in Pakistan, and settled there. This provided a fertile ground for the RSS and its associates. Gujarat's geographical location was significant as the province shared a long international border with Pakistan in the north along Kutch (Figure 3.1). This has always created fact-cum-fiction narratives about continuous Pakistani 'infiltration' into Gujarat and was exploited by right-wing Hindu nationalists.[12]

While Indira Gandhi's Congress (R) won the 1972 elections, the province witnessed a series of violent public agitations targeted at the incumbent government, led by upper-caste and conservative groups (Sanghavi, 2010). The first in 1974 called the Nav-Nirman (re-construction) movement was supposedly against corruption.[13] Initially started by students, it led to the resignation of the then chief minister, Chimanbhai Patel. It witnessed the participation of the Hindutva student group, Akhil Bharatiya Vidyarthi Parishad (ABVP), taking the lead in agitations. The Nav-Nirman movement was followed by the anti-Indira crusade of Jayaprakash Narayan in 1974, and the anti-Emergency agitation as Indira Gandhi declared a state of emergency across the country curbing civil and institutional liberties (Patel, 2002). The anti-Emergency agitation witnessed the large participation of members of the RSS and was a key moment in validating their political acceptance as they struggled in the name of democracy (Yagnik and Sheth, 2005). The weakening of the Congress during this decade was evident when the first non-Congress government was formed in 1975 by a coalition led by Desai's Congress (O) that was also joined by right-wing BJS. In Dholera, Chudasama and the likes were active in these agitations, creating a space for Hindutva politics slowly. RSS made some inroads into the villages as is evident from the fact that the BJS came second in the 1972 elections while the Congress (O) won the Dhandhuka constituency in 1975 (Table 3.1).

With repeated divisions in the party and a struggle against taller regional leaders who could challenge her authority, Indira Gandhi came to rely on her personal charisma more than ground-level organisations (Hart, 1976; Rudolph and Rudolph, 1987: 137). After she died in 1984, her son Rajiv Gandhi followed the style of personal charisma, disliking stronger leaders from the provinces, further weakening the grassroots organisation of the Congress. Kohli (1990) argues that since the 1970s, Congress nationally become increasingly populist, sharing with other political actors a kind of competing populism. It created space for communal appeals in the early 1980s, as the Congress party attempted to exploit cultural feelings, particularly of the Hindu majority. The RSS and its sister organisations were taking root across the country and both Indira and Rajiv Gandhi pandered to such Hindutva groups (Kohli, 1990). This legitimised Hindu nationalism opening a public political discourse for it. Thus, the vacuum created by the decimation of grassroots-level Congress was ready to be filled by RSS, a strong cadre-based organisation.

Moment Three: KHAM Politics

A major electoral strategy framed by the Congress in the late 1970s alienated Gujarat's middle class (and upper castes) and paved the way for the firm entrenchment of Hindutva ideology. Referred to as the KHAM strategy, Congress forged an alliance of Kshatriyas, Harijans, Adivasis and Muslims, together constituting about two-thirds of Gujarat's population. A motley group who never shared power gave Congress massive wins in the 1980 and 1985 provincial elections with three-fourths of the total seats each time (Table 3.1). Madhavsinh Solanki, a leader from a lower-caste Kshatriya caste, became the chief minister each time after the elections. However, the exclusion of the higher castes/upper classes from the corridors of political power led to their alienation, causing them to fight back soon after.

The challenge came from the upper-caste constituencies. As Sud (2012: 188) has argued, this challenge 'against the widening of democracy, as well as a potentially redistributive state' has been the sort of 'elite revolt' that Corbridge and Harriss (2000) earlier theorised. The alternative to KHAM was Hindutva and neoliberalism that the upper castes eventually embraced to control both politics and the economy of the province. Kohli (1990) argues that the KHAM model, despite its electoral success, brought along governance failure. There were also inherent tensions between the groups within KHAM. G. Shah (1996) argues that strategies such as distribution of party tickets and offices, poverty alleviation programmes, reservation for lower castes, and pro-poor activities of leaders gave the party a firm support base temporarily. However, with the declining influence of these leaders within the party, the backward groups eventually joined different formations.

After winning the elections each time (1980 and 1985), Solanki reopened cases of land ceiling avoidance along with reservations for backward castes in government jobs and educational institutions. The potential beneficiaries were from the KHAM groups, and the losers were upper castes. On each occasion, the province witnessed massive anti-reservation agitations led by the upper castes, resulting in open riots, especially in 1985 (Shani, 2005). The anti-reservation agitations led by the upper-caste constituencies had an avowed aim to dislodge Solanki and the Congress-led social and political formation KHAM in general. It also catapulted the combination of Brahmins, Vaniyas and Patidars to achieve upper-caste unity (Patel, 2002). In 1985, it started as riots between upper- and lower-caste Hindus over the government's new reservation policy. However, within weeks, the conflict took a religious colour as it turned into violence between Hindus and Muslims, with a key role again played by Hindutva organisations (Shani, 2010b).[14] According to Shani (2010b: 496), the violence of 1985 'marked the rise of Hindu nationalism to power in Gujarat'. The Sangh Parivar's indirect support during the anti-reservation movements and later explicit mobilisation around Hindutva ensured its ascendance amongst the upper-caste constituency. Several national-level events also helped Hindutva activities in Gujarat. For example, the Vishwa Hindu Parishad (VHP) used the Ramjanmabhoomi programme (see Kohli, 1990) to spread its wing while the RSS worked to occupy the political space left open by the Congress's growing irrelevance through a range of activities, including social work. The Bharatiya Kisan Sangh took over the farmer leadership, replacing age-old organisations such as Gujarat Khedut Samaj.

In Dholera, with the strong backing of the hitherto marginalised Kshatriyas, the Kolis, Congress won Dhandhuka in 1980 and 1985 by massive margins (Election Commission of India, 2020). However, as Darbars were upper castes, they were not among the beneficiaries of Solanki's policies. Already displeased at losing some of their land and traditional influence, they viewed Solanki's policies with suspicion. The anti-reservation agitations of the 1980s and other failures of the Solanki government provided a platform to groom an anti-Congress constituency. At the same time, for Darbar youths, disillusioned with the loss of their traditional influence in society, the voluntary work of the RSS that involved tasks such as supplying aid to villages after a natural calamity gave a sense of leadership (Thachil, 2014). Hindutva organisations provided help to Hindu families during the communal riots in Ahmedabad and after the 2001 earthquake in Kutch (Simpson, 2013). Such actions helped them gain the support of new communities. Similar examples are given by other scholars such as Berenschot (2011a) and Breman (2004) from the urban centre of Ahmedabad. Ramakumar (2017) gives a very good analysis of how the New Farmers movements of the 1980s were infiltrated by the RSS and how in the current decade, due to the agrarian crisis in the countryside, youth are being attracted to the RSS. The upper-caste coalition that emerged in Gujarat emboldened the BJP. The party decided to play an 'exclusively rabid Hindu card' in municipal elections after 1985 (Patel, 2002: 4833). The outcome was positive for the BJP as it won municipal elections in Ahmedabad, Vadodara, Surat, Rajkot, Bhavnagar, Jamnagar—the major cities that constitute a quarter of the population of the province (Patel, 2002: 4833). Following this, BJP founder L. K. Advani's Ram Rath Yatra in 1989–1990, that passed through large areas of Gujarat, left behind a long trail of communal violence.[15]

At the national level, as the Mandal Commission's recommendation for reservations in jobs and educational establishments for OBCs was accepted in 1989 by the federal government, India witnessed nationwide protests by upper-caste students, showing cleavages within the Hindu population.[16] From the Gujarat experience of 1985, the Sangh organisations were armed with the skill of managing such anti-reservation agitations, supporting them first and then turning them into an anti-Muslim agitation. Following the exact template at the national level, they initially supported these anti-reservation protests, while trying to shift the debate by raising the issue of Ram Janmabhhomi and uniting all Hindus under one flag to fight for the religion. Shani (2010a) argues that manufacturing Muslims into a viable threat to India and to its Hindu majority in the 1980s was related to growing caste tensions. This insecurity was particularly amongst the minority upper castes about the growing assertion of the lower castes, which threatened to upset the Hindu moral order (Mehta, 2010). Although, from a very different context and period, Simpson (2013) describes how the discourses of anti-Muslim entered the reconstruction process of post-2001 Kutch, ultimately helping Hindutva organisations and leaders to gain ground.

Over the subsequent decades, the RSS and BJP increased their support amongst 'lower' castes. Their growth amongst 'lower' castes since the 1990s has attracted the attention of many scholars who connected this vital shift to a 'politics of recognition' (Berenschot, 2011b; G. Shah, 1996; Shani, 2007; Yagnik and Sheth, 2005). While the Hindutva organisations presented a unified platform of all Hindus and shifted their opposition towards reservation policies in the 1980s, the 'lower' castes turned to the 'BJP out of a desire for social recognition, since they hoped to gain respectability and social mobility' (Berenschot, 2011b: 385). In addition, another class-based argument proposes that deindustrialisation and subsequent informalisation of labour in the 1980s in cities such as Ahmedabad, which resulted in a scramble for jobs and resources, enabled Sangh organisations to tap into the increased precarity that occurred simultaneously along with heightened communal tensions (Breman, 2004). With the background of joblessness, general precarity and the recurring religious riots, Hindutva groups took on the role of service providers, helping them make inroads into the 'lower' castes who were hitherto not aligned with the Hindutva project (Berenschot, 2011a; Shani, 2007; Spodek, 2011).

Moment Four: Liberalisation and Modi

The BJP combined with Janata Dal of Chimanbhai Patel (who left the Congress) to capture power in 1990 although the coalition broke after a year in power. However, the BJP won the provincial elections in 1995. As India opened its economy through policies of liberalisation, the BJP warmed up to the idea of a liberalised economy, shunning their previous incongruent economic policies. Keshubhai Patel, a long-time RSS leader from the Patidar caste, became the chief minister of Gujarat and brought a clear Hindutva agenda into the politics of the province. For example, he removed the ban preventing government employees from becoming active RSS members and filled the various educational and employment bodies with RSS personnel (Simpson, 2006: 341). A strong OBC leader from the BJP, Shankarsinh Vaghela, rebelled and went on to become the chief minister. But the next election in 1998 put the BJP firmly in power after which they have never lost a provincial election in Gujarat. Keshubhai's non-performing government failed miserably in dealing with the damaging earthquake of 2001. This led to Modi being installed as the chief minister. Taking forward the agendas of Hindutva and liberalisation, Modi continued to win elections as the BJP created a hegemony.

The marching together of Hindutva and liberalisation in the 1990s is aptly summarised by the interesting pattern Sud (2012: 33) alludes to: 'From 1995, three of Gujarat's five chief ministers—Keshubhai Patel, Shankarsinh Vaghela, and Modi—owe their political rise to the RSS while the non-RSS chief ministers: Dilip Parikh and Suresh Mehta are industrialists.' Even the two most recent chief ministers, Vijay Rupani and Bhupendra Patel, have worked with the RSS for a long time. When Modi was at the helm of the government from 2001, the association of Hindutva and liberalisation became more glaring. With a close overlap of business and politics, what we see was the 'Gujarat model of development'.

During the liberalisation era since the early 1990s, economic reforms in Gujarat have pushed up the GDP rate significantly (Dholakia and Dholakia, 2015). The reform era policies of the provincial government furthered the privatisation agenda that had been slyly in place in Gujarat since independence as Hirway and Mahadevia (2005) argue. For example, the Gujarat Infrastructure Agenda 2010 published in 1995 by the first BJP government laid down a blueprint for the privatisation of infrastructure (GIDB, 1999). A direct outcome of the vision document was the framing of the Build-Own-Operate-Transfer policy, providing a legal framework for private participation in the financing, construction, maintenance and operation of infrastructure projects even in sectors such as health, water supply and sewerage, and education (Hirway and Mahadevia, 2005). Similarly, the New Industrial and Incentive Policy 1995–2000 laid out concessions for industries that were willing to set up their own infrastructure. Direct investments made by industrial units in fixed assets, such as residential colonies, hospitals and schools for employees were eligible for tax incentives (Dholakia and Dholakia, 2015).

As the Dholera SIR project is essentially about creating a thriving future city, let us look at why urbanisation is so central to Modi's visions. Amongst the bigger provinces in India, Gujarat at 42 per cent is the fourth most urbanised province in India (Census India, 2011). Since liberalisation, the focus on urbanisation has increased dramatically. The national policy discourse has also changed since the 1990s as the emphasis shifted from balanced regional development to an urbanisation strategy in which cities and towns were being seen as growth centres and destinations for domestic and international investment that was discussed in the previous chapter (Desai, 2008). Following this pattern, provincial governments, including Gujarat, made significant reforms in the institutional architecture of urban and infrastructure governance. Along with the private sector, transnational institutions such as the World Bank and Asian Development Bank became involved (Mahadevia, 1998). For example, the Ahmedabad city authorities introduced road development and beautification projects such as the 1995–1996 redevelopment project of C. G. Road, delivered through a public–private partnership. The municipal corporation contributed 10 per cent of the cost while a private company put forward the rest in return for advertisement rights on the road for seven years (Desai, 2008). Large-scale infrastructure and beautification projects followed, including the Sabarmati River Front development, Kankaria Lakefront development and Bhadra redevelopment projects along with transportation projects such as the Bus Rapid Transit System, Ahmedabad Metro or the Ahmedabad Suburban Railway (Desai, 2008).[17]

One of the key laws that has been used for such infrastructure or residential projects is the Gujarat Town Planning and Urban Development Act (GTPUDA) that provided the Development Plan–Town Planning Schemes (DP–TPS)[18] mechanism. It was revived by Ahmedabad municipal chairman Surendra Patel, an RSS member and BJP treasurer during his tenure from 1997 to 2005. Its usage multiplied when 224 draft TP schemes were prepared during 2000–2016—compared to the twenty-four schemes during the 1976–1999 period (Mahadevia et al., 2018). This suited the real estate lobby that emerged as a potent force in the 1980s, highly represented by the Patidar community that sponsored many of the agitations of the previous decades. One key link of the real estate lobby to the BJP was Surendra Patel who himself was a Patidar. The troika was completed by the presence of the architecture and planning consultancy, Environmental Planning Collaborative, led by a Patidar, that received the commissions for most of these projects.[19]

These urban transformations, however, have come to represent an elitist vision of developing cities, such as Ahmedabad, termed 'world-class' that could attract more investments while catering to BJP's core aspirational constituency of the upper castes and middle class (Mahadevia et al., 2018). While the middle class stood behind the state and its aspirational projects, the projects were equally controversial for evicting substantial numbers of urban poor citizens. This created what Mahadevia called the 'schism of high growth and poor employment for a very large section of the population, high growth and low food consumption of a section of the population, and high investments in urban infrastructure and inadequate attention to the housing of the urban poor….' (2014: 374). Despite this, the voting patterns suggest that the BJP had a greater advantage in urban areas (Mahaprashasta, 2017; G. Shah, 1996; Tiwari and Verma, 2017).

Coming to power against the backdrop of the Gujarat earthquake of 2001 that ravaged part of the province, taking close to 20,000 lives, Modi's initial few months witnessed another set of mass deaths, this time with the state being hand in glove with the culprits. One of the most widespread and brutal communal riots in India took place in 2002, referred to as the Gujarat communal riots, which led to the deaths of approximately 2,000 people, the majority of whom were Muslims, while several hundreds of thousands were displaced (Sud, 2012).[20] The communal riots witnessed the heavy-handedness of the administration and Modi was criticised globally for his complicity (Patel, 2002; Varadarajan, 2002). However, winning the provincial assembly elections that followed the anti-Muslim riots with an increased majority in December 2002, Modi made significant efforts to attract investments into the province. One important institution for this was the biennale Vibrant Gujarat Global Summit (VGGS), an event to promote Gujarat as a safe investment destination for corporations and investors. Through VGGS, the government was looking forward to reviving the confidence of both domestic and foreign investors and the first event in 2003 led to the signing of hundreds of memoranda of understanding (MoUs) (Mahadevia, 2005). Interestingly, this approach towards a neoliberal development model had a dose of Hindutva. In 2003, when launched, the event was consciously scheduled during the important Hindu festival of Navaratri that is widely celebrated in Gujarat. That year, it was celebrated by the provincial government as the International Navaratri Festival, spending millions from the state coffers. The idea was to show normalcy as every citizen comes out on the streets to participate in the festivities and 'speak for themselves and dispel the propaganda that the state is unsafe' (Chief Industrial Adviser to the government quoted in Desai, 2008: 77). This process also had parallels in Dholera. The first major neoliberal policy was the Dholera Port launched in June 2002 soon after the riots (Projects Today, 2006). During this period of heightened communal tension, Hindutva organisations such as VHPs were making inroads into the villages of Dholera. This is discussed in Chapter 4.

Over his thirteen years as Gujarat's chief minister, winning three provincial elections, Modi has been held up both as the poster boy of Hindutva as well as of development. During the period, the economy of the province grew close to double digits continuously. Support and admiration for him on the development front, and for his unapologetic slew of neoliberal policies, was expressed vigorously by a larger Indian upper and middle class, corporate elites as well as economists such as Jagdish Bhagwati or Arvind Panagariya. This became the Gujarat model of development, the era 'from 2002–2003 to 2011–2012 during which Gujarat experienced a quantum jump in its growth rate' (Hirway, 2017). Modi's interpretation of neoliberal policies drove it forward. Hirway (2017) argues that the growth strategy had three major components: 'quantum jump in infrastructure to facilitate the inflow of corporate investment; quantum jump in (business-friendly) governance to address the requirements of corporate units; and unprecedented rise in incentives and subsidies to the corporate sector to attract investments' (Hirway, 2017). The result was a 'highly dualistic economy with a small high-tech, high-income, high-growth sector and a large informal and traditional sector' (Hirway, 2017).

Beyond the close to double-digit economic growth during this period, it resulted in a significant withdrawal of the state from many spheres of development. When it comes to spending on social sectors as a percentage of provincial GDP, the Reserve Bank of India's (2016) annual report ranks Gujarat amongst the worst (fifteenth) in a list of eighteen big provinces. It spent just about 5.9 per cent, as against the national average of 7.4 per cent of provincial GDP (R. Shah, 2016). The cuts in allocations for social sectors have continued since the 1990s as the report by Reserve Bank of India (2006) showed. The Reserve Bank of India's (2020) analysis of 2019–2020 provincial budgets reports that the share of spending on education is down to 1.46 per cent of the province's GDP, from an earlier 1.87 per cent in 2014–2015. In similar ways, its healthcare expenditure stands at 0.7 per cent of the GDP, amongst the lowest Indian provinces compared to an all-India average of 1 per cent (Reserve Bank of India, 2020: 55). With respect to labour, beyond the decrease in formal jobs, most jobs were created in the informal sector with some of the lowest average daily wages, declining during Modi's rule.[21]

On the other hand, several instances of land grabs from farmers by the state and corporations emerged.[22] The development model perpetuated alliances between the state and upper caste–middle class along with the corporate sector.[23] Jaffrelot (2019) analyses the influence of the Adanis and Ambanis on the Gujarat government and their personal rapport with Modi. Data reveals that these relations have transcended many typical examples of crony capitalism (Guha Thakurta, 2015; Jaffrelot, 2019). At the same time, liberalisation policies vis-à-vis Modi, himself an OBC, created new upwardly mobile groups that Modi called the 'neo-middle class' (Jaffrelot, 2015a). Such groups who moved to cities (for various reasons such as failure of agriculture or loss of land to corporations) and aspired to improve their living were a key vote bank for Modi. They have consistently ensured a strong voter turnout and regular wins for the BJP in urban constituencies.

Unequal Development: Connection with Neoliberalism and Hindutva

Going back to where we began, why despite double-digit growth rates, has 'vikas gando thayo chhe' (development gone crazy)? Why did this movement garner such public support when Gujarat has supposedly been amongst the most developed provinces, where according to scholars such as of Bhagwati and Panagariya, the Gujarat model of development has addressed issues of poverty, health, education or unemployment? We find that with the rise of Hindutva and neoliberalism in Gujarat, unequal development is simultaneously both the cause as well as the result of their ascendance.

Historical accounts point towards the significant unequal development that goes back to the British era when roads were built and railway lines were laid down. Regional inequalities were evident in the core–periphery dichotomy in almost every aspect of life (Hirway, 1995; Patel, 1991). Peripheral regions such as Saurashtra and Kutch reeled under severe under-investment for decades. The Nehruvian developmental state was to address some of these inequalities; however, it was circumvented by various lobbies. Apart from geographical inequalities, there are sectoral inequalities, most glaringly between agriculture and industry, especially with respect to production and the workforce they employ (Hirway, 2017). Contributing 10–15 per cent to GDP, agriculture employs half of the workforce while only 16 per cent of the workforce was employed in the manufacturing sector, contributing one-third of the GDP. There are also huge disparities within the agricultural sector. Canal-irrigated areas are concentrated in the core. Most districts of the periphery are still drought-prone and depend on groundwater for agriculture and domestic use. As these areas increasingly face a water crisis, the local population seeks seasonal employment in cities (Hirway and Mahadevia, 2005). Farmers in the core areas have often diversified their economic interests and are relatively well networked in political circles. Beyond the regional inequalities in agriculture, there is also the factor of caste. Small and marginal farmers belong largely to

OBC groups (GoG, 2016). This was certainly an outcome of the failure of land reforms of the 1950s and 1960s in the core region where wealthy and upper-caste communities circumvented the policies on land. In Dholera too, large landholdings remain in the hands of the Darbars even above the land ceiling whereas Kolis remain marginal farmers.

The core–periphery dichotomy inevitably played out in the trend of industrialisation and urbanisation. Historically investment had been heavily concentrated along the Golden Corridor (Mahadevia, 2005; Patel, 1991). Similarly, urbanisation remained concentrated in the core represented by Gujarat's three largest cities—Ahmedabad, Surat and Vadodara. Although the periphery has known urban centres such as Rajkot and Bhavnagar built by the princely kingdom, two-thirds of the total urban population in the province live in the core (Mahadevia, 2005). While the core has half of its population living in urban areas, the corresponding figures in the periphery are less than one-third. Notably, even the communal riots had a core–periphery dichotomy as most of these took place along the Ahmedabad–Vadodara–Godhra–Surat corridor (Golden Corridor). An excellent study by Shinoda (2002) buttresses the unequal development thesis along caste lines, which found that Brahmins, Banias and Patidars were owners in all types of industries, especially in capital-intensive fields, with a higher concentration in central Gujarat.

In the post-liberalisation period, although there was a chance to address some of these inequalities, what the peripheral regions received were mostly capital-intensive, resource-extracting or high-polluting industries, which furthered existing inequality. While the natural resource-rich coastal regions of Saurashtra and Kutch became the hub of large and medium industries, the new export-targeted capital-intensive industries are islands of modern production amidst an impoverished hinterland (Mahadevia, 2005). At the same time, with the help of government policies, these industries alienate land from the farmers while water resources are diverted to industries. Job creation has taken a major hit as the average investment per project in large and medium industries has gone up while the average employment per project has fallen. Emblematic of this problem is the Tata Nano plant whose arrival was celebrated as a major coup of Modi's policies. The factory that received subsidies amounting to billions of rupees barely employed a few hundred and was ultimately shut down.[24]

The outcome of the decade-long asymmetrical growth that was the Gujarat model of development was seen in the National Sample Survey Office data of 2018 that itself became controversial after the Modi government decided not to release it. The report found that unemployment reached a forty-five-year high nationally, while in Gujarat the rate of unemployment rose more rapidly than in other Indian provinces—from 0.5 per cent in 2011–2012 to 4.8 per cent in 2017–2018 (*Economic Times*, 2019). The number of jobless youths rose exponentially both in rural (from a mere 0.8 per cent in 2011–2012 to 14.9 per cent in 2017–2018) and urban Gujarat (from 2.1 per cent to 10.7 per cent) (*Economic Times*, 2019). These changes had an impact on the Patidar and OBC youth agitation between 2015 and 2017 for the very campaign of 'vikas gando thayo chhe'. The Patidar community that led the anti-reservation agitations of the 1980s against the Congress were now on the streets against the BJP government despite having the chief minister and the finance minister from their own community, demanding reservations. Similarly, the constituency of urban OBCs, the neo-middle class that stood solidly behind Modi, now turned against the BJP government.[25]

With recurring agitation-based politics that was also targeted at Muslims, religious tensions and conflicts stalled a genuine political debate on economic policies over the years, especially during Modi's tenure as the chief minister. While many of the reforms were introduced by stealth, elections were often on the issue of support for or rejection of Hindutva, and not on the government's performance or the right kind of development policies (Mahadevia, 2005). Modi has used communal, anti-minority, sub-nationalism or Hindutva planks in each of the three provincial elections he has won. The first time when elections were fought on the platform of development, that is, the 2017 elections, the BJP barely managed to cling on to power. The charismatic Modi saved the day for the BJP as he fought again on the grounds of Gujarati Asmita,[26] coming up with fictional stories of how a Gujarati (himself) has been targeted by the Congress by joining hands with enemy Pakistan (Naqvi, 2017).

The fact that the Gujarat government has been decreasing social expenditure is well in tune with the minimal state that the Sangh Parivar has always cultivated (Corbridge and Hariss, 2000; Jaffrelot, 1996). Hindutva actors rejected the Nehruvian state because of its attempts at reforming society—when, for the Hindu nationalists, the existing social order had to prevail (Jaffrelot, 1996). This social order was essentially elitist with the upper caste–middle class alliance. This social order was essentially elitist with the upper caste–middle class alliance. Over the years, the BJP has retained this social basis but has also developed links with big corporate houses (Jaffrelot, 2019). This explains why an unequal development model continued to survive and why there has rarely been a healthy debate about unequal development or the Gujarat model of development.

Following Mahadevia (2005), unequal development helps further both Hindutva and neoliberalism. Both neoliberalism and Hindutva are ultimately exclusivist in nature (Mahadevia, 2005). This was clear from the post-liberalisation policies that furthered unequal development across sectors, geography, caste or religious segments. This unequal development excludes large groups of people from the ambits of development. Like Hindutva, the Gujarat model of development (or liberalisation policies) is not about equity (Mahadevia, 2005). Since it is in the interests of the political and economic elite (who are mostly upper castes) to preserve the prevalent economic order, they seek refuge in a social ideology that legitimises the status quo. Hindutva ideologies in all their manifestations have never questioned caste and class inequalities. The social order that is envisaged by Hindutva and neoliberalism both converge on the belief that one has to be satisfied with whatever endowment one has from birth. Neither Hindutva nor neoliberalism is interested in the redistribution of wealth. The outcome of these dynamics was the starting point of the chapter: 'vikas gando thayo chhe'.

It was presumed that rapid economic growth would lead to improved well-being of the population as a whole. However, as the chapter has shown, this has not yet happened and is less likely to happen in the near future as the situation worsens further. As we have seen, the Gujarat model entailed high growth numbers for the economy through a close business–politics–bureaucratic alliance that ran the state coffers dry, ultimately resulting in the non-delivery of many of the social provisions with which the state was tasked. Taking this debate forward, the next chapters will unfold the realities of the actually existing state (AES) at the ground level.

Notes

1. 'Patidar' is a landed caste spread across the province of Gujarat and a significant diaspora spread over Europe, North America and Eastern and Southern Africa. They were hired as tenants by the landlords and princely states to farm large tracts of land of which ownership post-independence was transferred to the Patidar tenants through the land reforms. Post-independence, the community has diversified into secondary and tertiary sectors and has continued to influence the province's politics. In Dholera, although only one of the twenty-two villages has a Patidar majority, their financial and political strength has ensured a key role.
2. Refer to Sud (2017) for a summary of these agitations.

3. See Breman (1974, 1985, 1996, 2002, 2004), Hirway (1995), Rutten (1986, 1995), G. Shah (1970, 1974a, 1974b, 1975, 1996, 1998a, 1998b), Shinoda (2002) and Streefkert (1997).

4. Through economic liberalisation, an infrastructure-based development model—first the coastal Saurashtra, and later Kutch—was included in what came to be called the 'Silver Corridor'.

5. These include Gujarat Industrial Investment Corporation, Gujarat Industrial Development Corporation, Gujarat State Finance Corporation and Industrial Extension Bureau.

6. This does not mean that farmers were less influential before the green revolution. In fact, farmers in Gujarat were at the forefront of the fight for independence under Gujarati leaders of national prominence such as Mahatma Gandhi and Vallabhbhai Patel. The green revolution increased their financial strength, many of whom also diversified their surpluses. See Gidwani (2008).

7. Kshatriya is one of the four social orders of Hindu society constituting the ruling class often associated as the military caste. The traditional function of the Kshatriyas is to protect society by fighting in wartime and governing in peacetime (Oxford English Dictionary). Refer to G. Shah (1975) for an analysis of Kshatriya groups in Gujarat. See note 12 in Chapter 1 for a detailed note on caste.

8. Not to be confused with the Dholavira port of the Indus Valley Civilisation, the remains of which are located in the district of Kutch. The other port of the Indus Valley Civilisation is Lothal, 35 kilometres from Dholera.

9. A *sarpanch* is the head of the village-level local self-government in India. S/he is the main point of contact between the village population and the government officials.

10. For details on the 1969 riot and events, refer to G. Shah (1970) and Jaffrelot and Gayer (2012).

11. Romila Thapar (2000, 2005) deals in great depth with the subject of such imagined and real foreign aggressors through an analysis of the historiography on the destruction of the Somnath temple by Mahmud of Ghazni. Also see Pandey (1992), Van der Veer (1994) and Yagnik and Sheth (2005).

12. Scholars such as Shani (2005) have questioned this thesis, arguing the absence of incidents of religious violence until 1969, to be followed only in 1985 after which they became a recurring affair. Shani (2010b) brings up other issues like the control of bootlegging in the 1980s as key factors in which some of the killings were disparate incidents that did not have communal motives.

13. Several commentators such as Bhagat-Ganguly (2015), Jones and Jones (1976), Sanghavi (2010), G. Shah (1974a; 1974b; 1976, 1987) and Yagnik and Bhatt (1984) have covered the agitation politics in Gujarat.

14. For details on the events leading to anti-reservation riots and then to anti-Muslim riots, see Engineer, (1985), Ghassem-Fachandi (2012), Sanghavi (2010), Shani (2005, 2007, 2010a, 2010b) and Spodek (1989).

15. *Rath yatra* usually refers to a public procession in a chariot. For details on these events, see Guha (2008), Jaffrelot (1996, 2009), Panikkar (1993) and Srinivas (1991).

16. For details on these events refer to Corbridge and Harriss (2000) and Kohli (1990).

17. The politics of these projects, the impact on the economic as well as the socio-cultural profile is covered by a range of scholars: Desai, (2008, 2012), Mahadevia (1997, 2003, 2006, 2014), Mehta (2016), Mehta and Banerjee (2017), R. Shah (2016), Spodek (2011), Yagnik and Sheth (2011).

18. For details on DP–TPS mechanism, see Chapter 7. Also see Ballaney and Patel (2009) and Jain (2019).

19. The same firm of Bimal Patel has gone national with Narendra Modi becoming the prime minister in 2014. It has received several commissions for public projects across the country over the last few years. This includes one of the most prestigious and controversial recent projects, the Central Vista Project in New Delhi (Trivedy, 2019). This project plans to significantly change the heritage area that houses the Parliament in New Delhi (referred to as Lutyens' Delhi after the architect Edward Lutyens), with proposals to construct a new office and residence for the Indian prime minister in line with the French Élysée Palace; a new parliament building along with other massive constructions (Bhatia, 2020; Kapoor, 2020).

20. For details of the events, refer to Human Rights Watch (2002), International Initiative for Justice (2003), Raza and Hashmi (2002) and Varadarajan (2002). Also see Jaffrelot (2012) for an analysis of the Hindutva-isation of state apparatuses in Gujarat, especially around the 2002 riots.

21. The book by Hirway et al. (2014) covers these aspects in great detail. Also see Hirway (2015, 2017), Hirway and Shah (2011), Jaffrelot (2015a, 2019), Mahadevia (2005) and Sen and Drèze (2013).

22. Bahree (2014), Lobo and Kumar (2009), Juneja (2015) and Sud (2009, 2012) cover instances of land grab.

23. Sud (2009) has made an argument in the case of Gujarat that it exemplified a 'business friendly' pattern, more than a 'market-friendly' economy, even after liberalisation. Kohli (2006a and 2006b) and Rodrik and Subramanian (2004) earlier made the case for India.

24. Refer to Guha Thakurta (2009), Jaffrelot (2019) and Outlook (2017) for details on subsidies, job creation and the meagre labour wages in the Tata Nano project.

25. See Hirway (2016), Kothari (2016), Mehta (2015) and Sud (2017) for a detailed analysis of the protests.

26. Asmita means identity or soul often used towards the idea of Gujarati self-pride. See Bobbio (2012), Jaffrelot (2016) and Suhrud (2008).

4

Development Neither Reaches
Us Nor Leaves Us

First, it was development, by ... canal water. We were ready to give away our lands. They took those.... Then they came up with the Kalpasar dam. Nothing happened.... But we had land to cultivate.... Now, we have roads, probably canal water soon. Everything. But no land to cultivate. This is the joke of development.... Development neither reaches us nor leaves us. It's an illusion.... After that, they almost built the Dholera port [*chuckles*].... But, this time, we ... were tired of development. So, they came to force development on us....

Bhaubhai was often sarcastic while discussing the possibility of the smart city project being delivered. The fatigue around development that the comments above highlight was largely because of its non-delivery. A Congress party supporter, he was critical of the current spate of projects in Dholera, resenting the role of private corporations and land speculation which, he argued, were the reasons for the region's under-development. According to him, if the government was so keen to develop a city in Dholera, 'it should have been modelled after Gandhinagar and not a private company-built city like in America'. A key member of Bhal Bachao Samiti, the farmers' group protesting against the smart city project, Bhaubhai often spoke about the importance of the 'sarkar' in delivering development since private companies would never care about the locals. This perspective of Bhaubhai contrasts significantly with Pradeepsinh, a local BJP leader:

I built the Hotel Vision Modi.... We all have a responsibility in the development of Dholera. That was my part. Farmers' part is to give up their land. And with the SIR, we have such a good development project here.... Go and see the number of [motor]bikes and cars in Dholera people have now. They have smartphones, this big [*gestures with his right hand*].... In 2009, we had just two banks here, now there are six banks, today we have 200 times more deposits.... You see ... newly constructed houses, ask them when these were built, they would tell you only after 2009.... It does not matter if the smart city is built or not. Our villagers have developed even before a brick has been laid....

During the hour-long interview in Hindi, Pradeepsinh used the English word 'vision' more than ten times, mostly stressing that one needs to have a vision to keep and multiply money. He would often underline the role of Narendra Modi in delivering 'development' and how the 'Modi-sarkar'[1] continues to do a great job for Dholera. For him, 'development' was inherently linked to Modi. Even if private companies were throwing money into Dholera, it was down to Modi's 'vision' and 'planning'. His use of the word 'vision' could also be linked to the hotel that he built and named 'Hotel Vision Modi', discussed in the next chapters.

In many ways, the 'development' projects have different meanings for different stakeholders. Bhaubhai and Pradeepsinh represent two significantly varying discourses around development. While the former spoke of the loss of land as an irony of development, the latter portrayed it to be villagers carrying out their 'part' in the development process, as if it was their duty to hand over their land. Compared to Bhaubhai's comments portraying development as a responsibility for the state to deliver, Pradeepsinh saw the project as essentially bringing in money to the area and giving locals a chance to develop. He argued that those who had the 'vision' could keep and multiply their money whereas the 'rest wasted the money on prostitutes, alcohol or gambling'. According to him, an individual's choice and ability shape whether they take hold of the chance for development.

It should be asked why, for such two very different individuals, development is so central in discussing the state. Scholars have pointed out that, over the decades, the sphere of the state has expanded in response to the political necessities of development (Corbridge et al., 2005). At the same time, development or welfare have been key sources for the state to create legitimacy, although the ways in which they have been planned and delivered changed over the years.[2] Beyond this legitimacy, development has provided the platform to reimagine the idea of the state, whether this was the Nehruvian version of socialism or the current era of neoliberalism. In this reimagining, certain actors such as Nehru or Modi become central, essentially riding on their ideas about development. As development ideas changed from a state-led canal project to a privately built city in Dholera, what is important within this is how the state, its constituents and its relationship with citizens have been significantly transformed. Discussing this, the chapter reveals the state in practice.

Re-imagining the State through Hindutva and Neoliberalism

Jessop (1990) argues that to implement its professed objectives, a new political regime usually undertakes a state project. In the desire to transform the social status quo, political forces need comprehensive institutional reforms and a certain reinvention of the state. As the institutions of the state are thoroughly reformed, the society in effect replicates the trend. Prakash (2003) argued that the new regime has two domains to capture: social and material. Hence, Nehru attempted to put socialist economic ideas at the centre to build a secular egalitarian society (somewhat unsuccessfully). In similar ways, the Hindutva group's project of 're-imagination of the state' or, in simple terms making India a 'Hindu Rashtra', involves the restructuring of the social domain by consolidating 'all social groups except the minorities for dominating electoral politics' (Prakash, 2003: 1602). This, in turn, would contribute to its objective in the material domain, that is, sanctioning certain castes or classes 'to own and control productive assets and sustain the existing hierarchy in social relationships through the control of state apparatus' (Prakash, 2003: 1602). This would ultimately help redefine the state into what the Hindutva forces would prefer: the Hindu state.[3]

Within Hindutva's reimagining of the state through development, Modi's approach is significant, having come up with an unapologetic brand of neoliberalism and Hindutva. His politics of Hindutva and ideas of delivering development through neoliberal policies have marched forward. As we saw in the previous chapter, Modi has been condemned for his administration's complicity in the communal violence of 2002 along with criticism of the economic policies for delivering growth at the cost of human development. However, he has gone ahead unabashedly with both. His policies have also been important in trying to create a new discourse of development, even if divisive. Kashwan (2014) postulated that Modi differentiates his approach to development from the Congress in a clear manner. His vision of market-led development is not based on an apologetic explanation of trickle-down theories. During an election rally in 2009, Modi said, 'For 60 years, the Congress Party has been doling out hens and goats in the name of tribal development; I want to ask you why my Adivasi brothers should not aspire for floriculture?'

Kashwan (2014) argues that although his development policies have rarely integrated Adivasis (or similar categories) into markets,[4] he manages to stir a debate or create an impression around their possible participation as market players. A quote on Modi's website during the 2014 election campaign said, 'Forget if you are rich or poor. All you need is faith in yourself....' (Kashwan, 2014). As BJP's campaigning has shown a clear championing of the neoliberal model in recent years, it is essentially tied to how the party wants to reimagine the idea of the Indian state.

Chapter 2 demonstrated how the state has moved away from the post-colonial state that followed the Nehruvian model of development at an 'ideational level' to the era of the post-liberalisation phase. Towards this, Sud (2012) has shown how the Gujarat state has moved from its policies of 'land to the tiller' to those of land liberalisation. This has been further accelerated during Modi's tenure, aptly shown by the fact that the Gujarat Industrial Development Corporation (GIDC) acquired 4,620 hectares of land from farmers in 1990–2001, which increased to 21,308 hectares in 2001–2011 (Hirway et al., 2014: 160–166). This was often at the expense of the state's agricultural capabilities while land was usually sold to industrialists at less than the market price (Jaffrelot, 2017).

Take the case of the Special Investment Region (SIR) Act of 2009 that marked a significant step in unapologetically courting corporations. The SIR Act intended 'to come up with a legal framework to enable the development of mega investment regions and industrial areas in the state' which will be 'global hubs of economic activity supported by world-class infrastructure, premium civic amenities, centers of excellence and proactive policy framework' (GoG, 2009: 01). In similar ways, the Gujarat Industrial Policy of 2009 was explicitly designed for making the province the most attractive investment destination in the world. Since land with the right kind of infrastructure is key to compete, the adequate provisioning and availability of land was urgent. This 'interweaving of ideas is seen not only in the discourse of the official state as a whole but also at the level of individuals within the state' as depicted by Modi in his argument regarding the market in the previous paragraph (Sud, 2009: 655). Interestingly for Dholera, such ideas were even carried out by the likes of Pradeepsinh or the many BJP supporters.

This chapter deconstructs the state through ideas of development while documenting the arrival of neoliberal development, an entry that emboldened the actors of Hindutva. Within the concept of the actually existing state (AES), this chapter deals with the first proposition that the AES is characterised by both formal and shadow elements. As Barbara Harriss-White (2003: 70) contends, the official part of the state has been hollowed out especially since the 1980s, being replaced by what she called the 'shadow state', a vast assemblage of brokers, political workers or crooks. In similar ways, in Dholera, the formal state and its shadow exist side by side, complementing each other's roles on occasion. The shadow elements are evident when formal state officials accept tribute, patronage or use their office to corner private benefits, whereas non-state actors use the shadow of the state to earn their livelihoods. In the process, the activities of the formal state are shadowed from within or from outside and by both state and non-state actors. This makes the state porous to the actors of society as well as businesses. This is why, to understand the state in Dholera, we need to look through the lens of the AES. To do this, the chapter looks at the changes that came just before and after the announcement of a series of development projects in the 2000s.

The Start of Neoliberalism Laced with Hindutva in Dholera

The Narmada Canal project of the 1960s did not trigger any major land sales in Dholera other than farmers losing land to the government for canal construction. Similarly, the next project, the Kalpasar Dam, initially mooted in the 1970s did not affect any changes in the daily lives of most farmers in Dholera. Both projects remained on paper for most of their history. What massively changed the complexion of land transactions in the region is the Dholera Port launched in 2002. However, as many of the locals claim and the land sale records in part prove, land sales started before the announcement of the project.

As discussed, Hindutva organisations such as the RSS took root in Dholera in the 1970s. In the 1980s and 1990s, the more militant groups such as VHP, Bajrang Dal or ABVP spread further in the region, especially among college-going students from the upper castes. Aside from college students, upper-caste youth visiting nearby towns and cities, which were rife with loose groups that had representations of these organisations, helped the spread of Hindutva ideologies. In fact, a Darbar leader from Dholera made this point: 'We should have listened to Bhupen Bhai (Bhupendrasinh Chudasama) and joined the BJP early in the 1980s.... You see the outcomes now. We are far behind the Patidars who were given the lands we ruled. They joined other higher castes to corner everything in the 1980s and 1990s....'[5] Similarly, the few Koli youths (such as Naranbhai, who features prominently in the later chapters) who had friendships with upper-caste peers or ventured out to nearby cities in search of jobs, were introduced to these organisations.

The Rath Yatras, the Ram Janmabhoomi movement and the frequent incidents of religious riots against Muslims in the last two decades of the twentieth century gave Hindutva organisations important space in the media and public discourses in the province. Although there has not been any recorded religious violence in Dholera, news of riots in bigger cities often spread like wildfire. With a biased press, this became easier,[6] essentially giving the Hindutva organisations a doorway to the villages of the region. This penetration was eased by the involvement of Hindutva groups such as the RSS in development works.

Although it was in discussion for a while, Dholera Port project was announced in June 2002 to be developed as a General Cargo port (Prabhune, 2006; Projects Today, 2006). The project first went to the construction company JK Cements who later formed a joint venture with the Adanis to build the port. Adani Group is an Indian multinational corporation whose founder, Gautam Adani, has faced allegations of crony capitalism due to his proximity to Modi. The Adanis had already been into the port business, having built and owned the Mundra port in the Kutch region of Gujarat. The project was ultimately transferred to the Adanis alone (Manoj, 2007). Later, a chemical industrial estate to be fronted by the GIDC was added. This was, however, met with protests by local farmers who filed a Public Interest Litigation at the Gujarat High Court arguing that the project would harm the wildlife sanctuary that bordered the proposed estate. It was the first instance when local farmers joined hands against state projects. This same group of farmers then went on to undertake their protracted struggle against the current Dholera SIR project discussed later in Chapter 7. After the high court raised objections, the chemical industrial estate project was shelved and not much is known.

When Modi came to power in 2001, Gujarat witnessed one of the most horrific episodes of communal riots that started in February 2002 with skirmishes continuing into the next couple of months. In June of the same year, the Dholera Port project was officially launched. Around the time when the project was launched, these villages were easily accessible to Hindutva organisations. The fear of the other was palpable, due to the widespread media coverage amid open support for Modi's acts by the vernacular press. As reflected in Vijayrajsinh's statement during an interview, 'The Sangh organisations, especially VHP, were mostly *saving* the locals from others' (emphasis added to highlight his sarcasm). Around this time, a new set of land buyers arrived in these villages. As farmers recollected during interviews, they were ignorant about the Port project. Vijayrajsinh first mentioned the presence of people associated with VHP in these land transactions:

> … Why don't you examine the role of the BJP politicians? I can show you the resorts and [Town Planning] schemes[7] around Dholera which are owned by [*mentions the name of two ministers*] or their sons…. And why just the BJP? Do you know Sinha [pseudonym], the VHP leader?[8] He is a doctor. His brother is also a doctor…. During the Gujarat riots, or may be a little before or after, when the Port was announced, these people frequented our villages. It was funny because they were here to buy land…. That is how they saved my village from the Mughals [*chuckles*].

In other villages, interviewees often pointed out how a motley group of businessmen from Ahmedabad came shopping for Dholera's farmlands during this time. They were mostly doctors and other professionals. It was not always clear whether the sale started before the announcement of the project. But it was certainly around the time when communal passions were high. In fact, Pradeepsinh, the local BJP leader, while arguing how the SIR project was helpful for the locals, blurted out something, which buttressed the same:

> … See all these doctors, lawyers from Ahmedabad came to give us money in Dholera. Earlier, they were charging us millions of rupees for our surgeries, court cases in Ahmedabad. Do you think if Modiji did not announce this project, we could have access to their money? Sinha Bhai brought a lot of his friends for our lands. I know they bought at a cheaper price, but it led to many new buyers from Ahmedabad….

When asked who Sinha was, he realised that he should not have mentioned the name and covered it up by saying he was a friend from Ahmedabad. More than the role of one or two Sinhas, it is important to see how the politics of Hindutva, and its actors by extension, fluently dissipated into real estate. It also illustrates the role of Hindutva actors in taking a neoliberal project forward. Although non-state actors, they draw their power from associations with the state. VHP has been instrumental in enabling the BJP to gain power at various levels. The organisation is often seen as part of the state, influencing significant policy directions of the government. Scholars have argued that along with the decline of the Congress party and the growth of regional parties, the rise of Hindutva has been an outcome of the gradual shift in favour of an increasingly market-driven economy that worked itself through the political system (Desai, 2011b: 358; Nielsen and Nilsen, 2016). It can certainly be argued as to which one predated the other, whether neoliberalism helped Hindutva or if Hindutva led to neoliberalism. However, what is certain is their interconnectedness. This is one answer to why Hindutva goes together with neoliberalism, a question this book attempts to answer. Here, the entry of the Sinhas into these villages was on the pretext of a Hindutva ideological project as people related them with the VHP and not with the Port project. However, their Hindutva was intrinsically linked with private commercial interests.

Ahmedabad International Airport and Its Ever-Shifting Locations

The development juggernaut of Dholera is often an unending puzzle with several projects thrown in, only to be cancelled or morphed into another one. For a long time, finding a site to develop a new Ahmedabad International Airport (currently Sardar Vallabhbhai Patel International Airport) remained a priority for the provincial government. Initially, there was talk of extending the airport at the existing site, but this was deemed unfeasible because of the lack of vacant land around it. Then, the site moved to Vadsar, around 20 kilometres from both Gandhinagar and Ahmedabad. Around 2007, it was moved to Fedara, located around 20 kilometres from Dholera SIR (TNN, 2008). In 2010, the site was again moved to the village of Navagam located around 8 kilometres off the Bhavnagar–Ahmedabad highway and on the north-eastern boundaries of the Dholera SIR closer to the sea (Figures 4.1 and 4.2; Arora, 2010). The relocation was met with objections from experts due to the low-lying area with major flood risks. Interestingly, in this journey through these potential sites, the fictitious airport has left a trail of real estate activities (Figure 4.3).

Relocating the Ahmedabad airport was further justified when the Gujarat International Finance Tec-City (GIFT City)[9] in Gandhinagar had to cancel its tallest building, the Diamond Tower because of its proximity to the existing Ahmedabad airport (Pathak, 2012). During an interview with Mishra (pseudonym), the governing body member of the Dholera Special Investment Regional Development Authority Directory (DSIRDA) who was also part of the apex body of GIFT city, subtly gave me evidence of the involvement of high-ranking politicians and bureaucrats in some shadow land deals of the projects:

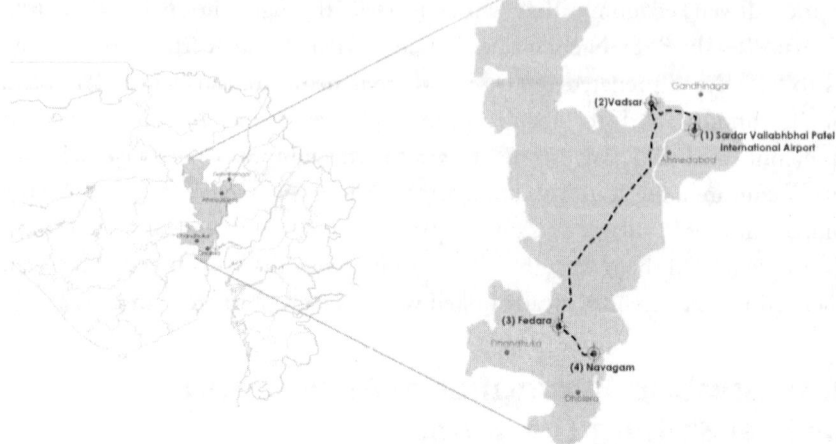

Figure 4.1   The journey for an alternative site for Ahmedabad International Airport

Source: Author.

Figure 4.2   The mud road leading to the current site of the Dholera International
Airport and the village of Nawagaon

Source: Author.

> The case of another International Airport for Ahmedabad has been there for
> a while.... Why did it go to a location, 100 kilometers from Ahmedabad after
> deciding on a nearby site.... You should check the owners of these real-estate
> projects. Get all the details, especially when they started. I am sure you will be
> puzzled and can never trace the real ones [*laughs*]. Go to the villages and ask the
> farmers or the Dalals: whom did they sold [*sic*] their land to....

Tempted by Mishra's advice, I spoke to some of the middlemen and farmers
in the area to inquire about the details of land sales. Fedara, the nearest village
on the highway from the new airport site, was on the highway connecting

Figure 4.3 Some of the real estate projects between Fedara and Dholera

Source: Author.

Dholera with Ahmedabad; it was 20 kilometres away from the north-eastern bordering village of the SIR. Similar to the frequent housing societies and resorts in the middle of nowhere along the highway, this 20 kilometre stretch is adorned with a number of hoardings amid farmland converted into residential plots. For a long stretch from Ahmedabad before arriving in Fedara, the highway remains barren. Suddenly from Fedara until the start of the SIR, there are a number of proposed real estate projects.

Tracing the documentary trail with respect to ownership of these projects is a tough and risky task as most of the projects are flooded with what is referred to as black money through *benami* (unnamed) transactions. In this, the price at which a plot of land is sold is often not shown on official papers, with mention of a much lower value. As most transactions of money take place in cash instead of bank transfers, there is no record to track them. In fact, some Dholera farmers claimed to be paid in gold biscuit bars to hide any official record. This would mean that the land, which was, for example, bought for INR 1 million per acre, would be registered in the Land Record office to be sold for INR 100,000. Hence, INR 900,000 was paid directly in cash (or in gold). The buyer's money of INR 900,000 in this case can be presumed to be untaxed and hence black. Thus, the buyer found a way to turn his black money into white (which is accounted for) by investing in land bought at the prevailing market rate but without recording the same. This is because the value of the land would be based at INR 1 million and not the INR 100,000 paid in records. With the absence of any capital gains tax, it is an extremely lucrative business. Real estate investments is a major sector absorbing black money and converting it into white.[10]

Newspapers around 2007–2009 started reporting that land was being acquired for an airport and government bureaucrats claimed that three top infrastructure companies, GMR Groups, GVK from India, and Changi of Singapore, were in the race for developing the project (R. Shah, 2008, 2009; TNN, 2009). At one point, the Adanis offered to entirely fund or even build the roads in the 30 kilometre stretch from the proposed airport to the seaport that they were to develop (TNN, 2008). A mini-Japan township project was also proposed between Fedara, the site of the international airport on one side and Dholera, the site for Adani's seaport on the other side (R. Shah, 2008). The reports further claim that this was a shot in the arm of the Modi-led government a week following the Tatas moving their factory to build Nano cars from the province of West Bengal to Gujarat (R. Shah, 2008). The government expected Japanese automakers to start factories across the province after a huge business delegation led by Modi visited Japan in April 2007 (R. Shah, 2008). The talk of building a Japanese township returned in 2018 although in a different site located next to where the Tatas moved their factory in 2008 (Ahmedabad Mirror, 2018). The Tata factory is redundant as production of Nano cars has stopped.

A middleman in land transactions, Mihir, helped me connect a few dots. Mihir spoke at length explaining how a BJP senior leader named Jain (pseudonym) was living in the town of Dhandhuka around 2005, before the 2007 provincial elections. Jain is currently a senior cabinet minister in the federal government whose henchman, Yashpalsinh, was a Dhandhuka native. Yashpalsinh's brother was Mihir's friend:

> Yashpalsinh [and Jain] both collaborated to buy land here.... Land was bought by Jain's son and Yashpal's younger brother.... They would pay the farmer, convert it into Non-Agricultural (NA) land [still in farmer's name] and then transfer it to a company. When they bought land in that area, the maximum price was INR 10,000–12,000 per *bigha*.[11] Mostly, INR 2,000, 3,000 or 4,000 per *bigha*....

After the 2007 provincial elections, which the BJP comfortably won, Jain got a set of powerful cabinet portfolios in the ministry. He then managed to get the

Fedara and Dholera projects on track. Before the elections, and hence before the announcement of the project, he already converted those agricultural lands to Non-Agricultural (NA) usage at a cheaper rate. After the announcement of the project, newspaper front pages were laden with these projects. Suddenly, these villages started witnessing government surveyors, which increased the hype. Mihir argues:

> The same land [which he bought for INR 2,000–12,000] was now worth INR 500,000 per *bigha* overnight. But forget that appreciation in price. Think about the NA converted land which was now being converted into [Town-Planning] schemes and sold in plots of 100–200 square metres. If NA [conversion] costs him INR 5,000 per *bigha* add INR 5,000–10,000 for the land, probably even lesser. It means for one square metre it's not even INR 5.… Most of the buyers are BJP leaders. You will not find any other party supporter in the land business.

Similar accounts from local land brokers were common. One broker, Ashok, who had associations with the BJP, discussed how he helped the party's leaders buy land in his village without realising that there was a big project coming. He regretted not keeping his own land. Later, he started brokering when land sales peaked further and the initial buyers such as Yashpalsinh disappeared. Land further into the interior villages, far from the highways was being sold. By then, Ashok managed to gain some information through his party links about the location of the upcoming airport. He bought two plots of land at almost ten times the price he had helped others buy. However, he seemed content as the land he bought near the new airport site was from the profit he accrued working as a broker in addition to building a two-storey house.

Politicians' business interests and the political interests of businessmen are emerging areas of research to which scholars such as Jaffrelot et al. (2019) and Sinha and Wyatt (2019) have contributed recently. Often, many of these deals entail crony capitalism if not outright unfair practices. Beyond situating some of these arguments, the prospective Dholera International Airport and its ever-changing location underline the role of profits that can be accrued in the production of such fictitious sites without delivering anything significant. The involvement of Jain in the above set of projects not only underlines how state actors corner benefits or how they are involved in private businesses but it also illustrates how state actors working in the shadows leave a trail of speculative real estate projects while going through the networks of Hindutva.

The state then becomes the arena through which the benefits of a neoliberal project are captured. In that case, party politics or Hindutva organisations help these networks. Whereas Jain comes from the formal state and draws his power from his state position, his practices are for private gains. He is here to maximise accumulation and not necessarily to further BJP ideologies or RSS works, although the latter is an outcome as material benefits often motivate the likes of Ashok to continue to associate themselves with the Hindutva groups. As Mihir claimed, most of the people in the land business are from the BJP, so one must come through a certain set of social capital or networks. Even if a person is not with the BJP, a history with the RSS comes in handy as the next vignette shows.

Travel of Neoliberal Discourses of Development from Kutch to Dholera

The previous vignettes documented how the AES is composed of the formal and shadow elements of the state and their role in taking Hindutva and neoliberal projects forward. It is also important to understand how neoliberal ideas of development travel. More importantly, we need to explore how surpluses generated from one site are invested in another, leading to a chain of speculative activities. Simultaneously, in the travels of such neoliberal ideas, often popular politicians or corporations become the binding force. The story of a few businessmen is documented here, who, based on their ideas and experiences of development in Kutch, their native region, have invested in Dholera's land. Beyond Modi, some of them also had the Adanis in mind who built the Mundra port in Kutch and made it a hub of business activities.

Prawn fisheries cropped up in Dholera around the 2000s and turned out to be a lucrative business in the vast fallow land near the sea. Businessmen from the region of Kutch used to come to the villages in Dholera during the prawn harvesting season. One of these businessmen was forty-five-year-old Shankar. In our first meeting, he repeatedly asked various questions about how the bureaucrats in Gandhinagar see the Dholera smart city project or if they are taking an active interest. A passionate Modi supporter, he had been with the BJP. I got to know more about Shankar's business since he had made a fair amount of money from land deals as a middleman in Kutch. In his role as a land broker, he was what Sud (2014: 597) called an 'aggregator', 'putting together small plots of land to produce a commercially viable unit' for the eventual buyer, mostly for incoming businessmen. Local informants claim that businessmen such as Shankar had bought vast amounts of land in Dholera, although many of them soon sold those. According to Shankar, he had witnessed similar incidents of rising prices in his native place. Anticipating similar growth, Shankar bought 50 *bighas* of land at a nominal rate compared to current prices. He used his connections in the BJP to get his deal done. On being asked how and why he bought that land, he said:

> Whatever money we have is from the land price increase in Kutch.... It is entirely Modiji's work.... Our land was not even fertile.... Worse than Dholera.... Modiji transformed the broken and fallen lands of Kutch. We were devastated by the earthquake. But see today. Labourers from UP, Bihar flock in to work....

However, his claim, 'Modiji will transform Dholera', was possibly to buttress his own faith in the prime minister, especially since all was not well with his investment. Since he bought land in Unai, the Port project has been forgotten. With the launch of the Dholera SIR project, the focus shifted to other villages such as Dholera. Although Unai village falls under the Dholera SIR boundary, it has had a complicated relationship with the authorities as it became the centre of farmers' agitations. Whether linked to the protests or not, Unai fell under the 6th Town Planning scheme. This means that it will be the last scheme to be developed. On top of that, most of the Unai land was in the agriculture zone, barring a fraction that was residential. Shankar's land also came inside the agriculture zone, which commands the lowest price and he may lose money if he decides to sell.

The entire Dholera SIR or the smart city project with a 920 square kilometre area is divided into six Town Planning schemes which are to be developed in different phases (although none of these deadlines has been met yet). Each of these schemes is then further divided into various zones such as residential, commercial, industrial and agricultural, among others. Based on the type of zones, a certain type of activities will be permitted. Since the speculation around residential or commercial real estate spaces is maximum, these zones also command the highest prices.

The travel of development ideas through Hindutva networks was further clarified by another businessman. Jugraj supported the Congress party in his native village although he has spent some time as a member of the RSS in the past. Harbouring political ambitions, he joined the Congress fold and won the *sarpanch* (see Chapter 3, note 9) election in his village. In Dholera, Jugraj bought land in a residential zone in the main village of Dholera as he wanted to play safe:

… I do not support the BJP, but I know Modiji does what he promises. And when I initially came to Dholera, the Adanis took over the port. I was very sure it'd be successful.… But I took my time. It was after the SIR project came that I got in touch with a friend in Gandhinagar revenue office. He was a Rajput. Although from the BJP, we were together in the RSS.… So, I just told Kunwarbhai [Kunwarsinh] that I need land from this village, and you cannot take any commission [*laughs*].

Kutch is the westernmost district of India and has remained backwards, owing to several factors such as location and geography, among others. The disastrous 2001 earthquake further worsened the situation. The mishandling of the earthquake was a key factor that put Modi in the chief minister's chair. Modi adopted a slew of neoliberal measures while involving private corporations and religious organisations in the rebuilding efforts (Simpson, 2013). Turning Kutch into a tax haven along with a slew of other measures such as availability of cheap land and electricity, Modi made it into a prosperous industrial region. A number of corporate houses moved to the region to start their manufacturing units due to the significant tax break (Simpson, 2013; Sud, 2020a). Just the two power plants of Tata and Adani brought GBP 4.5 billion of investments. Simultaneously, Kutch tourism with its beautiful white salt deserts was promoted and it became a tourist hub. With such a remarkable transformation from an arid wasteland into an industrial hub and tourist destination, Kutch is often held up as a showpiece of Modi's Gujarat model of development. Along with industries, hotels and resorts suddenly started dotting the landscape, which led to a sudden surge of demand for land, leading to massive land speculation. Thus, Kutchi land buyers, armed with memories of their own underdevelopment, saw the 'miracle' of (neoliberal) development firsthand that encouraged them to invest their surplus profits in Dholera.[12]

In the Dholera land market, Kutchis along with businessmen from other parts of the world inflated land value while ushering in new imaginaries and possibilities of profit. When looking at the experiences of the Kutchis in Dholera, who signify the provincial-level embrace of the neoliberal model of development, their referencing of Kutch is also key to driving speculations. The platforms used for land speculation are provincial, national as well as transnational circuits of capital and are not limited to just the Kutchis. For example, while interviewing a local BJP leader, I met his US-based retired uncle, who has a motel business in the US. He has bought land in the Dholera SIR as he saw a future in the idea:

> I left these lands, went to Bombay and then to USA [*sic*].... Modi is a great
> visionary. Once I knew it was launched by Modiji, I was very sure these lands
> would yield gold. See how much he is respected everywhere in the world....
> I have heard a lot about smart cities around the world. London, New York all are
> smart cities.... Modiji knows how to 'make' development....

Thus, he referenced cities from the West in order to legitimise the concept of
smart cities and to argue his faith in Modi's narrative of development. At the
same time, he referenced the Dholera of the 1980s when he left the place for
greener pastures abroad. Many similar accounts were presented by interviewees
where a relative of a respondent living abroad invested in land or advised the
locals to do so. Often the interviewees would make point out how their non-
resident relatives were well aware of 'smart cities' in other parts of the world.
Beyond the global examples, many underlined how Modi 'developed' Gujarat,
bringing in industries or building 'top quality' roads and airports across the
province. Some of these examples were developed during Modi's reign (such
as Sanand, Hansalpur) while others (such as Morbi) preceded him, but were
thrown in to make their arguments stronger. Each individual had their own
way of inter-referencing, and their own imaginations of development forged
from the legacy of economic development in Gujarat.[13]

Importantly, this has not gone unchallenged. As discussed in Chapter 3, the
2017 provincial Gujarat Assembly elections became a major battleground and
a referendum of sorts concerning this growth model. Whereas the Dholera SIR
project has been a major public relations tool for Modi during his successful
2014 prime ministerial campaign, the 2017 state assembly elections saw radio
advertisements of the opposition Congress party which mocked the government
sitting idle on Dholera farmers' lands for ten years and its failure to build the
proposed Dholera airport in as many years. As development discourses are
inevitably linked to Modi, his critics point towards the same argument. Talking
about crony capitalism under Modi, Paresh Dhanani, the leader of opposition
in the provincial assembly (2017–2022) from the Congress party, pointed out
to me that Modi has helped corporations dry out the state's resources and there
was no new job creation.

Another Congress leader, Lalji Desai, was equally critical of crony capitalism,
which, according to him, has caused the state's development to rot. He calls it
the 'Modani' model, Modi plus Adani, which snatched resources away from
the public and placed it into the hands of a few industrial houses. Hence, Lalji
argues that 'the two main agitations in Gujarat over the last few years, the

Patidars and the OBC [Other Backward Classes] ones or even the Adivasi or the farmers' agitations, are all outcomes of the reverse gear that the economy has taken which led to loss of employment opportunities....' The 2017 Gujarat election fought on development minus Hindutva proved to be a major test for the BJP and the Modi-led development model. The BJP hung on to power with a reduced majority as Modi's development took a hit. An election outcome is not necessarily a referendum on one single issue (such as development) since a host of other considerations such as caste matter. However, the protests by some of the traditional BJP supporters dented a blow to the neoliberalism-led Hindutva bandwagon, and the government went back to launch policies which were a disjuncture from neoliberal prescriptions (discussed in Chapter 7).

Metamorphosis of Capital and Land

Mitchell (2002: 19), in one of his most influential essays titled 'Can the Mosquito Speak?', illustrated how 'capital can circulate and, by combining with further forces, go through metamorphoses into other forms.' He showed the metamorphoses from 'money into property and labour, property and labour into sugarcane, sugarcane into processed sugar or alcohol, and back again into money' (Mitchell, 2002: 33). In the process, resources and arrangements that were used by the capitalist, Abbud, who was behind these metamorphoses in Egypt, did not come alone from him as he used an intricate network of power, resource and money that flowed and mutated forms. The previous sections depict a similar metamorphosis of power, money or religion in Dholera with networks spread well beyond it. However, to limit the phenomenon to VHP leaders, the Kutchi businessmen or even to the federal minister would be misplaced.

According to Mitchell (2002), to personify or link these circulations and forces to particular individuals is too simple, although such individuals at times secure control of certain elements and may even claim to represent those elements. Throughout these vignettes, which are from the early years of a spate of neoliberal projects coming to the Dholera region, we witnessed both state and non-state actors use the state for personal benefits. Such use of the state takes place from within the state space and/or from outside. At the same time, it is done by both state and non-state actors. This makes the state porous to the actors of society as well as businesses. The porosity of the state shapes and, at the same time, is shaped by the disjuncture in economic or cultural ideological projects. Hence, it brings the very idea of development to the centre. Interestingly, more than ideology, accumulation remained key as Harriss-White argues 'the state is [also] used by the intermediate classes for accumulation rather than for legitimation' (2003: 47).

There are some key observations around the central themes of the state and development. First, in the 1990s, there was a change in approach by the provincial state as well as the federal government to adopt a host of policies which marked a break from the previous Nehruvian era. For example, until then, infrastructure construction as well as its day-to-day running was the domain of the state. So much so that even the export-processing zones, first established in Kandla in Gujarat as early as 1965, were all set up and owned by the government (Kundra, 2000). However, in the 1990s with the BJP government in power, as discussed in Chapter 3), policies started changing. It marked a significant departure towards encouraging complete private involvement in various sectors, including infrastructure. The contrasting views of the development of Bhaubhai and Pradeepsinh in the introduction to this chapter demonstrated how these ideas are diffused at the level of even the villages. It is necessary to underline here that the stepping back of the state or the inching forward of non-state actors precedes the BJP in Gujarat.[14] However, there is a further proliferation of these phenomena across the province with Hindutva and economic liberalisation.

Second, the policies of infrastructure delivery by private sectors made the state more porous to society. As it opened up newer avenues of shadow activities, it also gave scope for newer actors to make claims to the state or resources. Hence, within this, whereas the likes of the Adanis are given cheaper land, Hindutva or caste alliances open up the field for newer actors such as VHP workers or Kutchi businessmen. In many of these cases, accumulation matters more than ideology. So, Hindutva acts as a way of opening up spheres of accumulation, an introduction card to a large extent. This is applicable to all cases, be it the Dholera port or the international airport in multiple locations. It helped a host of state and non-state actors using their position within the state or their influence due to their proximity to state institutions to corner personal benefits. For non-state actors such as the Sinhas or the Kutchi businessmen, this proximity was usually through Hindutva organisations. Sinha and his friends entered the villages with ambiguous identities. While their association with the VHP impressed upon the villagers their attempt to work with Hindu society, their commercial interests were unknown. In the same way, Jain, a ruling party politician, used his influence in state organisations to possibly launch the airport project at a certain site where he had bought vast swathes of land.

Third, linking the state at an ideational level with the projects of neoliberal development is how ideas of such development travel from one site to another, increasing their legitimacy. Be it the Kutchi businessmen, the US returnee or other non-residents, they found references to the smart city project or the Port project at the provincial, national or transnational levels. Their business was driven essentially by neoliberal ideas of development while using Hindutva networks. These neoliberal ideas travel from one place to another with their intended or unintended impacts. Such referencing is heavily linked with the likes of Modi or Adani.

This brings forth the last and most important point: approaches to development can be used to reimagine the state. These narratives of development enable leaders such as Modi to launch a project which reorients the values and ideologies that the state has towards development projects. The state's journey from the Nehruvian socialist model of development to the current neoliberal model, which in Gujarat came to be expressed through the Gujarat model of development, is testimony to how the state is being reimagined. In this re-imagination of the state, the project of Hindutva would address the social domain while an economic model is needed to address the material domain. Here, neoliberalism seems to have suited the Hindutva flagbearers. Thus, the two projects by which the BJP was able to reimagine the state are Hindutva and neoliberalism. Gujarat became the 'Hindutva laboratory' (Spodek, 2002) where the BJP has been partly successful in creating a hegemony attempting to get rid of the vestiges of Nehruvian socialism and secularism in the province. These developments have allowed a leader such as Modi to capture the institutions of the state and reimagine and represent it through discourses of neoliberalism. However, when it comes to the delivery or implementation of such neoliberal development, which in itself is exclusionary, we encounter people such as Jain or the brothers of the VHP national leader. Development with Hindutva legitimation provides the platform for these state or non-state actors to capture the institutions of the state.

The interconnectedness between the two projects is present at multiple levels. In the villages, VHP workers invest in land while possibly introducing themselves through their Hindutva networks. At the provincial level, Modi overlaps the Vibrant Gujarat investment summits with the Hindu festival of Navaratri, spending millions from state coffers to celebrate it as the International Navaratri Festival. Aggressive neoliberal policies that were coupled with equally aggressive Hindutva practices gave Modi or the BJP the breathing space and the platform to revisit the idea of the state. This is where, at the ideational level, economic liberalism meets political illiberalism. Although illiberal Hindutva shares little in common with the Washington Consensus, the former favouring an exclusivist societal order whereas the latter prefers a free market, there is a strong measure of agreement in their shared disdain for dirigisme or the idea that states can directly empower poorer people (Corbridge, 1999). This is why Hindutva and neoliberalism go together.

The newly emerging interactions between the state and businesses in infrastructure projects, lubricated by Hindutva, within the backdrop of neoliberalism, cannot be explained through the existing scholarship. Studies often fail to explain the continuing rise of an exclusivist majoritarian ideology, that is, Hindutva, in rural areas or amongst farmers. While scholars such as Chacko (2018a, 2018b), Chacko and Jayasuriya (2017) or Nilsen (2019) have provided analysis through various frameworks at the macro scale, the chapter provided an explanation based on the everyday interactions of the state and society at the micro level through both societal as well as economic logic. Current scholarship also lacks the intimate stories of how the actors and practices of Hindutva and neoliberalism come together. This chapter illustrated how the state and its development projects become a platform for cultural or economic ideologies to prosper as formal state and non-state actors who are part of the AES become bound together. At the same time, it is important to understand how strategies of the AES force it to depart from its own professed policies. Documenting instances when neoliberal development discourses travel from one place to another, the chapter depicts how neoliberalism moves forward using existing caste and Hindutva networks.

Notes

1. By 'Modi-sarkar', Pradeepsinh referred to the Modi-led government or state. It may even mean 'Mr Modi' as 'sarkar' can be used to refer to a person in higher position. Refer to note 1 in Chapter 2 for an explanation on 'sarkar'.
2. Other than Scott (1998) in his book, Seeing *Like a State*, where he illustrates an expansion of state capacity to extract further information on the society, scholars have covered India in great detail. See Corbridge and Harriss (2000), Corbridge et al. (2005) and Gupta and Sivaramakrishnan (2011), among others.
3. See Jaffrelot (1996) for detailed insights on the Hindu state.
4. In Chapter 3, how Modi's policies have rather been detrimental for marginal communities like Adivasis was illustrated. Also refer to Hirway and Mahadevia (2005), Hirway et al. (2014) and Jaffrelot (2015a).

5. This claim by the Darbar leader active within the RSS is significant as data has shown that Rajput communities across the province have lagged behind other upper castes (Patel, 2002; G. Shah, 1998a).

6. The biased role of the vernacular press starting with the 1969 riots has been mentioned by many scholars (G. Shah, 1970; Shani, 2007). The reach of newer media like video cassettes to towns and villages extended this.

7. 'Scheme' is often used to refer to real estate projects. It comes from the Town Planning schemes in the cities and towns of Gujarat. For Town Planning schemes, see Ballaney and Patel (2009) and Jain (2019).

8. The interviewee mentioned the real name as well his national level post in the VHP.

9. Gujarat International Finance Tec-City (GIFT City) is a partially completed central business district in Gandhinagar. As of 2023, fintech firms and banks, including HSBC, JP Morgan and Barclays, have offices.

10. See A. Kumar (1999) for a detailed take on the black economy.

11. *Bigha* is a traditional unit of measurement of area of land. 1 acre = 2.5 *bigha*s. It is used across various Indian provinces although the sizes and measurements vary.

12. Although they see Kutch's underdevelopment through a certain lens, it does not mean that the likes of Shankar were living in poverty and suddenly benefitted from a neoliberal project. They must have had enough money to buy and sell land in the first place, other than the social capital to get into the business of land. Shankar was a Rajput, which explains why he jumped into the land business.

13. In saying this, I am careful to not argue that this has been 'development for all'. In most cases, such industrialisation or delivery of infrastructure has benefitted a select few, especially the upper echelons (Hirway et al., 2014). We discussed this in the previous chapter.

14. A number of scholars have shown that this was very clearly the case of Gujarat's political economy from the 1970s until the 1990s. Some of them would include Breman (1985, 1996, 2004, 2007), Hirway (1995, 2000, 2002, 2003), Hirway et al. (2002), Rutten (1986, 1995), G. Shah (1975, 1976, 1996), Shinoda (2002) and Streefkert et al. (2002).

5

Mimicking the State

Vijayrajsinh, the leader of the protesting farmers in Dholera, often complained about how people from the BJP have captured the *mamlatdar*[1] office (Block Development Office). According to him, they do not let any work happen without approval from the local BJP leaders. He claimed that the *mamlatdar* advised him to speak to the local BJP head to expedite the process of converting his agricultural land to non-agricultural land. Furious at this, Vijayrajsinh preferred to wait instead of talking to a 'stupid' from the BJP.

In the initial days of fieldwork, I viewed these stories usually targeted against the RSS or BJP with suspicion. After all, Vijayrajsinh was fighting against the BJP government in his opposition to the Dholera SIR project. However, spending time, one could witness the ubiquity of middlemen, brokers inside the government offices, and how each one of them was associated with the Hindutva organisations. Thus, these 'men' from right-wing Hindu nationalist organisations were part of the everyday state. For example, interviews with *talati*s working in and around the Dholera SIR villages that witnessed a massive spike in land prices underlined it. The *talati*s are government officials at the lowest echelons of bureaucracy in rural Gujarat tasked with duties such as maintaining crop and land records of the village, collecting tax revenue and irrigation dues in addition to delivering government-led development projects. In private, they agreed to have brokered land deals for private buyers, in many cases by using their past networks in Hindutva organisations. While their task as officials was to act as conduits to bring the state closer to citizens, their moonlighting was entirely against such a novel idea.

Similarly, in land deals, there is a ubiquity of private intermediaries usually referred to as *dalal*s (brokers). Broker is used here to refer to the private agents or intermediaries who are not officially associated with the state. Under middlemen, I include both brokers and government officials who moonlight.

The omnipresent middlemen and their affiliation with Hindutva organisations become the basis of my second proposition on the AES—that a number of actors work in both the shadow and formal spheres of the state simultaneously and constitute the AES. Through the ability to manipulate their proximity to the state, society and other non-state organisations, they shape the entity of the state and its delivery of services to citizens. Whereas government officials may represent the formal state, brokers have increasingly penetrated the formal state spaces. In working within or outside the state spaces, middlemen (both private brokers and government officials) create a shadow space within the state, in which they work. State officials, in turn, through their moonlighting practices enlarge this shadow. In Dholera, both the brokers and moonlighting officials constitute the AES. What binds these actors of AES, however disparate, is their affiliation with Hindutva organisations.

Middlemen, Development and the State

Scholars have taken the failure of democratic norms and institutions outlined in the Indian Constitution to be the reason for an 'omnipresent, but feeble' (Kohli, 1990: 6) state that has led to the ubiquity of middlemen in India. They have been variously termed *pyarveekar, dalal,* broker or political fixer by scholars and their functions vary (Jeffrey and Lerche, 2000; Manor, 2000; Oldenburg, 1987; Reddy and Haragopal, 1985; Sud, 2014a; Witsoe, 2012). They, as Sud (2012) argues, are part of the landscape of imperfect, inaccessible states. This relationship has been explored through client–patron forms, leading Chandra (2004) to call India a 'patronage democracy'. Guha (2014) and Mosse (2001) have elaborated on how the historical background of Indian society can be argued as a precursor to the current system of middlemen. Witsoe (2012) points out that the role of brokers often reflects the ways in which the boundaries between state and society are blurred within everyday state practices. Bailey (1960) described the broker as a new class of individuals with the skills and knowledge necessary to allow villagers to interact with a newly independent Indian state. Thus, Witsoe (2012) argues that when viewed 'from below', brokers are an essential part of many people's experience of the state. Hence, understanding the way the brokers work would necessitate a suspension of the notion of the formal boundaries between state and society, something we theorised through the scholarships of Abrams and Mitchell (to list a few) in Chapter 2.

Both before and after India's independence, middlemen played a key role in the land revenue systems as they brought the state closer to those it governed (Sud, 2014a). Hence, the current set of middlemen in the land market in the post-liberalisation era is not unique. However, since 1991, state retrenchment and increased privatisation have generated new spaces for these middlemen as they coordinate activities between state, market and the society, actively shaping the relationships of the state and the market with the citizens. As footloose capital looks for hitherto untapped or under-exploited sites of production, the importance of these middlemen has further increased (Sud, 2014a). These men do the work of searching and purchasing land on the ground for domestic or international corporations and become the local anchors (Sud, 2014a; Levien, 2011) to aggregate vast numbers of small land holdings buying from disparate farmers and streamlining them for large buyers. Thus, they are an important component of capital accumulation in land.

Importantly for the chapter and the book at large, the presence of these actors demonstrates the blurred boundaries of the state, and such middlemen represent the porous interface between the state and society (Berenschot, 2011a). They highlight how state sovereignty is questioned or, at least, is fragmented. There is a symbiotic relationship as these actors on one hand are necessary for citizens to access the state. On the other hand, politicians need them to access citizens. Although their ubiquity has been researched as a marker of corruption (Jeffrey and Lerche, 2000; Oldenburg, 1987), their key role in bringing the state closer to the people by linking rural clients with government bureaucrats and politicians has also been pointed out. They are termed as agents of benevolence, goodwill and increased equity, 'lubricants' of Indian democracy who enable citizens' access to government resources (Corbridge et al., 2005; Krishna, 2003; Manor, 2000; Simon, 2009). Berenschot (2011a) highlights a missing link in the middlemen scholarship: Hindutva. He finds that middlemen who are active in the BJP or RSS play a key role as patrons of lower castes, delivering state resources in return for their votes.

Contrary to some scholarship underlining the 'benevolence' of middlemen, or their ability to act as a lubricant in Indian democracy, their practices in Dholera do not bring the state closer to the people. Rather, middlemen corner state resources and even private investments and become a barrier between people and the state. This is because their own survival is reliant on maintaining this distance.[2] The chapter shows how this distance is sustained through the practices of certain actors with associations to Hindutva, and how they take forward the neoliberal project in rural areas. The middlemen in Dholera deal especially with land, their role in land administration and transactions being of greater relevance to this book.[3] It is important to ask here whether middlemen's furthering of neoliberalism is conscious or coincidental. In the stories recounted later in this chapter, many of them may never have heard the term 'neoliberalism'. In that case, do they play an important part in Dholera's neoliberal phenomenon? Yes, is the answer here. While many of the middlemen may not be actively aware of their role in the process, the realisation of phenomena such as real estate transactions, privatisation of commons, financialisation of hitherto farmlands or building of real estate township projects would have never been possible in their absence.

The practices of middlemen are studied through several broad questions. How does the AES in Dholera function at the ground level when a neoliberal project is launched?[4] Who are the key actors and how do their practices shape the AES? What are the cultural associations and existing social norms and networks that help such practices? As middlemen straddle smoothly between the formal and shadow spaces, their movement is lubricated by the networks formed through societal, cultural and economic associations. The chapter analyses their practices and impact, asking how they affect the delivery of development and citizens' access to the state.

Beyond their ubiquity, why are middlemen so important to disaggregate the state and the AES in particular? Why should the study of everyday practices of these actors (officials or brokers) illuminate how a state that facilitates a majoritarian cultural ideology comes together with a transnational economic philosophy? This requires an explanation of the formation of the state and its relationship to society. As discussed in greater detail in Chapter 2, Abrams argued that the state is a multi-layered entity and it 'comes into being as a structuration within political practice' (1988: 82). This entity starts as an implicit construct or an idea, and then takes shape, and becomes embedded in society through everyday practices before acquiring an overt symbolic identity. The entity, both its image and practices, are produced when the actors (and institutions) who represent the state interact with society. As the state is continuously in touch with society and never isolated, it is constantly made and remade through changes in society. However, this is not a one-way process. As the state comes into existence through these practices, existing societal hierarchies or relationships could give rise to newer ones. The everyday practices of middlemen are important to understand the changes which a project such as Dholera SIR can bring to the entity of the state and society and their inter-relationships.

In seeking to enhance their legitimacy and effectiveness, middlemen make concerted efforts to mimic key symbols or practices of the state. I use the idea of 'mimicking the state' to depict how they imitate the formal state to gain legitimacy. At the same time, they do not attempt to create a parallel state and limit their activities strictly to proving their association with state institutions. Nandini Sundar (2014) also uses the term 'mimetic state' while examining the tactics of the state and Maoist insurgents in India. She finds that both the state and Maoists mimic one another in order to improve efficacy and gain legitimacy. Whereas the book draws from the mimicry discourse by Bhabha (1984) on the colonial state, it does not go into disaggregating the concept.

Two related arguments emerge from the assessment of the everyday practices of middlemen and are explored through two relationships. The first is the relationship between middlemen and the state. One of the most common practices of middlemen is their mimicry of the state. To be successful, they are dependent on the ability to appear like the state. The hard work put in presenting themselves as the state or at least state-like is underlined by their frequent attempts to exhibit their proximity to state institutions, to ministers or to bureaucrats. Second is the relationship of these middlemen with Hindutva organisations. The everyday Hindutva, the banal or mundane form of it, provides a network that connects these actors even if they come from diverse backgrounds with disparate state or societal associations. Through these practices, Hindutva is strengthened, riding on the project of liberalisation.

The 'Foot Soldiers' of RSS in Everyday Lives

Naranbhai (pseudonym), a local BJP leader in Dholera, in Manor's (2000: 817) classification would be called a political fixer, described as 'political intermediaries between the localities and powerful figures (bureaucrats, politicians) at high levels'. He started life as a worker in a diamond-polishing factory in nearby Bhavnagar. Returning a few years later, he opened a small workshop to polish diamonds and looked after the family farm. He was a classmate of Pradeepsinh (pseudonym), a local Darbar strongman and an important BJP functionary. Of late, collaborating with Pradeepsinh and others, Naranbhai has made a huge fortune in land deals and invested the surplus to diversify his businesses. He accepted that he had brokered more than 1,800 acres of land over the last ten years. When asked about his networks in BJP and RSS and if those are useful for his land business, he said:

> I cannot compare but I think BJP party meetings are more useful businesswise…. Here, we speak about each other's wealth, profession that is very useful…. So many 'Sahebs' have gotten in touch with me after the meetings and I have sold them land.

The acknowledgement that he benefitted from the BJP and RSS meetings is important. Brokers such as Naranbhai use their networks in these organisations to take their private businesses forward. For example, a typical deal that Naranbhai undertook had this route: he would get a referral from a friend in the RSS or BJP about a prospective client. To identify a potential seller, he would use his network within his village or approach an RSS or BJP worker from another village. Then, his connections at the revenue department who in all likelihood have some association with the RSS or BJP would help complete the transaction. Simpson (2006: 339) similarly noted that the membership and networks of many Hindutva organisations coincide, so that 'a merchant may be a member of his caste association, professional guild and the Rotary Club, and enjoy the influence of his comrades in each'. These networks also overlap with local governments, party politics, commerce and religious committees.

　Once, while we were chatting, Naranbhai received a call on his mobile. After ten–fifteen minutes of persuading the caller, he picked up his motorcycle and I perched on the pillion precariously. On our way to the village that was a ten-minute drive, Naranbhai told me:

> Someone has excavated two *bigha*s of his [the caller's] land and supplied the soil to L&T [Larsen & Toubro][5] in the Activation Zone…. Everyone knows the contractors who are supplying soil [*he mentioned a few names who were regulars at the BJP office*]….

Such incidents, usually small fights, within the village or involving different castes were commonly mediated by the likes of Naranbhai. Negotiations by middlemen fill a crucial gap and may be a source of rent-seeking for them. Their involvement can solve such issues quickly without the involvement of the police or court (Berenschot, 2011a). As we arrived, twelve–fifteen people had gathered and were quite agitated as this was the third case in a month's time. The region of Dholera is low-lying and close to the sea. Most constructions require enormous earth filling. Since the start of construction at the Activation Area,[6] there has been a scarcity of soil in Dholera. Naranbhai tried his best to convince the crowd:

I will ensure that you get your compensation.... However, do not pursue a police case. We all know that the Darbars are in control of the entire police and court.... You have lost the land and you will end up in jail....

Sensing that the matter was getting out of control as the crowd was still restless, he offered to call Pradeepsinh (the local BJP strongman) and resolve the matter. After the call, Naranbhai explained that Pradeepsinh had assured that the farmers would be compensated and that going to the police would not help. The crowd now seemed convinced. With the impending Gujarat assembly elections of December 2017, Naranbhai saw an opportunity to remind them that he is their leader:

I am your *sevak* [servant].... I will not let injustice happen to you. If you do not get anything, I will buy those few *bigha*s of land. Is that okay?

Although Naranbhai was not fighting the election, his nephew Rambhai lobbied hard for the BJP party candidature. Moreover, Naranbhai was a dedicated foot soldier of the RSS and needed to garner votes for the BJP (Berenschot, 2011a). Pradeepsinh had brain surgery and was avoiding phone calls. A ten–fifteen-minute conversation with him was doubtful. On our return, when asked if he actually spoke to Pradeepsinh, he smiled without answering.

From the vignette, two important issues emerge which are connected to the two relationships mentioned earlier: between middlemen and the state, and middlemen and Hindutva. First, middlemen are not always the benevolent agents who bring the state and its resources to villagers, instead they may block citizens' attempts to approach the state. In his traditional avatar as the political fixer, Naranbhai may have helped these people in accessing the state, including approaching the police. However, despite the crowd's insistence, Naranbhai stopped them from filing a case. He instilled in them fear of the police, thus presenting the state and its institutions as anti-Koli and hence anti-people. The state was made to appear too distant, too hostile while he, the RSS or BJP functionary, was by their side or at their home to resolve their issues. After all, Naranbhai was not any middleman, but one embedded in the BJP or RSS (a point which Figure 5.1 [*right*] clearly demonstrates).

He stopped them from accessing the state not because this would be a difficult process for the Kolis but because this may affect his hold on the village or complicate his relationships with other Darbars. In this way, middlemen such as Naranbhai block people's access to the state, something that earlier established them as leaders ensuring the continuity of the

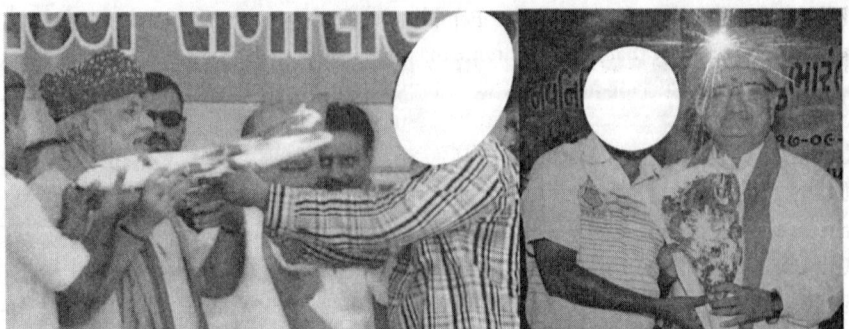

Figure 5.1   Middlemen with provincial- and federal-level politicians

Left: Pradeepsinh giving a replica of an aeroplane to Narendra Modi when he visited the region during the 2017 election campaign. The aeroplane is symbolic of the Airbus factory that was the focus of the SIR around this time.

Right: A picture of Naranbhai with Bhupendrasinh in his drawing room.

Source: Author.

patron–client relationship. In this process, do the subjects perceive Naranbhai as the one who guarantees them justice more than the state? Yes, is the more likely answer. Naranbhai assured the villagers that they would be compensated. Although the authenticity of the call is in doubt, he managed to convince them that a BJP or RSS worker could be trusted more than state institutions.

However, the main reason for the actions of middlemen is financial as well as political. This validates the argument that middlemen's businesses have a strong connection with networks in Hindutva organisations. Harriss-White's (2003) proposal of the shadow state has similar traits where the market, society and the state are not separate but flow seamlessly into one another. Here, Naranbhai has business partnerships with many Darbar contractors who dug soil from the farmlands. These contractors are BJP members and Naranbhai cannot afford a scenario in which BJP leaders are openly perceived to be aggressors against Kolis. Hence, to maintain his political, social and economic capital, he promised the Kolis that he would buy their land if he could not ensure compensation. Now, this was a smart deal. It would ensure his patronage without any financial loss. Starting as a modest middleman, Naranbhai has bought swathes of land in these villages. He has built his own land bank, buying from fellow villagers who sell at times of distress, as he was sure that prices would increase. Therefore, buying four to five *bigha*s of land and then selling them later is part of his business. A buyer from another city would not be concerned about the land digging.

Village Officials' Use of the State and Hindutva Networks

Scholars have discussed the possibility of studying the state through everyday bureaucratic practices (Gupta, 1995; Gupta and Sharma, 2006; Mitchell, 1999). Many ethnographies of the Indian state have focused on the bureaucracy and the everyday performances of state institutions (Gupta, 1995; Mathur, 2015; Qureshi, 2015). To understand how states are constituted or are substantiated in people's lives, one must move beyond the macro-level institutional analyses of the state and undertake an ethnography of local bureaucratic practices and their encounters with citizen subjects (Bouchard, 2011). This may include following government officials in their role as a state official or as a private citizen when s/he interacts with citizen subjects or with an international agency, as the state in its everyday form cannot be disconnected from macro-processes and structures (Joseph and Nugent, 1994). The first part of this, a bureaucrat's interaction with citizens, is clearly visible in this chapter whereas in the next chapter, the bureaucrat's interaction with international agencies is analysed. At the same time, even if lower-level officials in this chapter do not meet personnel from international agencies, their role in smoothening the functions of such agencies cannot be ignored. Through their practices, these officials create the preconditions in which the flow of international capital or knowledge takes place.

The next vignettes are about two village officials, who are part of the formal state but also switch into shadow roles using the networks of Hindutva organisations, delineating how the AES functions. Government officials in their state roles undertake a host of bureaucratic exercises that create a state effect (Mitchell, 1991). However, through practices that are beyond their official roles, they continue to create the state effect whether intended or otherwise. This deconstructing of the state or the AES through informal practices contribute significantly to an understanding of the coming together of the agents of liberalisation and the actors of Hindutva.

A *talati* in Gujarat works under the local government keeping village records and implementing various development plans and projects. As s/he works with the revenue office, a *talati* has access to the land records of the village. At the same time, s/he is also aware of the socio-economic demographics of each household. Each of them is powered with documents knowing the bureaucratic nitty-gritty, which often baffle individual buyers or even a less powerful broker. Most of the *talatis* in Dholera villages accepted to have moonlighted as land brokers. The number of deals that they have been involved in until now ranged from ten to 'countless'. When asked where they meet their prospective clients or discuss land deals, they were upfront in their acceptance that they had private offices. None of them lived in the villages of Dholera due to a 'lack of basic infrastructures such as good schools, hospitals'. However, such distances often gave them enough ambiguity to carry out these extra jobs. Depending on the quantity and quality of business each *talati* used to get, the sizes of the offices varied.

I met Ajit (pseudonym) at the office of one of the *sarpanch*'s (head of the village-level local self-government, note 10 in Chapter 3) whose family headed the Congress party in the area. Ajit was the *talati* of a few important villages and belonged to the powerful Darbar community. The villages under his supervision are centrally located and command high land prices vis-à-vis political strength. Ajit's presence at the *sarpanch*'s office was not very surprising because the *talati*'s role required coordination with the *sarpanch*. However, on the day of our next meeting, he asked me to come to the BJP party office adjoining a local highway restaurant. I frequented the office during my fieldwork to interview some BJP leaders or middlemen associated with the party. I was surprised to find Ajit there, as I did not expect a government official to be sitting in a political party office.

For our next meeting, he invited me to his home where I was taken to his small office adjoining the drawing room but with separate access. As I followed him, Ajit removed his sandals and looked at me, implying I should follow suit. The otherwise modern office had a small statue of a female deity raised on a laminated wooden platform hinged in one corner of the room. I asked him why he built the office. He answered:

> Earlier, I used to meet them [clients] outside my office in Dholera. However, I felt that people started snooping.... Then, I started meeting them in the village market. Here, I had all the resources: land records, maps, photocopy, printers. Moreover, I could see that the clients trusted me easily because of my office or because I was known in the market as the local *talati*.... Even someone coming from Mumbai would be comfortable if he is dealing with a government employee than a *dalal*. One Baroda party just said to me: 'I have faith in you'....

According to him, the Congress leader was a Darbar and they are on good terms, because of their Darbar lineage. Narrating that his father was an RSS *pracharak*,[7] he mentioned how he worked with the RSS in the tribal districts of Gujarat and travelled to other provinces to undertake 'development' work before he got the job of *talati*. Those networks still help him as he gets business from them. Being a Darbar, he was always preferred by other Darbars for any official work and went on to argue that even Congress leaders have RSS connections.

Ajit's siting of offices and use of networks in the RSS or BJP illustrate how state officials mimic the formal state where they undertake their non-state practices while using networks of Hindutva. Three aspects are important here. First, the importance of a state position is discernible. The client earlier asserting, 'I have faith in you' reflects where Ajit's power comes from. Other *talati*s similarly acknowledge the importance of their state roles in the overcrowded market of brokers in Dholera. Their official position with the state ensures extra trust, as they are vulnerable to complaints in addition to having an intricate knowledge of the bureaucracy.

Second, Ajit spoke about the loss of some business after he moved his office to his residence, 30 kilometers from his workplace. Compared to the days when he was moonlighting seated in his state office or the marketplace, he claimed to have lost momentum. In the market or at his state office, he was known as the government employee and clients trusted him more due to this proximity. At home, physically far from the office, he lacked social capital. Hence, geographies of the state space matter, not just the state position of the official.

Third, the role of the RSS as the lubricant in the success of mimicking the state is noticeable. Ajit's long association with the RSS led him to call it a development organisation, arguing how his state role is very similar to what his role in the RSS stood for. These Hindutva networks still fetch him business. In that case, if Dholera SIR is a project of neoliberal essence, then the likes of Ajit are conduits in the circulation of finance and knowledge in the speculative real estate market through the networks of Hindutva.

Another *talati*, Sailesh (pseudonym) was from a nearby district belonging to a lower caste. A week after our first brief meeting in the village under his supervision, I saw him in an office in the Hotel Vision Modi (HVM) (Figure 5.2). After I requested a detailed meeting, he invited me to the same office at HVM. HVM is a recently built five-storey structure at the entrance of Dholera. Standing near the Ahmedabad–Bhavnagar highway, HVM was strange if one considers its usage. The ground floor had a teashop that was the most active place, an ATM that was permanently shut, a printing and photocopy shop and a couple of similar shops. The DSIRDA local office where the town planner sits once or twice a week occupies two big halls on the first and second floor. These two floors also have a number of offices providing real

Figure 5.2   A front view of the Hotel Vision Modi

Source: Author.

estate-related services. Both Naranbhai and his nephew Rambhai, BJP leaders, were amongst those with offices here. A few rooms on the third and fourth floors of the building also provided overnight accommodation. Therefore, various spaces accessible to the public from a tea stall to a government office sit alongside private real estate offices involved in speculation. Pradeepsinh (BJP leader) who owned the building named it after Modi as he felt an 'obligation to dedicate something to Narendra Modi who has done so much for them by announcing the SIR project'. He wanted to show the world that Dholera has more to offer than mud and thatched roof houses.

On the day of our meeting, Sailesh invited me to a shiny air-conditioned office in HVM with sleek furniture and a small female deity placed on a corner platform, very similar to Ajit's office. After assurances of anonymity, Sailesh acknowledged that he owned the office. He started narrating his personal story: how he moved from a nearby district, how tough it was to gain contacts here being an outsider from a 'lower' caste and how his connections in the RSS helped him. To set up this office, he borrowed money from Pradeepsinh. On why he chose this location, he replied that the building was at the centre of everything. It was next door to the SIR office, close to the sub registrar or the *mamlatdar* and close to Rambhai or Naranbhai from the BJP who have helped him immensely by forwarding business. When asked why the RSS was so important when one could not even see an office of the organisation, Sailesh smiled:

> RSS does not need an office. Every temple is its office. Every Gram Panchayat can be their office. Every highway hotel is their office. They just need their men to be leading these [places].… So, if I have RSS connections, even if it is Congress or BJP, I will be getting my business done.…

This partly explained how the *talati*, Ajit, was working smoothly with the Congress *sarpanch* while frequenting the BJP office. As we were chatting, two men arrived from Mumbai. They mentioned how a certain *panditji* (priest) from Mumbai suggested the name of the local head of some 'sanstha' (organisation) in Ahmedabad who knew a bureaucrat in the revenue department who gave him Sailesh's number. According to him, he preferred Sailesh because he was a government official and hence was more responsible. Later, Sailesh confirmed to me that 'sanstha' referred to a local branch of the RSS. The conversation moved swiftly to finalise a deal and visit the sub-registrar's office to 'inform' and 'request' the officials to hasten the process. Finalising the price, the clients asked Sailesh about the survey number of the plot of land they had just bought, claiming that he knew someone in Gandhinagar to find the location of his final plot.[8] Sailesh smiled broadly and said:

> Should I take you to the government office in two minutes which will tell you best where your final plot will be? It is just opposite my office. The Dholera SIR office is around the corridor.…

Both the visitors appeared puzzled (and equally impressed). Sailesh then explained that his office was located at the centre of everything: sub-registrar office, DSIRDA local office and *mamlatdar* office.

The two vignettes illustrate the practice of mimicking the formal state using Hindutva as the lubricant. The state is mimicked by both categories of middlemen, the private brokers as well as the moonlighting officials. To mimic the formal state successfully, Sailesh sited his private office in the HVM, and hence physically closer to other state institutions such as the SIR, *mamlatdar* and sub-registrar offices. All these offices deal with land-related matters. The attempt here is to appear like the state, and hence mimic the state. This was clear as Sailesh boasted in front of his clients regarding how they were at the best property office.

The practices of the *talati*s help explain the two key relationships: (*a*) middlemen and the state; and (*b*) middlemen and Hindutva organisations. Both Ajit and Sailesh used the state in more than just these ways. Due to their position as the village *talati*s, they are presumed to be more responsible than a private broker. This official role of the *talati* ensures an embedded life in the villages, which plays a key role in making these deals easier. Other than swift access to land-related records of these villages due to their state positions, the *talati*s are well versed in the vicissitudes of every family. Spending a day or two every week, they know the socio-economic conditions of each household: which man is looking actively to sell land to marry his daughter off, who is drowning in debt or who lost a lot of money in gambling dens along the sea. Such knowledge is important in finding land that is prone to sale.

The other relationship is between the middlemen and the Hindutva organisations. The formation and use of their networks, and the material implications on the idea of the state are noteworthy. There is a symbiotic relationship between the *talati*s and the BJP or RSS members where both gain from each other's presence. Sailesh rented the office space in HVM to use not just the proximity to the state but also the RSS. He borrowed money from the owner of HVM who is a BJP leader. He is next door to Rambhai or Naranbhai's offices, BJP or RSS office-bearers. It also allows an individual such as Naranbhai to maintain and exhibit his proximity to the formal machinery of the state. The likes of Sailesh, the *talati*, help Naranbhai, the broker and BJP or RSS member, by fast-tracking his official work. Sailesh, the lower-caste *talati*, coming from a different place, uses the networks of Hindutva to cope with and penetrate existing social relations. Thus, the middlemen's mimicking of the state and their embeddedness in the BJP or RSS are inextricable from each other in the AES. These practices of state officials and brokers create what Mitchell (1991) argued is the state effect (Figure 5.3 shows an ongoing deal outside a government office).

What then is the outcome of these newer formations of the state on common citizens? Does this web of *talati*s and other middlemen block the state from citizens? Jayesh (pseudonym) spent a year running around revenue offices and middlemen to convert his agricultural land along the highway into non-agricultural use. This is although he was ready to pay a bribe at the revenue office. He requested help from Sailesh, the *talati*, but to no avail. Naranbhai, the middleman and BJP/RSS member, told me that Jayesh never approached him because he has been a Congress supporter and went with the anti-SIR farmers' protests. That was the reason why this routine work was stalled.

Figure 5.3   Middlemen's activities in Dholera

Left: A conversation between one of the interviewed middlemen (*second from left*), the Ahmedabad-based client in a grey polo shirt and the farmers. This took place just outside the sub-registrar's office while I was in the middle of the discussions when the final clauses of the deal were being brokered.

Right: An office of one of the land brokers cum real estate dealers along the Ahmedabad–Bhavnagar highway. Notice Modi's picture on the office front signage. Modi's pictures are ubiquitous in such office or shop front signages in the region.

Source: Author.

Thus, in the state, which has come into effect through the practices of these actors and the bureaucrats with a strong Hindutva connection, services are exclusionary. Whereas the reasons for the delay were not entirely clear, Jayesh's active participation in the anti-SIR protests or non-association with Hindutva organisations made matters worse. As Das and Poole (2004: 245) argue, 'it is this illegibility of the state, the unreadability of its rules and regulations' that allows the oscillation 'between the rational and the magical to become the defining feature of the state' in such spaces. Does this mean that the newer forms of the state are exclusionary? Perhaps yes as the state is being captured and cornered by agents of an exclusivist philosophy—Hindutva.

At the same time, its ubiquity both inside and outside state spaces has also made it nothing spectacular. This is extremely surprising when we consider that the murderer of M. K. Gandhi, the father of the nation, had been affiliated with the RSS. As Sailesh mentioned, the RSS does not need an office and every temple is its office. In fact, every state office is their office too, and hence they are part of the everyday life of the state. In the vignettes mentioned earlier, Hindutva in Dholera is noticeably present and/or absent through its mundaneness, what scholars have termed as 'neo-Hindutva' (Reddy, 2011), 'banalisation of Hindu nationalism' (Jaffrelot, 2015b) or 'banal Hindutva' (Jeffrey et al., 2017) that makes Hindutva practices seem ordinary.

In these forms, Hindutva has a clear disjuncture between its ideologies and practices. What was significant to V. Savarkar, the founding father of the ideology, may not be reflected in the practices in Dholera. However, what is most important is how it has entrenched the state and society. In Dholera, there has not necessarily been an increase in Hindu religiosity, compared to the 'state–temple–corporate complex' that Nanda (2009) talks about due to the coming together of globalisation and Hindutva. However, in the everyday state and society of Dholera, there is a discernible political and economic angle of Hindutva that does not bare (maybe, does not need to) its exclusivist religious or cultural ideology. The political angle delivers votes whereas the economic angle delivers material benefits to its followers.

Importantly, the banal Hindutva in practice in Dholera takes on board existing kinship or caste configurations. Hence, Ajit, the upper-caste *talati*, combined his Darbar caste networks with his past associations with Hindutva to make a smooth movement between opposing political parties or between the state and society. For Sailesh, an outsider from a lower caste, Hindutva provided a perfect network to make some inroads. Thus, the two *talatis*, with contrasting backgrounds, use Hindutva to further their material gains. The practices of Hindutva or its banal forms in Dholera are illustrated when *talatis*, the government officials, drink cups of tea, play cards or spend hours chatting at the local BJP office. In the process, the state official straddles multiple roles: a *talati*, a broker and an RSS member (officially or otherwise).

Such banal forms of Hindutva are an outcome of deeper roots spread by the RSS over time. Many of these middlemen in their youth have attended the weekly RSS exercise camps without necessarily knowing what the organisation stands for. For them, taking part in such sessions was more about keeping yourself fit and less about fighting the 'anti-Hindu' forces. Thus, the mimicking of the state coupled with banal Hindutva takes the project of neoliberalism forward. Hindutva has provided a political, cultural or social platform for neoliberalism to penetrate these villages. At the same time, the Dholera SIR, the neoliberal project, provides a route to material gains to lubricate the wheels of the Hindutva chariot. Hence, Hindutva has been further entrenched into the state and society due to the chances of material gains that the SIR project has brought with it. This has resulted in the penetration of the state not just by the transnational actors of neoliberalism in Gandhinagar but also by the small-time middlemen in Dholera. Thus, going back to Abrams (1988), the image of the state that the practices of these men create signifies the AES.

The construction of Vibrant Dholera Summits

Ahmedabad-based Dilipsinh (pseudonym) was often considered Bhupendrasinh's (the powerful BJP cabinet minister's) right-hand man. One afternoon, he accompanied the CEO of DSIRDA, Sharma (pseudonym), who was inspecting the construction progress of the Activation Area. Whenever Sharma was on his official visit to Dholera, Dilipsinh accompanied him. Dilipsinh's proximity to Bhupendrasinh, BJP as well as to Sharma channelled such authority in Dholera that anyone could be misled into taking him as a political office-bearer or a senior government officer. As I too could not ignore the impression of someone from the state, I asked him about the progress of the project or investors' interest in Dholera. He said:

> We should be in a good position by the end of next year [2018] when the Activation Area will be ready.... See, Sharma frequents the place and we will hold L&T if they do not deliver on time....
>
> [*On the drop of interest amongst investors*] We used to hold these investors' meetings.... We modelled it on the Vibrant Gujarat [Global Summit]. We received amazing responses.... All these *mamlatdar*s, *talati*s, revenue officials and even a few police officers are asked to attend so that any issue faced by the buyers can be resolved.... The buyers used to bring their documents and get verified. There were transfers of land in a few minutes.... As they say 'single window',[9] we did something similar.

On being asked further about the investors' meet, he told me that since buyers face issues due to bureaucratic delays or fake brokers, the real estate developers in Dholera instituted the Dholera Developers and Investors' Summit (DDIS), more commonly the Vibrant Dholera summit. Held annually, it was attended by government officials and buyers could have their documents verified by officials or could get land transferred. The next summit was organised in Ahmedabad soon after the December 2017 provincial elections. It drew a wider audience and cabinet minister and Dholera native Bhupendrasinh attended as the chief guest. Dignitaries included officials of the Gujarat Infrastructure Development Board (GIDB) and the country deputy head of INFINITY (pseudonym) who delivered PowerPoint presentations on the benefits of investing in Dholera (Figure 5.4). INFINITY is a multinational engineering firm that is tasked with looking after the entire programme of the project. The minister, during his lecture, mentioned Dilipsinh's name, underlining how he was keeping track of the progress of the project. There were familiar faces from the villages:

Figure 5.4   Photograph of Dholera Developers and Investors' Summit. GIDB officials, INFINITY staff and Bhupendrasinh are seated on the stage during the event.

Source: Author.

some middlemen, including Naranbhai, real estate dealers and local government officials. Naranbhai invited me for tea outside. Two officials joined us, and when asked what they were doing here, a revenue official responded:

> … We cannot say no [to the officials or the politicians].… We have to work in these villages, with these leaders, with this party. In addition, we do get to know some new people and may get business.… However, I do accept that as a department, it is our responsibility to make things easy for buyers.…

The Dholera investors' summit and the presence of government officials can be interpreted as an instance of the state walking extra miles to help businesses, a facet of the neoliberal state. However, is this the formal state or its shadow? At the same time, is this the state which cuts short the usual bureaucratic procedures to woo prospective investors? People associated with the formal state participated in fulfilling private tasks that involved their official positions. The reasons behind the participation of the village officials could be many: the compulsion to follow the unofficial orders of a senior official, associations with BJP or RSS or to keep the likes of BJP leaders Pradeepsinh or Bhupendrasinh happy to undertake their own set of shadow practices. Moonlighting officials need the patronage of local BJP leaders, as illustrated in the case of the *talatis* earlier.

At the same time, while village officials acknowledge that they must serve the land buyers or make the process smoother, the event cannot be defined as an exercise of the formal state or a collaboration. It is worth noting that not all the practices in the shadow of the formal state are illegal. The DDIS event is not illegal. It, however, works in the shadow of the state. Hence, it is an exception where the state actors joined non-state actors to woo prospective investors. The AES actors also include the staff of INFINITY who are not part of the formal state. Thus, as expected, the network, which worked in the village to deliver a neoliberal project, goes higher up.

Second, this is a platform where the non-state mimics the state in order to undertake shadow activities. The investors' summit is an imitation of the successful model of the Vibrant Gujarat Global Summit (VGGS) where corporations from around the world gather in Gandhinagar every two years. In Chapter 3, I have elaborated on how the biennale VGGS became a major institution in reviving the image of Modi as a market-friendly leader. Hence, to appear like the state, the association of real estate dealers from Dholera mimics a platform that has acceptance at multiple levels of the state or amongst business fraternities. Further, with the use of their influence in the BJP and the government machinery, they could bring not just a tall cabinet minister but also a host of government officials. Although the event did not have an official tag, officials from the revenue department were ready to provide the single window service to private land buyers.

These networks of state and non-state players in the AES are an outcome of the actually existing neoliberal project from which I borrowed the term 'actually existing state' (AES). Neoliberalism is carried forward through disjuncture between ideologies and their everyday political operations and societal effects (Castree, 2006). Neoliberalism in practice takes myriad forms (Ong, 2006). It may enable state expansion in certain spheres although the idea is against its very foundational ideologies (Wacquant, 2009). In Dholera, whereas the state policymakers[10] argue for the state to hollow out, the practices of these officials show how the AES instead is drawn out. Hence, when neoliberalism came to Dholera, it used the platform provided by middlemen who were also members of Hindutva organisations. Thus, the everyday practices of Hindutva or neoliberalism significantly differ from their ideologies. The marriage of convenience between Hindutva and neoliberalism has been possible because of the inconsistencies between their ideologies and practices, helping to explain the continued rise of Hindutva with the coming of a neoliberal project to the rural areas of Dholera. This understanding of neoliberalism or Hindutva synchronises well with the proposition of the AES as each of them is signified by the everyday realities of how they function on the ground compared to theories and ideologies.

The SIR project comes at a time of shrinking government budgets in welfare and other provisions when the previous windows of brokering and patronage have started to shrink as explained in Chapter 3. It was clear that the province has witnessed significant state withdrawal from many spheres. In that case, the sudden increase in middlemen and their shadow practices is clearly an outcome of the Dholera smart city project. Similar to how these middlemen managed to access the state for citizen subjects, they continue to do so while consolidating personal, familial and political gain. However, their mimicking of the state becomes a barrier between the state and its citizens, demonstrating what state retrenchment could mean for smaller towns and villages in the neoliberal era. The launch of an infrastructure project first led to a massive spike in land prices, resulting in a diverse set of shadow state practices. In this shadowing, the men in the middle combine tasks usually linked with brokers or political fixers by working within and between the state, society and market. They transform how neoliberalism functions at the ground level. New business transactions have taken place through new political alignments usually stitched through Hindutva forces without necessarily undermining existing caste, kin or religious dynamics.

We saw the state's interaction with citizens, largely, has long been monopolised by these actors. In doing so, we found the spread of Hindutva not just amongst the trident-wielding, dedicated, idealistic workers but also among those who are not necessarily strongly aligned with its ideologies. As the state in Gandhinagar or New Delhi is allying with private corporations, actors working in its shadows at the ground level too are appropriating the state. What binds together these myriad disparate actors—the politicians, the government officials, the middlemen with allegiance to the BJP or Congress party—are the Hindutva organisations. Thus, the shadow state overlaps with these organisations. While Modi earns political capital speaking at various forums about the Dholera smart city from within the 'formal' state, the shadows continue their own practices—both with and without the blessings of the formal state. In this, how liberalisation and Hindutva go hand in hand on the ground and how the various layers of the state—formal and informal—feed off one other was illustrated.

Notes

1. A *mamlatdar* is a gazetted officer of the provincial government and is the head of a block, consisting of about fifty or more villages.
2. Oldenburg (1987) pointed towards this and many later scholars theorised along that line.
3. Baka (2013), Levien (2018), Searle (2010) and Sud (2014a) have discussed middlemen involved in land deals.
4. The case of the Dholera SIR representing neoliberalism is covered in Chapter 2. Scholars have covered similar projects rightly depicting their neoliberal tenets. For cases on India, see Banerjee-Guha (2008, 2010), Goldman (2011), Levien (2011, 2013a, 2018) and Sampat (2008, 2010). For Dholera smart city or the SIR, Bhandari (2015), Datta (2015) and Sampat (2015c, 2016) cover the debate.
5. L&T, or Larsen & Toubro Limited, is an Indian conglomerate, with business interests in engineering, construction, real estate manufacturing of capital goods as well as information technology and financial services (Forbes, 2019). Activation Area is the 21 square kilometres within the Dholera SIR that is being developed to be sold as land parcels to corporations.
6. See note 6 in Chapter 1. Activation Area is the 20 square kilometre zone that the government has developed to jumpstart the project.
7. *Pracharak*s are full-time workers or volunteers of the RSS.
8. In Chapter 7, the process of Town Planning Schemes in Gujarat is explained. In brief, the authorities acquire plots of land (called Original Plot or OP) in a certain area after notifying it, usually on the outskirts of an urban region. After putting infrastructure like roads and electricity in these plots, the original owner is returned a new plot of land, called the Final Plot (FP), which is 40–60 per cent of the OP. Although a reduced size, the price of the new plot or FP is significantly higher due to the new infrastructure as well as the fact that it now falls within the municipal boundary. The balance land is used by the authorities partly for developing the infrastructure with the rest sold to generate revenue.
9. 'Single window' refers to a facility that allows multiple parties involved in transactions to lodge standardised applications with a single entry point to fulfil all related regulatory requirements.
10. In Chapter 6, I describe two of the high-ranking bureaucrats who advocate cutting down the red tape and minimising state bureaucratic staff by outsourcing state functions.

6

The Entrepreneurial Shadow State

Tripathi (pseudonym), a senior officer in the Town Planning department, was scathing in his attacks on the DSIRDA, acknowledging errors in the SIR Act and its implementation in Dholera. This admission was significant, as he had chaired many meetings where crucial decisions concerning the planning and implementation of Dholera SIR (or Dholera smart city) were taken. Knowing that I was from a UK-based university, Tripathi proudly spoke about his own son, a graduate in town planning from a reputed UK university. He then called his son, Rutul, who was seated in a room within his office. Tripathi's large office had adjoining cabins, which were spacious enough to act as regular offices. After a brief introduction, we moved to an adjacent cabin where his son was seated. As we conversed about different things, life in Gujarat or the UK, I realised this cabin was effectively his son's de facto office for the planning and architecture consultancy services he offered. According to him, he often attended to his clients here as he was learning the trade from his experienced father. Even though he started his consultancy very recently, he had an envious portfolio of projects.

Unsurprisingly, he did not acknowledge how the location of his own office inside his father's office fetches him business. In a society where patronage, favours and bribes are rampant, clients who visit or seek favour from Rutul's powerful father, would often be obliged to hire the son. As Harriss-White (2003: 89) noted, 'The shadow state spills into the lanes surrounding state offices and ... officials' residences.' The shadow elements of the state here physically spill into and are found inside the state offices undertaking private business. These are vivid images of the formal and shadow elements of a state working in tandem with one another.

As we disentangle the various facets of the AES in practice, this chapter gives a picture of state policymaking and the institutional architecture that set the stage for the implementation of the Dholera project. While the previous chapter examined the practices of the actors of the AES in the villages where the SIR project was being implemented, this chapter looks at the level of the provincial capital where the policies of such projects are framed. It studies the special purpose vehicle (SPV) called the DSIRDA tasked with delivering the Dholera SIR project (see Appendix 1 for the composition and organisational structure of DSIRDA). The main office of the DSIRDA is located in Udyog Bhawan (Industries' Building) in Gandhinagar, the provincial capital. Specifically exploring its functioning, board members and its staff, both in their roles inside and outside the state, the chapter brings attention to how the practices of the shadow state transform the newer institutions of the state. The office space also houses the staff of INFINITY (not the real name), a private consultant involved in the project. Their physical presence on the same floor of the government-owned DSIRDA tells the story of how the neoliberal Indian state is porous at multiple scales.

While scholars have covered the Gujarat state's overlap with the private from a range of perspectives, this chapter illuminates how personnel and institutions undertake shadow practices due to the pressure on the state to become more entrepreneurial while also trying to corner benefits for themselves. Hence, the reasons are not just neoliberal logic but also personal motives. It builds upon two different sets of concepts, state entrepreneurialism and shadow state, to argue how they are interconnected, thereby contributing to newer understandings of the working of the state in the neoliberal era, especially within the context of urban entrepreneurialism. The chapter brings into focus the salience of caste and kin networks in the quotidian operations of the shadow state. It contributes to our understanding of the shadow state by showing the micropolitics of caste and kin networks shaping state agendas in the neoliberal era. This shadow state conceptualisation advances our understanding of such micro-practices differing subtly and elaborates on other scholars such as Harriss-White's (2003) original coinage of the shadow state.

At the level where policies are framed, the state is presumably more formal with the least interference of, and overlaps with, society. In fact, the location of institutions such as DSIRDA in Gandhinagar in itself is interesting. Far from the chaos of society, the planned city of Gandhinagar is an island largely bereft of everyday state–society interactions. For a villager from Dholera to come, find and interact with the state in Udyog Bhawan or Gandhinagar is at best a dreadful task,[1] so much so that farmer protests are not allowed to enter the precincts of Gandhinagar. Thus, Gandhinagar as the seat of the state's legislature or executive sits like the proverbial state in theory, far removed from the chaos of the rest of Gujarat. Studying the AES here to see the impact of its practices on the idea of the state, the chapter is in conversation with what Gupta and Sivaramakrishnan (2011: 5) called the attempt to find 'new way(s) to conceptualise the Indian state after liberalisation'. This is done by showing how Hindutva and liberalisation are entrenched at the higher echelons of the state.

It is debatable if one can draw a clean break from the past to show that the state here is entirely different. As mentioned in Chapter 4, through various policies, strategies and actions, Modi has clearly shown his attempt to build the 'New Gujarat', reimagining the idea of the state that would show a clear departure from the previous Nehruvian or Congress-led state and a break from the past under his leadership. Projects such as Dholera SIR are physical manifestations while pushing to build a more energetic and entrepreneurial state through organisations such as DSIRDA. Modi took on board neoliberal competitiveness or entrepreneurial expectations of the state and made them into a reality—starkly different from images of the state of the past. Even if one argues these to be continuities in practice, he has tried to create the narrative of generating and emphasising newness.

The Entrepreneurial Shadow State

This chapter focuses on the third proposition of the AES. As the smart city project attracts both support and resistance, the formal and the shadow state work together to smoothen business deals or to diffuse anti-SIR protests. These interactions are present at multiple levels of the state. As services are outsourced, blurred boundaries between formal and shadow elements illuminate how the state's relationship with society and market is being redefined. This chapter makes two key inferences about the state. First, policies of liberalisation have affected how actors from shadow spaces appropriate the state and take up the role of the state, often becoming its face. Second, the actors of the AES undertake a host of shadow practices to take forward the project of neoliberalism. Whether their practices escalate the speed with which projects are undertaken is one matter, but in the process a number of usual bureaucratic procedures are skipped. These shadow practices of formal state actors take place due to the entrepreneurial zeal of the state, a key facet of neoliberalism.

At the same time, such shadow practices often have an element of corruption. The shadow state and the practices discussed here may or may not be categorised under corruption. Here, the term 'shadow' is used under broad categorisation to document the presence of an apparatus or a field where various blocs struggle to corner material gains without debating which of those is/are illegal. Some of these practices can be obvious corruption while others are extra-mile steps taken by state actors for ease of doing business. In that sense, one can argue that the concept is closer to Partha Chatterjee's (2002) political society that described a parallel field of governance in which claims are advanced based on morality rather than legal rights. While this is not the case under the shadow state in the article, the two concepts exist only in relation to the state as they both implicate public servants in informality, and they have a profound influence on the city. However, this article focuses on the state and elites' practices.

So, is the state a field of competition and conflict or is the state itself a field of struggle? Poulantzas's (1978) scholarship on the capitalist state is particularly relevant here as he argued that the principal political role of the capitalist state is organising the power bloc and disorganising the popular masses. Its 'different apparatuses, sections, and levels serve as power centers for different fractions or fractional alliances within the power bloc and/or as centers of resistance for different elements among the popular masses' (Jessop, 1999: 48). Hence 'the state here is the strategic field formed through intersecting power networks that becomes a favourable terrain for political manoeuvre by the hegemonic fraction' (Jessop, 1999: 48). It is through constituting this terrain that the state helps to organise the power bloc, and thus the state is a field where competing interests ultimately struggle for power. In similar ways, instead of looking at the shadow practices of the state as a marker of corruption, we look at it as a reaction to the pressure from the power blocs. The practices that many of the state actors undertake are motivated by disparate intentions.

Following the neoliberal policies of 1991, provincial governments often proposed spatial policies seeking and competing for domestic and international investments from private sectors. Tax breaks, subsidised resources (such as land or water) and provision of physical infrastructure were central to those policies which are part of the state's attempts at urban entrepreneurialism. To deliver neoliberal, market-friendly policies, to become more entrepreneurial and to compete against each other for private investments, the Indian state at various levels reformed its institutional architecture, making it more market-oriented through institutions such as SPVs (DSIRDA is an example here). They became part of the delivery of governance mechanisms too, beyond the implementation of just a certain project. Such distinctive characteristic of this form of state intervention is referred to as state entrepreneurialism when state agencies or certain bureaucratically run public sector units indulge in risk-taking and profit-maximising activities (Chen, 2013; Pow, 2002). Studying the Chinese local state's role in planning that has seen a profound shift towards state entrepreneurialism, Wu (2018) defines it as state engagement with the market through institutional reform as it demonstrates a greater interest in introducing, developing and deploying market instruments and engages in market-like entrepreneurial activities. Projects such as Dholera are physical manifestations pushing to build a more energetic and entrepreneurial set of state or semi-state organisations.

A growing literature has looked at state entrepreneurialism in India, including in enclaves such as SEZs and SIRs (Das, 2015; Datta, 2015; Goldman, 2011; Kennedy, 2013, Kennedy and Sood, 2019; Sood and Kennedy, 2020). The shadow nature of the phenomenon has also been examined, such as the outsourcing of state functions to private groups and consultants (Kennedy and Sood, 2019; Sami and Anand, 2021). Hurl and Vogelpohl (2021) provide a global perspective. The case of Dholera SIR here adds a new dimension by illuminating the existence of an increasingly blurry boundary between the state and non-state actors who are key stakeholders in the private sector. It demonstrates how public officials occupy non-state spaces for private benefits using their official positions, while private-sector actors function as de facto state representatives for their own benefits.

In all, the Gujarat model of state-entrepreneurialism reflects a mode of governance which goes the extra mile to suit the market and private interests characterised by motives of personal benefits delivered through caste and kin relations. It is important to note here that when it comes to the case for competition in the neoliberal era, provincial governments in India have competed for investment in the pre-liberalisation era as well. Often referred to as the Licence Raj, provinces regularly lobbied the central government in New Delhi for a greater share in the Five-Year Plans (see Kohli, 2009; Sinha, 2005). There are also many instances of favouritism for designated corporations during that period (Kohli, 2009; Sinha, 2005). Thus, neoliberalism's introduction is not the only factor for competition amongst provincial governments nor the ubiquity of shadow state practices.

Making the State Efficient and Entrepreneurial: Neoliberalism and Bureaucracy

Scholars have demonstrated that under neoliberalism, the Indian state has not withered away (Levien, 2018). Instead, the state has adopted newer forms as the traditional bureaucracy now coordinates with groups such as NGOs that promote development through notions such as self-reliance (Gupta and Sharma, 2006; Mathur, 2015). However, the size of bureaucrats has been trimmed down in many provinces. Outsourcing of jobs and contracting private companies is rampant. These companies often hire staff at significantly reduced salaries. Such appallingly low remuneration and labour conditions are outcomes of Modi's tearing down of whatever labour laws existed to protect some of the basic rights and wages. Earlier, we saw such outsourcing and a decrease in the number of government officials even in the villages of Dubai.

The role of bureaucrats in Gujarat in taking the project of neoliberalism forward is considerable. Newspaper and magazine articles in Gujarat often mentioned the role of some of the key bureaucrats in the success of institutions such as Vibrant Gujarat. These same bureaucrats were moved to the Prime Minister's Office in New Delhi after Modi won the national elections in 2014. However, critical academic scholarship which could tell us how entrenched neoliberalism is amongst these bureaucrats or reveal their impact on the ground is missing. While the initial reaction towards economic liberalisation amongst high-ranking bureaucrats was mixed (Das, 2005), by the end of the 1990s there seemed to be consistent support amongst the higher levels of bureaucracy about the role of neoliberal policies in advancing India's economy. Many of these bureaucrats have become cheerleaders for these policies (Chatterjee and McCartney, 2019; Das, 2005; Mooij, 2005).

Since the staff of INFINITY and DSIRDA shared the same office (Figures 6.1 and 6.2), I once asked Pandey, a senior manager at DSIRDA, about his views on the overlap of the roles of INFINITY and DSIRDA. He had this to say:

> Importantly, here we have government officials who work for eight hours a day continuously. That is because they see the INFINITY people, seated in the same office, [work] for ten hours a day.... We need to learn the ethos from the private sector and then we can become efficient and entrepreneurial. Whatever organisational structure and system we are developing for Dholera, there will be a brand of corporate–government culture. We are not strictly government because if we follow government rules and way of working, nothing can happen.... We have to become entrepreneurial.... [Therefore,] having INFINITY inside has improved our speed, made us more efficient and productive....

Figure 6.1 (*Left*) The reception area in the DSIRDA office. The 'corporate culture' that Pandey wanted to develop was ably supported by the office interior, which is distinct from the usual government offices, even the ones on the same floor in Udyog Bhawan.

Source: Author.

Figure 6.2 (*Right*) A delegation from Suzuki going through the model of the proposed Dholera SIR at the DSIRDA office

Source: DSIRDA Twitter profile.

There seemed to be an agreement on this among other civil servants. Sharma, the head of DSIRDA, an Indian Administrative Services (IAS)[2] official, argued similarly when asked about the impact of sharing an office with a private consultant:

> I see it as a very positive development. Firstly, we do not want government departments to swell too much. That talk is everywhere. [The government needs] to cut down on size and expenditure. It is better to outsource, to achieve higher efficiency. [Secondly,] there is a perception that government departments are very bad and not managed properly, and private sector is good … we are engaging world-class consultants to create a world class city…. In the future, however, it will also lead to capacity building of government organisations….

Both these views clearly represent on-the-ground perspectives on a state under neoliberalism—pared down, efficient, such as the corporate sector. Two key arguments supporting neoliberalism emerge from the above quotes. First, neoliberal ideologies of competition and efficiency have played a key role for the state in the recruitment of INFINITY. Sharma is happy to outsource state responsibilities to private consultants to increase efficiency. Second, another reason given for INFINITY's presence is the need for the public sector to mimic the private sector and become more efficient, for example, in terms of the number of working hours. Earlier we saw how non-state actors were mimicking the state, it is the private sector being mimicked by state actors in Gandhinagar.

Both interviewees foresaw a key role for INFINITY to restructure the state from within, pointing out how INFINITY could 'professionalise', 'corporatise' and/or make the state 'more efficient',[3] through its effect on state organisations.

Similarly, Pandey underlined the need to make the state more 'entrepreneurial' and Sharma expressed the same view. The case of making the state more entrepreneurial is again a neoliberal tenet. State entrepreneurialism refers to a policy which attempts to leverage support for increased private sector involvement, and a more business-like way of running (Chen, 2013). In the infrastructure and urbanisation sectors in particular, such an endeavour is usually made through institutions such as parastatals, SPVs. In working towards such state entrepreneurialism, Sharma found a key role for INFINITY by delivering 'world-class' practices to the countryside of Gujarat. In the longer run, INFINITY in his view would contribute towards the capacity building of DSIRDA. Such statements provide evidence of a more tangible outcome of engaging with such firms, namely, the lasting impression on the zeal of the state to be entrepreneurial.

The State–Non-State Conundrum: The Case of INFINITY

Beyond making the DSIRDA's staff work for longer hours, the outcome of INFINITY's involvement was rather different from what Sharma claimed. Analysing the practices of the AES here, it is worth noting that everyday practices inside the state office reflect a negotiation of state versus non-state relations. Raj, a key member of staff from INFINITY, was a regular face inside the DSIRDA office, advising a host of government officials from the DSIRDA team while taking care of his own work for INFINITY. He was also the front man in dealing with a possible investor visiting the DSIRDA office. For a high-profile investor, his boss, Srivastava (pseudonym), INFINITY project lead, would do a similar job.

Whereas this could be an understanding between INFINITY and DSIRDA in managing daily affairs, such practices instead involved INFINITY staff acting on behalf of the state, creating an impression that they were part of the state. This was evident from interviews with visitors to the DSIRDA office. Frequent visitors named the staff of INFINITY as being amongst the 'high-ranking officials who are very good at getting things done'. They could rarely differentiate between the INFINITY staff and the bureaucrats of DSIRDA. Many of them considered Srivastava to be the head of DSIRDA and the only 'constant' presence whereas 'people such as Sharma keep coming and going'. Srivastava exuded 'confidence, power and continuity....'

Srivastava represented a centre of power in the office other than Sharma, CEO of DSIRDA. As the interviewees mentioned, Srivastava was the mainstay since 2013 whereas the DSIRDA CEOs (who were generally government bureaucrats) were transferred or promoted regularly. Sharma, for instance, was transferred exactly two years after he joined as the head of DSIRDA. For a long time, the post remained vacant or was delegated to officers as an additional responsibility. Discussing the role of Srivastava in the project, Raj said:

> It is because of Srivastava sir that the project is still on…. He is decisive and knows whom to pressurise and how to handle the bureaucrats. I will give you an example: getting the water for Dholera…. We kept revolving around five different sources and were back to square one after a year or two. Then, we had a meeting with the principal secretary and Srivastava sir made sure that all those five bureaucrats were summoned. He told them that 'if you are not giving me water, I can get other sources but do not mess around with me. You will be transferred in two years. Someone new will come to ask me to start it again'…

My impression of Srivastava from our short interview was no different. Assertive, often using the language of a state bureaucrat or politician, he spoke about the importance of the project for India and Gujarat:

> … The country needs the [Dholeta] project. It will give a sudden boost to the economy. You must have seen Mr Modi stressing its importance. The key aspect is the size and scale of Dholera. It is bigger than Singapore. Mr Modi wants this to be realised as soon as possible, and we are putting in our best efforts. He is behind us….

Interestingly, whenever INFINITY or DSIRDA staff visited the site in Dholera, the local real estate developers often paid enthusiastic visits, in which they were unable to differentiate between INFINITY and DSIRDA. For these developers, 'they are all from Gandhinagar'. Gandhinagar to them was the seat of the state that delivers business, or at least by associating with it one can acquire business. These property developers' websites and social media profiles are adorned with photographs of company bosses with INFINITY or DSIRDA staff or with other business delegates visiting Dholera. Both INFINITY and DSIRDA staff, including Srivastava and Pandey, attended the Dholera Developers and Investors Summit 2018 of the local property developers' association (in Chapter 5). A number of property developers queued up to click pictures with them.[4] One of them responded to my question on why the staff were important, referring to the pictures on his website: 'They make our projects legitimate. These are "big" government officers, big people. And our customers then find us easy to believe....' This endeavour to prove proximity to the state draws us back to some of the conclusions of the previous chapter, especially regarding 'mimicking the state'.

The position of INFINITY and its staff or the perception that businesses have of them raises a fundamental question: are these corporate actors part of the AES? This is especially significant in the post-liberalisation context when existing bureaucratic structures have collaborated with new actors, such as these private corporations. INFINITY's staff are not part of the bureaucratic structure of DSIRDA but work from the same space. Although INFINITY is different from the middlemen of Chapter 5 in being appointed by the government, INFINITY too straddles the formal and shadow spaces of the state. In working simultaneously from both inside and outside of the state spaces, INFINITY mediates relations between the state and businesses. What it has provided to the DSIRDA office beyond its consultancy is an anchor to hold the many aspects of the project together. Through these practices, they have become part of the AES.

The Governing Body of DSIRDA: Politicking and Breaching of the State

As the state tries to become more entrepreneurial and lure investors, the actors of AES undertake a host of shadow practices. Earlier we saw how the formal and shadow elements of AES flow into one another smoothly and how their movement creates a new image of the state as well as new state actors who constitute the AES. These new actors blur the lines between formal and shadow elements in light of a large infrastructure project, as we witness the state's changing relationship with society and the market or business. They underline the importance of ongoing practices in the shadow state, and how these practices occur even at the highest echelons of the state.

Mishra (pseudonym) is one of the board members of DSIRDA.[5] Once as he was talking about constant political pressure on the members to move forward without particular care for details, he described certain events during the initial stages of the smart city project. While looking into the details of the companies, which signed memoranda of understanding (MoUs) with the government,

I came across one company, which was registered under the name of Dholera even before the announcement of the project. Mishra told me about an interaction with one senior bureaucrat, Saha (pseudonym), after a board meeting around November–December 2008 that helped me understand the case. The Dholera SIR project was being finalised around this time and a conceptual 'Master Plan'[6] had just arrived from Halcrow, the UK-based consultants:

> … At the meeting when we were shown the 'conceptual master plan' … for the first time, Saha said: 'We will implement this.' I said: 'The plan has to be worked out. It is still sketchy.' [Saha said:] 'Sir, whatever you have to do, you can do later. You please approve it today. Write your complaints, we will look into it [*sic*]. However, if you are going to sit on this or reject, I am going to lose my job tomorrow….' [I said:] 'But this is incomplete. Even the zones are not complete.' He went on: '… We can arrange some funds for your institute [*takes the name*]…. Or else I will have to change the board. You will not be on the board from tomorrow…. Vibrant Gujarat is in two months' time. We have the investors from Singapore … are [*sic*] on board. Where will we give them lands from if this is not approved?' The board approved this….

The Vibrant Gujarat (Global Summit [VGGS]) 2009 was held in February 2009 where the Dholera SIR project was launched by the government. During the summit, there were three main companies which signed MoUs with the government, one of which was a Singapore-based company whose owner floated a couple of companies around 2008. This company was to be allotted 1,219 hectares in Dholera. This new company with Dholera in its name was registered with the Registrar of Companies Kolkata in 2008.[7] If Dholera SIR was first announced to the public in 2009, it was strange that a company named after it already existed months before the launch of the project. Mishra subtly answered this by explaining what Saha told him in 2008 about the Singapore-based investors ready with the money.

Similar incidents of exceptions are quite widespread. The state of exception is so common that they come across as routine (Das and Poole, 2004). For example, the government launched the Dholera port project in 2002. Surprisingly, a company named 'Dholera Port and Special Economic Zone Limited' was already registered in 1998. This was much before anything was heard about the Dholera port project and, more interestingly, even before the concept of SEZ was in place. From the analysis of land sale records of the Dholera SIR region, it was clear that the first set of sudden sales or outside buyers arriving in Dholera began around 2000, and soon after the port project along with an industrial estate was launched in 2002. Offices of real estate companies started mushrooming around 2000. Hence, peak land sales started before the announcement of the project, underlining the insider information that must have been used.

However, such exceptions in the name of ease of business have been commonplace in the Indian state, both historically and in the current scenarios. As argued earlier, the era of Licence Raj is wrought with favouritism (Sinha, 2005). In the neoliberal period, however, as scholars (Ong, 2006; Sood and Kennedy, 2020) have shown such exceptions have also received an official mechanism. The observations raise questions about whether these practices signify illegality, corruption and also why I prefer to call them shadow. These 'exceptions' are an outcome of the entrepreneurial zeal which the state needs to inculcate to become more 'efficient' or 'professional' as the DSIRDA bureaucrats earlier argued.

However, this entrepreneurial zeal has resulted in a series of shadow practices by the state as many actors with such information used them to corner personal benefits. The passing of information to businesses, possibly by bureaucrats, is one case in point. Whether these practices escalate the speed of project delivery is one matter, but in the process a number of usual bureaucratic procedures are skipped. The informal luring, threatening or arm-twisting to approve the planning drawings of the project illustrate how shadow practices are undertaken. While the obligations of a neoliberal ideology may compel the state or its personnel to become 'competitive' and 'entrepreneurial', the state undertakes shadow practices and becomes the 'state of exception' (Ong, 2006). At the same time, this is also motivated by private interests, as the next section will document.

An Official's Use of Caste, Kinship and the State

A salient feature of the AES is the network of caste, and kin relationships that often thrive shadow practices. Shadow state practices overlap with caste and kin networks, and understanding these networks is key to illuminating the practices and disentangling the idea of the state. Scholars have pointed out that the state is no neutral arbiter when it comes to the social relations of caste or kin (Harriss-White, 2003: 191). Following neoliberal policies in the 1990s, the state or the market never attempted to abolish or transform such existing relations. Rather, it 'encourage(d) them to rework themselves as economic institutions and to persist' (Harriss-White, 2003: 191). As both caste and religion are practiced in a flexible manner, they 'generate exclusive, networked forms of accumulation and corporatist forms of economic regulation' as we see below (Harriss-White, 2003: 191).

Mihir was previously a muscleman cum middleman operating in land deals. His role usually involves brokering a land deal and charging a fixed sum from the buyer (usually never more than 5 per cent in his case). However, when he comes across obstinate sellers, using muscle power is 'part of the job'. He argued that the nature of the work was such that every land broker had to be a muscleman or at least hire someone. Once he vividly explained his first major deal: a 'collector' from Gandhinagar was buying land for a company named 'Suzlon' that deals in wind energy and planned to set up an SEZ in Dholera. By 'collector', Mihir referred to an administrative position as the following discussion will clarify. I quote a section from our discussion:

> Mihir: ... This company [Suzlon] wanted more land from that area.... Being a Patidar,[8] he [Kaushik Dhanani] is the main person of the then the minister's daughter [*takes name*] in Dholera. In our first meeting in his office, he gave me the list of all the land, and I was stunned. He knew ... its ownership history.... What happens is companies like Suzlon cannot buy such a massive tract of land. They hire people like Kaushik.... They ask Kaushik to buy it as he is responsible, being a government official.... Then, Kaushik needs us to buy the land on the ground....
>
> ... So, after a couple of months ... Suzlon decided not to get into the mess.... We bought a Honda City car [from the token money]. Kaushik started his projects in Ambli with the same money probably.
>
> Author: Which project?
>
> Mihir: ... Smart Township [*name changed*] next to Dholera Hotel [*name changed*] on the highway.... I am not sure about the real owner but [a certain] minister's relative is definitely there....

Kaushik Dhanani is a senior manager at GIDB, the apex authority of DSIRDA. Before moving to Gandhinagar, Kaushik was a land revenue official in a sub-district neighbouring Dholera when the SIR was launched. His position in the land revenue department was important, as he was the custodian of all the land records of the fifty or so villages under the sub-district's administration. Any land transaction has to pass through his office. Kaushik then moved to Gandhinagar as a deputy collector in the Revenue Department. This was followed by his elevation to GIDB where he had an impressive profile.

For a graduate of chemistry, he was a chief town planner with GIDB and was the CEO of DSIRDA, and hence a member of its Governing Board members. He was also the CEO of another SIR authority for a brief period.

While this set of promotions in such a brief span is remarkable, Kaushik's moonlighting is no less extraordinary, illuminating the intricate working of the shadow state taking caste and kin networks onboard in neoliberal India. Real estate dealers in Dholera often claim that the Smart Township project (mentioned earlier) has been very successful in the region. The informants argue: 'It belonged to Patidars and second, they have connections in the ministry and the SIR office.' In a society where caste is a consistent marker of personal, professional or political relationships, Patidar buyers first went to Kaushik. Second, their connections in Gandhinagar gave buyers additional faith. The project was supposedly owned by the daughter of an important minister, who was a Patidar.

Kaushik's private office dealing with these projects was in a sector in Gandhinagar where he undertook his shadow role while his government position at GIDB/DSIRDA was barely 3 kilometers away. The Registrar of Company's records show the details and the address was where Kaushik's residential office was located. On the website of Smart Township, MoUs worth billions of Indian rupees signed with the Government of Gujarat during the biennial VGGS were uploaded. At the 2015 VGGS, when Anandiben Patel (a Patidar) was the chief minister, the website claimed to have signed MoUs worth INR 36 billion, which dipped to INR 8 billion in the VGGS 2017 by the time a new chief minister was in place. Along with its own projects, the website regularly uploads recent pictures of the progress of the construction of SIR undertaken on behalf of the government. This often created ambiguity and made Smart Township appear like a government-promoted project. At the Gujarat Patidar Business Summit 2018 held in Gandhinagar, Kaushik's company participated actively and drew immense interest being the only representation from the much talked about Dholera smart city.

However, of late, Kaushik has been facing heat from various sides after a new chief minister came to power in Gujarat. A departmental inquiry was launched against him although information has not been divulged. This was further corroborated by a number of complaints against Kaushik and Smart Township, which appeared online on multiple websites that report consumer complaints. Complaints ranged from being cheated to how Kaushik used his connections to suppress the voices of the complainants. One buyer, who worked as a small businessperson in Ahmedabad, complained of being cheated as there was not much progress in the township.

Many local brokers and developers unabashedly mentioned how the blessing of certain relatives of ministers is key to Kaushik's project. These networks are hard and risky for researchers to break into, while finding a documentary trail to prove it is near impossible. Yet the evidence mentioned earlier suggests that these claims are not completely unfounded. The minister's daughter has been caught in a massive land fraud in a nearby district for getting government owned land at a discounted rate. One cannot ignore the fact that when the chief minister was a Patidar, Kaushik's company signed MoUs worth more than four times compared to two years later when the Patidar chief minister was replaced. At the same time, Suzlon Energy Limited, for which Kaushik was buying land, was owned by a Patidar. A bureaucrat such as Kaushik blurs the line between the state and non-state. He enabled a large private company to aggregate land, and for that, he used his position at the revenue department or later at the GIDB. To target a specific seller, one needs to know the survey numbers and ownership details that Kaushik automatically had access to.

Kaushik drew power from his Patidar kinship networks to undertake his shadow practices. Hence, within these dynamics involving the shadow state, manifesting neoliberalism, traditional caste and kin relations play an important role. David Mosse (2020) has argued that current economic and political forces have simultaneously weakened and revived caste in ways that defy easy generalisation. Historically accumulated 'caste capital' is flexible enough to 'suit new institutional orders and opportunity structures' (Bandyopadhyay, 2016: 36–37). Similarly, Harriss-White (2003: 176–200) argued that under a market economy, caste continues to be a 'social structure of accumulation' for Indian capitalism. Kaushik's moonlighting that blurs the public–private or formal–shadow boundaries sums up the neoliberal entrepreneurial state, be it in Gandhinagar or Dholera. Importantly, these fuzzy boundaries of the public–private or state–non-state are not just an outcome of their poor categorisation but arise from the shadow practices of state actors such as Kaushik who constantly unmake these boundaries. Caste, kin relationships become the logic through which shadow practices are undertaken that also take the project of neoliberalism forward.

Going back to where we started the chapter, as services are outsourced, blurred boundaries of the state help theorise how the state's relationship with society and the market is being redefined. Two key ideas around the AES emerged. First, policies of liberalisation have affected how new entrants into the state's bureaucratic architecture appropriate the state and often become the face of the state. Second, these new actors of the AES undertake a host of shadow practices to take forward the project of neoliberalism. These shadow practices by formal state actors take place due to the demand of the entrepreneurial zeal of the state, a key facet of neoliberalism. Not only do state actors advocate the intrinsic virtue in private entities participating in public affairs but bureaucrats also use a neoliberal argument to explain why the public sector needs to learn from the private. However, the evidence indicates that private corporations have strengthened state capacity in minimal ways; instead, they have in fact appropriated state spaces.

The boundaries between the state and society or state and non-state actors have always remained fuzzy. However, if the movement between state and non-state is as fluid as seen in the previous chapter, why do we still label the entities, formal and shadow, separately? I find Fuller and Harriss's (2001) argument relevant here that even if the state–society boundary is fluid and negotiable to social context and position, material boundaries such as the wall of a government offices exist however blurred and porous. At the same time, for a majority of the citizens such as the farmers, the AES, for all its shadow characteristics, remains inaccessible.

Notes

1. Interviews with many farmers from Dholera revealed their unsuccessful attempts to reach the DSIRDA.
2. IAS is the premier civil service of India. Members serve the Government of India as well as the provinces.
3. The words commonly appeared during the interviews with both Pandey and Sharma.
4. Not all of these photographs could be published due to copyright issues.
5. I am withholding further details of his position to maintain anonymity.
6. See note 2 for 'Master Plan'. By 'conceptual' master plan, Mishra referred to the sketchy nature.
7. I withhold the full name here. These records can be accessed officially for a small fee from the website of MCA21 and operated by the Ministry of Corporate Affairs of India (http://www.mca.gov.in/).
8. Patidar is a landed caste. This was explained in Chapter 3, note 1.

7
Protests, Neoliberalism and Hindutva amongst Farmers

In September 2016, around 2,000 farmers led by the Bhal Bachao Samiti[1] (Protect Bhal Committee, henceforth BBS) and Sagar Rabari from Gujarat Khedut Samaj (Gujarat Farmers' Society) gathered in front of Hotel Vision Modi, the local office of the DSIRDA. Many of these farmers were recently served notices to vacate their land for the project. Farmers were particularly angry because, in December 2015, they managed to get an order from the Gujarat High Court which directed the DSIRDA to maintain the status quo and not acquire any land from farmers until the matter was duly heard (Express News Network, 2015). However, ignoring the court order, DSIRDA kept sending these notices.

As farmer leaders were negotiating with DSIRDA officials, the crowd outside grew restless. Some women farmers forced their way into the office, and the rest of the crowd followed. Once the women were inside, the matter suddenly snowballed into a commotion as the crowd broke down furniture, tore maps hung on the walls and threw away official files. It continued for almost an hour as nobody seemed to be able to control the situation. The officials then offered to negotiate farmers' demands, including an immediate stop to notices. Other demands such as shutting down the local DSIRDA office were to be taken up with senior officials in Gandhinagar. However, none of these promises were delivered.

Before this incident, another huge protest meeting was organised in Dholera in 2015, under the banner of Koli Samaj (Koli Society). Although close to 10,000 women and men attended, it did not yield much beyond the show of strength (*Top right* in Figure 7.1). In fact, a few months after the Koli Samaj meeting, when the BBS farmers planned a *padayatra* (march on foot) rally from Dholera to Gandhinagar, only a few participated. It later transpired that many of the farmer leaders were persuaded by individual caste leaders

Figure 7.1   Photographs from the anti-SIR rallies between 2012 and 2016

Source: Sagar Rabari.

(both Koli and Darbar) to skip the event. In July 2017, the Activation Area in the SIR project was in full swing with farmers regularly served notices to vacate their farmlands. According to a DSIRDA bureaucrat, many farmers 'voluntarily' accepted compensation.[2]

Despite the imminent dispossession of land and livelihood, it was difficult to find either resistance or consent as predominant themes in the subjective expressions of the farmers. Instead, what emerged was ambivalence and aspiration. Interestingly, the same group of Gujarat Khedut Samaj leaders managed to get thirty-six of the forty-four villages removed from another Special Investment Region project in a 100-day-long agitation against the same government in 2013 (Duncan and Agarwal, 2017). This was a rare incident when Modi, as the chief minister of Gujarat, accepted demands from protestors. The picture one gets by studying the protest in Dholera is of a resistance that fails to keep momentum after every major protest event.

Notably, these soon to be dispossessed farmers continued to vote for the ruling BJP, which has openly backed the project since its launch in 2009. To understand the weak protests, it is important to analyse the continued prominence of the BJP party in rural Gujarat. This is significant because weak resistance and the party's strong electoral performance are connected.

In the 2017 provincial Gujarat elections, when the BJP faced a stiff challenge from Congress, it managed to win only 63 out of the 140 rural seats (down from 77). However, in the 2019 Parliamentary elections, BJP won 61 per cent of rural votes compared to 44 per cent from the 2017 provincial elections (Bansal, 2019; D. Kumar, 2017). This remained the trend: whenever the BJP has lost some support, it has managed to bounce back in the next elections.

This brings Gaventa's (2019) arguments into context: 'Why in a situation of glaring inequality where one may intuitively expect upheaval, does one instead find, or appear to find, acquiescence? Under what conditions and against what obstacles does rebellion begin to appear?' (cited in Bernstein, 2020: 3). Raising those questions for Dholera, how do we make sense of these events: a farmers' resistance against a project that threatens to dispossess them loses momentum after every major protest. Why do farmers who face land dispossession support and acquiesce to a right-wing project and locals continue to vote for the same BJP party? And second, linked to this is another key question: why and how does a neoliberal capitalist state make welfare provisions to subaltern classes?

In answering these questions, we see the coming together of neoliberalism and Hindutva, also contributing towards our understanding of the rise of authoritarian populism in rural areas of India. The continued rise of authoritarian populism in rural areas across the globe over the last few decades makes the study extremely important (Scoones et al., 2018). Here, the fourth proposition of the AES—that in everyday practices the AES constitutes and is, simultaneously, constituted by intricate linkages between economic and cultural ideologies—is particularly relevant. Through its formal and shadow elements, AES is a great facilitator of the marriage between 'liberal' neoliberalism and 'illiberal' Hindutva which we see later in the chapter. An explanation of how the two economic and cultural ideologies come together to help each other, and how they may depart from their own macro-ideologies depending on the context, significantly contributes to the analysis. It fleshes out how Hindutva has effectively superseded earlier styles of political action amongst farmers, most notably the New Farmers Movement (Brass, 1994). This is not to claim that the Hindutva groups have replaced farmers' movements across Gujarat. There are still various land rights movements and farmers' protests led by progressive platforms.

The anti-SIR protest in Dholera is led by the BBS, formed by representatives of the twenty-two villages that come under the SIR to coordinate the movement. 'Bhal' is the traditional name of the Dholera region. The same protest platform was used to successfully challenge the government that earlier launched a chemical estate in the vicinity of a national park. Protests started in 2010, although a strong resistance was noticeable by 2012 with a simultaneous peak in land sales. BBS has sub-committees in the affected villages representing both Koli and Darbar castes. Water from the Narmada via canals remains a long-term demand of the farmers and has been clubbed with the fight against the SIR. Slogans by the farmers of BBS include 'SIR hatao, Bhal bachao' (Take back SIR, save Bhal) or 'SIR hatao, Narmada laao' (Take back SIR, bring Narmada). The Gujarat Khedut Samaj coordinates similar protests at the provincial scale. Although the movement has not been strong enough to repeal the project, the farmers managed to get an order from the high court to maintain 'status-quo', essentially stopping any land acquisition until the matter is duly heard (Express News Network, 2015). Table 7.1 documents some of the key events.

Table 7.1   Key events in the farmers' resistance movement

Year	Event
2009	Dholera SIR launched
2010–2011	Bhal Bachao Samiti (BBS) is formed again. Petition against the SIR project at the Gujarat Hugh Court
2012	Gujarat Legislative Assembly election. A Koli from BJP wins the Dhandhuka constituency
2013	Another Special Investment Region (SIR) Mandal Becharaji is cancelled after a 100-day long intense farmer protests led by Gujarat Khedut Samaj
2014	Federal election and Narendra Modi becomes prime minister of India
2015	Koli Samaj meeting in Dholera against the SIR project
2015	*Padayatra* rally from Dholera to Gandhinagar
2015	Gujarat High Court orders status quo and stops further land acquisition
2016	Local office of DSIRDA torched in Dholera (narrated in the introduction to this chapter)
2017	Narmada canal distributaries construction starts in Dholera
2017	Gujarat Legislative Assembly election when Bhupendrasinh scraped through from Dholka constituency. In Dhandhuka, a Koli from Congress wins.

Source: Author's reconstruction of events from interviews and archival research.

Resistance and the Actually Existing State (AES)

Despite living with the knowledge that the loss of their land was imminent, Dholera farmers were not always vocal in protest. While some farmer leaders were actively protesting, most farmers could not be mobilised. On occasions, even farmer leaders would miss important demonstrations or meetings. Following James Scott (1990), this absence of contestation should not always be seen as acquiescence or support for the Dholera smart city project. It is by paying attention to the negotiations made in everyday life, to what people do and say, that we can see how 'counterhegemonic consciousness is elaborated' (Scott, 1990: 200).

This is especially true as there are sporadic protests, a sustained fight at the high court by a few farmers, or everyday incidents such as government officials being banned from entering villages. In that case, what is important to understand is why this same resistance has been unsuccessful in maintaining a sustained momentum. We need to understand the everyday interactions between the state and society, and the key role economic policies and the socio-cultural project of Hindutva play in these villages. A type of dominance has been created over the years as Hindutva groups have infiltrated state organisations at multiple levels as we saw in previous chapters. They often act as gatekeepers to the state, playing a key role in citizens' access to the state.

The scholarship on the phenomenon of state-led land acquisition received significant attention in the 2000s, especially through the concept of 'land grab'.[3] While diverse in nature, the scholarship largely uses David Harvey's (2005) framework of 'accumulation by dispossession'. However, in critiquing accumulation by dispossession, Levien (2013b: 15; 2018) points out that despite Harvey's acknowledgement of state force, it ignores the obvious reliance on state force'. Capital cannot automatically find 'outlets in land or in any other asset' (Levien, 2013b: 15) and is painstakingly moved (Searle, 2010). The state becomes an important enabler through various strategies, including the use of force and the scholarship on land grab covers many of those dimensions.

The political reactions to 'land grabbing' from below are vastly varied and complex, ranging from 'resistance, acquiescence or incorporation' as Hall et al. (2015) sums up. The scholarship on resistance to 'land grab' is influenced particularly by concepts such as 'countermovement' (Polanyi, 2001 [1944]), 'hegemony' (Gramsci, 1971) or Scott's (1985) 'weapons of the weak'. According to Scott (1985: 29), resistance takes diverse overt and covert forms such as judicial challenges, social movements or even ordinary scuffles and these are illustrated in the scholarship. Scott (1985) proposes that peasants calculate the risks of their actions in coming up with far more rational behaviours as a range of factors such as their own safety, ethnicity or local politics come into play.

Within this, the scholarship on the Indian rural resistance against similar phenomena offers an interesting perspective due to the centrality of its electoral politics. Resistance is often channelled and made to work through both 'social movements' as well as 'political associations' (Levien and Agarwal, 2020). Scholars such as Chatterjee (2004, 2008) have argued that the poor wield their power through their vote as they engage in political negotiations with authorities. Similar ideas were developed by Benjamin (2008) and Anjaria (2011).[4] Baviskar (1995) critiqued the focus on the farmers vs the state narratives in her study of the impact of the Sardar Sarovar Project. This was followed by a significant scholarship in the 2000s that commented on a similar reductionist approach to the debates of farmers vs state or farmers vs corporations (Balakrishnan, 2013; Levien and Agarwal, 2020).

However, underlining the role of the state in making land deals happen, Levien (2012: 12) proposes that the 'broker state' has facilitated a 'market-oriented compensation policy'. Such policies fracture villagers, ultimately 'undermining any basis for collective action' (Levien, 2012: 12). In other cases, such as in the province of Tamil Nadu, Vijayabaskar (2010) argues that the state has been rolling out policies for a while to encourage peasants to quit farming. Dholera farmers' protests can be placed within these bargains where they have occasionally managed to push the state to take their demands onboard due to democratic compulsions. At the same time, what is novel in Dholera is the extra determination of the AES actors who take caste, religious or political associations onboard to weaken the protests.

Beyond electoral politics, the Indian case is particularly interesting due to the success of farmers' protests in blocking major projects over the past two decades (Levien and Agarwal, 2020). Nielsen et al. (2020) find that 'the ability to cultivate and appropriate the new political spaces opened by the anti-dispossession movement ... correlated strongly with historically produced caste and class relations...'. The aspects of castes, class and religion-based politics provide a key entry point to understanding the complexity of these resistances as well as the counter-resistances that could be run by similar groups or even by the AES or organisations associated with AES (Roy, 2011a: 272).

This chapter contributes to this scholarship through two key arguments, which are also part of the framing of the AES. First is the prevalence of Hindutva politics through which actors of the AES negotiate with the state and society to help diffuse these protests. Their practices may include contradictory steps ultimately aimed at creating acquiescence. This is the disjuncture in Hindutva. It 'represents a constellation of forces, not all of which draw energy from the RSS–Jan Sangh–BJP lineage' (Yadav, 2017). In fact, Brass's (1994) work on similar overlaps in northern India is of particular relevance here. Second, through a host of economic measures that may signify a departure from the basic tenets of neoliberalism, the actors in the AES negotiate farmers' resistance and help the neoliberal project to continue. This brings to the fore the economic logic of the diffused protest. In his book, *Give a Man a Fish*, James Ferguson (2015) analyses redistributive neoliberalism in which the state has taken an active role in the process by handing out direct cash to citizens. While not argued by Ferguson, the strategies by the AES in Dholera can be seen as an attempt to keep neoliberalism on track by negotiating some of the resistances, which may arise due to the extreme impact of neoliberal policies.

Hindutva Politics: Caste Solidarity vis-à-vis Contradiction, Elite Co-Option

As farmers were losing their land to the project, it was not that the smart city project (the raison d'être for the loss) or the loss of their land 'was such a terrible thing that everyone forgot their usual squabbles in order to focus on remaking the world' (Simpson, 2013: 5). Existing patronage and caste fights found their way into the language of the daily lives of villagers in their opposition or support of the project. Within this, Hindutva politics has assimilated a host of practices to mitigate protests by farmers in Dholera or to ensure support for the BJP. Desai (2015) studying the rise of the BJP among the lower caste population in the city of Ahmedabad pointed towards the 'desire' and 'ambivalence' that mark subaltern political subjectivities (also see Balakrishnan, 2019; Cross, 2015). In similar ways, Hindutva actors using the state or its institutions in Dholera managed to create a sense of ambivalence as well as hope and aspiration towards the neoliberal project. This ambivalence made it difficult to find either resistance or consent as predominant themes in the subjective expressions of the dispossessed (Desai, 2015).

As we saw in the earlier chapters, caste remains a significant indicator of economic, social as well as political relations in India, particularly in rural areas. In a review of the role played by caste in 'India's land wars' (Levien, 2011; Steur, 2015), Nielsen et al. (2020: 684–685) describe how 'caste consistently mediates land transfers in present-day India by pre-empting, undermining or fueling processes of social contestation'. Earlier, we saw how the project of Hindutva has successfully replaced the Congress system of patronage by empowering lower caste leaders amongst the Kolis. However, this does not mean that Kolis led the Hindutva organisations. In fact, the top echelons of Hindutva organisations remain with the Darbars who hold considerable financial power. Kolis generally became the foot soldiers of Hindutva groups (Berenschot, 2011a).

Many Kolis have managed to become the *sarpanch*[5] of their villages. When land transactions began in any village after the announcement of the Dholera SIR, the *sarpanch*es took the lead in supporting the project. When the BBS, the farmers' group, petitioned in the high court against the project, every *sarpanch* from these twenty-two villages signed letters explicitly mentioning the support of their villagers towards the project. One narrative successfully established amongst the villagers has been to transfer the blame for the loss of land to previous Congress governments at the federal level that launched the Delhi–Mumbai Industrial Corridor (DMIC), which supposedly necessitated the Dholera SIR project: 'Modi had no other option but to agree [to the project].' Hence, the neoliberal policies due to which farmers were going to lose their lands became associated with both BJP and Congress, despite the fact that the latter has been out of power in Gujarat since 1995. Also, Dholera SIR was not launched because of DMIC. Jenkins (1999) makes this argument of obfuscation at the macro scale in his 'reform by stealth' argument that neoliberal reform went through in India as the 'blame' was shifted between federal and provincial governments.

Coming back to caste, until 2007, the elected members of the legislative assembly (MLAs) in Dholera belonged to upper-caste groups. However, during the 2007 provincial assembly election, the Koli community, which is close to 70 per cent of the local population fielded a Koli local who stood as an Independent and went on to win the seat. The Koli Samaj, an umbrella group of the Koli community, supported him. The BJP quickly understood the group's sentiments and ceded space by fielding a local Koli in 2012 who defeated an upper-caste candidate from Congress. Hence, the Koli farmers voted for a party that launched and implemented policies to dispossess them of their land within three years. When BJP fielded the Koli candidate in 2012, one informal agreement was that the Kolis would not coordinate with upper-caste Darbar farmer leaders in BBS or Khedut Samaj. In return, some of the Koli majority villages were to be taken off the SIR project. Post-election, the BJP did not respect the promise. The Koli Samaj then held the massive anti-SIR meeting in Dholera in 2015 (Figure 7.1, *top right*). This meeting coupled with the high court directive ordering a status-quo a few months later boosted the confidence of the anti-SIR protesters amongst the Kolis. However, the ultimate aim of getting the project cancelled remained a distant dream.

In 2017, Koli leaders in the anti-SIR movement, BBS, planned to organise a rally before the election to send a strong message to the ruling government. This time, the Koli Samaj stepped back. One of the local Koli Samaj leaders spoke about the pressure from senior Koli BJP leaders from Gandhinagar not to go openly against the government closer to the election: 'I received a call directly from a minister from Bhavnagar. He asked us to not do anything until the elections....' Although organisations such as Koli Samaj claim to be apolitical, they are often arm-twisted by the BJP. Even during the anti-SIR meeting of 2015, which was clearly anti-BJP or anti-Modi, leaders of Koli Samaj rarely criticised either in their lectures. They would criticise a specific policy, a state official or a BJP cabinet minister, but shied away from an anti-Modi agenda. The leaders from the protesting group, BBS, often pointed out how Koli Samaj leaders use such social networks and platforms as a step to gain a place in the ruling party. Whereas the Koli Samaj advised constituents to vote for the BJP in 2012, there was no clarity in the 2017 elections. Hence, by negotiating contradictions through caste solidarity or by conceding political space to the 'lower' caste, Hindutva politics mitigated the anti-SIR protests from becoming a strong force.

In one of the protesting farmers' meetings in September 2017, it was decided that the BBS would campaign against Bhupendrasinh Chudasama, the Darbar BJP leader and a Dholera native. Bhupendrasinh, MLA from a nearby constituency, was a powerful BJP cabinet minister, holding multiple important portfolios. BBS planned to defeat the strong incumbent minister and increase the pressure to cancel the SIR project. With an anti-BJP wave across rural Gujarat, it seemed plausible. As news about the plan broke, Darbar community elders summoned Darbar farmer leaders within the BBS and convinced them not to go ahead. One of them later narrated:

> We prepared everything. We even had two [*candidates named*] 'Bhupendrasinh Manubha Chudasama'. If these candidates had their names in the EVM [electronic voting machine], there was no chance that Bhupendrasinh could win. He was there in that meeting.... [They] promised that Bhupendrasinh would get the (SIR) project cancelled after the election. Although, I do not believe him, others said yes and we cancelled our plan....

These BBS leaders were promised the cancellation of the project after the election. The incident was significant because by ensuring that the anti-SIR Darbar leaders do not campaign against Bhupendrasinh, a definite defeat was averted. Bhupendrasinh won by a margin of just 327 votes (Elections.in, 2017).[6] Second, by managing the anti-SIR protestors using caste solidarity, the Hindutva actors ensured a loss of face for the Darbar farmer leaders as the BJP did not keep the promise of cancelling the SIR project. This led to many Kolis from the BBS questioning the wisdom of the Darbar leaders of BBS, as they felt cheated, thus creating a rift amongst the protesting farmers. Similarly, the summoning of Vijayrajsinh and other Darbar leaders from the BBS just before the *padayatra* was important as it diffused the agitation that was planned to build a sustained momentum against the SIR. Vijayrajsinh and his associates in the BBS were asked 'not to empower the Kolis further....' Many of the Darbar leaders went missing on that day and, in the end, were alienated from the BBS altogether. There are many similar incidents mentioned during interviews by opposite caste groups. Caste solidarity and/or animosity often trumped the resistance against the SIR.

The BJP also changed tactics and lured many farmer leaders by offering them tickets to fight local elections. One such leader was Bhimsinh. In 2015, during my fieldwork, he was a staunch critic of the SIR project. In fact, in a 2014 report in *Frontline* magazine that highlighted the protesting farmers, Bhimsinh was photographed sitting with the farmer leader, Sagar Rabari from Gujarat Khedut Samaj (see Katakam, 2014; Akhtar, 2023 for figures). However, in 2017, Bhimsinh was a changed man after he unsuccessfully fought the local village council election on a BJP ticket. He now supported the project, explaining how the SIR will bring development to Dholera.

Not very different was the curious case of Kunwarsinh, the general secretary of the BBS, the protesting farmers' group. He was always critical of the smart city in public. Surprisingly, for a farmer leader, his main business was real estate. When the Dholera SIR project came, his family, which controlled the opposition Congress party in this area, swiftly took up land brokering. With the massive sum earned as brokerage, he started a few real estate projects in Dholera and nearby places. More surprisingly, in private, Kunwarsinh often came across as a supporter of the SIR project:

> ... How will Dholera progress if not through SIR? We have all become richer because of the land business not because of ... farming. We gave up farming ages ago.... I do not meet the BJP leaders.... However, I support Modi. He is doing

great for India and we Indians are getting our respect in the world…. He is the
Hindu Hriday Samrat [King of Hindus' heart]….

Thus, even within the resistance movement, there are leaders supportive of the
neoliberal project and/or its ability to deliver development. He often posted
Modi's lectures on his social media accounts. At the same time, Kunwarsinh
praised Modi as the king of Hindu hearts, a title given to him by right-wing
groups. Such appeal eclipses ideologies of support or opposition towards the
SIR project, ensuring the continued electoral success of the BJP. What works
for Hindutva politics is the presence of these leaders who can help undermine
the class-based unity amongst the Darbars and Kolis exploiting the caste
contradictions that existed historically.

In similar ways, aspiration and hope created through construction and
real estate activities brought in a semblance of economic development,
manufacturing legitimacy of the project. The activities due to the project
created an impression of progress while also delivering some economic benefits
to a certain section. The highway on which these villages were located has been
widened to four lanes after the project was announced. Concrete buildings
started appearing as real estate projects were launched. With the enormous
increase in land prices, many farmers came out of their cyclical debt. Although
locals continue to undertake seasonal migration to nearby cities in search of
employment, the construction and infrastructural investment provided some
opportunity for upward mobility. A farmer stated, 'I could never imagine that
I could come out of my debt. But having sold half of my land, I have paid
back [the loans], built a pucca house, a car for the family and have some fixed
deposits in the bank….' Around the same time, many of the villages along the
sea, which remained neglected by the state until now, have seen significant
improvement in basic infrastructure such as roads and potable water.

These infrastructure improvements are often argued to be associated with
the SIR projects by BJP leaders during interviews. This is not true since such
basic infrastructure comes through various rural development schemes and
is not connected with the smart city project. Second, inequality has, in fact,
increased, as most of the land sellers from the lower castes have not reinvested
the money that they received from selling their land wisely. These people now
undertake year-long migration to nearby cities as they do not have land to
cultivate, compared to the seasonal migration earlier. Scholars have similarly
argued that the lack of resistance could be due to 'aspirations' and 'hope'
that such projects may evoke (Cross, 2014). Both Balakrishnan (2019) and

Cross (2014) found that lower castes view these projects as 'a space of promise and hope' and 'a great leveller'. Gürel et al. (2019), Levien (2018), Sud (2009) and other scholars have similarly documented instances of the breakdown of protests in the Indian contexts by variegated groups and how some land sellers support the infrastructure project, while others may not.

Within the local population, a section emerged such as the Bhal Vikas Manch (Bhal Development Forum) which staged demonstrations showing their support to projects. Some villagers even blame the anti-SIR protestors for posing a threat to their development. Such narratives were especially popular among BJP or Modi supporters. The smart city project also resonated with the narrative of the sub-national identity of Gujarat. One local businessman (unclear political affiliation) expressed his support of the project: '... we will have schools, hospitals, airports similar to Ahmedabad. We will not be forced to travel to Ahmedabad for small medical issues.... If the solar farm comes up, then Dholera will supply electricity to the world. Gujarat will remain the number one province in India.' Appeal to sub-national identity has shaped the expectations of informed villagers and helped form consent. Adaman et al. (2019) have documented a very similar set of nationalist sentiments around a mining project in the Turkish context. Appeal to sub-national identity has shaped the expectations of informed villagers and helped form consent. An important factor in Modi's successful election campaigns as the chief minister of Gujarat was his ability to appeal to such sub-national identities (Bobbio, 2012; Jaffrelot, 2016).

Disjuncture in Neoliberalism

Whereas the Dholera SIR project is a representative case of neoliberalism in the definitions of Harvey (2005), some of the policies and welfare measures that the provincial government has recently adopted depart from this understanding of neoliberalism. Both Venugopal (2015) and Wacquant (2012) categorised the scholarship on neoliberalism broadly into two groups. The first takes neoliberalism as a given doctrine and focuses on the hegemonic economic conception as scholars like Ferguson (2010: 170) pointed out how 'in perhaps the strictest sense, neoliberalism refers to a macroeconomic doctrine.' Chang (2003: 5) similarly describes neoliberalism as 'born out of an unholy alliance between neoclassical economics and the Austrian-Libertarian tradition'. The second approach identifies neoliberalism in the real world and focuses on the disjuncture between neoliberal ideologies and their practices (Brenner and

Theodore, 2002: 352). It considers neoliberalism not as an 'end-state' but as a process—and as a project embedded in the context, 'produced within national, regional, and local contexts defined by the legacies of inherited frameworks, policy regimes, regulatory practices, and political struggles' (Brenner and Theodore, 2002: 349). It is fraught with contradictions and negotiations in the pursuit of market-driven transformation. At the same time, being embedded in the context, neoliberalism should not be seen as a unitary top-down force as it is constituted by situated practices. Hence, many of the practices and policies that are adopted by the AES in Dholera signify the disjuncture in practice.

The distinctive configurations of market-oriented programmes are shaped by the way in which these programmes collide with existing institutional landscapes to produce distinctive forms of 'variegated neoliberalisation' (Chacko and Jayasuriya, 2018). In this approach, the focus is on the ongoing political and social processes, rather than a specific set of policy templates. I explore these negotiations that shape and constitute neoliberalism in these rural areas, displaying a disjuncture between what is proffered and what is practiced. Beyond the strategies of Hindutva politics, the AES actors have delivered material benefits to farmers to mitigate their protests. It simultaneously allowed the BJP to balance the needs of poor voters, wealthy core constituencies and movement ideologues.

The 2017 Gujarat provincial election results alarmed the BJP due to the electoral loss in rural areas across the province. While they clung to power, BJP was only able to win 63 seats out of the 140 rural seats (down from 77) whereas the opposition Congress party won 71 seats. Overall, they polled 2 percentage points less than Congress in rural areas compared to 7 points higher if the urban areas were included (D. Kumar, 2017). The incoming BJP government reacted to this shrinking vote with a slew of measures targeting rural areas. In the 2018–2019 provincial budget, the government sanctioned INR 192.1 billion to be spent on new electricity connections for farmers, and another INR 401.1 billion for electricity subsidies. Crop loans were to be provided at 0 per cent interest (*Financial Express*, 2018). In the 2019–2020 budget, similarly, significant allocations were made towards agriculture (*India Today*, 2019).

Since 2012, several Dholera farmers received benefits under the scheme named Sujalam Sufalam. Through the scheme, the government funded 60 per cent of the total cost of building water reservoirs for farmers in dry areas. Dholera farmers were particular beneficiaries of the project, and most interviewers acknowledged that the cabinet minister, Bhupendrasinh, had an important role to play in this. They received the funding soon after the 2012 assembly elections when the protest movement against SIR projects across the province gained momentum.[7] The timing was important from another perspective. Around 2013, Modi started his campaign for the Indian prime ministerial post. Thus, strategies were required to quell any possible future protest in the countryside of Gujarat as Modi projected himself as someone who gave the best of the deals to farmers and corporations.

The Sujalam Sufalam scheme is interesting from two perspectives. First, such welfare projects are against the basic neoliberal tenets of cutting down on public subsidies and expenses. Following Washington Consensus' (Williamson, 1990) policy prescriptions, governments around the world have been cutting welfare budgets. The Gujarat provincial government has been at the forefront of such policy measures, withdrawing funding from most social sectors over the years (Reserve Bank of India, 2020: 55). Contrasting the trend, the Sujalam Sufalam project is a departure from neoliberalism similar to what Ferguson (2015) suggested through 'redistributive neoliberalism' or what Brenner et al. (2010a) referred to as 'opportunistic moments, workarounds and on-the-hoof recalibrations'. Interestingly, this departure was intended to deliver the neoliberal project of Dholera smart city in the longer run. Second, while the Sujalam Sufalam scheme funded 60 per cent of the cost, to cover the remaining 40 per cent, the government appealed to religious and social institutions to contribute. Many of the farmers received funding from religious groups such as the Swaminarayan temple. This furthers another neoliberal tenet (Kaya, 2015), underscoring how neoliberalism finds a marriage of convenience with right-wing ideologies such as Hindutva.[8]

Scholars have mentioned the increasing friendliness between Hindutva and the Swaminarayan sect.[9] In fact, Swaminarayan temple priests, over the years, have vocally supported BJP and asked the sect's majorly Patidar supporters not to vote for the Congress in the 2017 assembly elections (Express News Service, 2017). Involving such religious or social groups to contribute to developmental projects is a feature of neoliberalism in practice, as Kaya (2015) has shown in the case of Turkey. Bhattacharjee (2019) and Simpson (2013) have demonstrated the increasing friendliness between various Hindutva organisations and the Swaminarayan sect in the rebuilding of the Kutch region in Gujarat after the 2001 earthquake. Importantly, most of the beneficiaries were now BJP supporters. During interviews, they opposed the SIR project due to imminent dispossession but also acknowledged that they did not attend protest meetings. They now claim that it would be immoral to go back after taking financial help from religious groups. Thus, the welfare services by these religious groups have weakened the farmer protest and simultaneously, ensured votes for the Hindutva party. Hence, both neoliberalism and Hindutva helped each other proliferate in these villages.

Thachil (2014) argues that the delivery of welfare measures helped the BJP gain new supporters while preserving its core constituency. One donor of Sujalam Sufalam, a local upper-caste businessman who made it big from land business in Dholera, saw this donation as a way to give back to his 'poor' or 'backward' neighbours. Similarly, a BJP leader claimed that he donated land to construct water reservoirs for his villagers because this is what Hinduism taught him. The involvement in the welfare projects of Hindutva organisations helped address upper-caste youth's disillusionment with the loss of their community's traditional influence in society (Simpson, 2013). Thus, Sujalam Sufalam brought new supporters into the Hindutva organisations without antagonising traditional upper-caste voters. This is fascinating when compared to the massive agitation by upper-caste youths against affirmative actions, especially the Mandal Commission. The Mandal Commission that proposed reservations for lower castes in late 1980s negatively affected the prospect of the Congress party as the upper castes that stood to lose deserted the party unlike the BJP now.

The second contradictory policy decision taken by the BJP government, especially due to the influential role played by Bhupendrasinh, was to bring back Dholera under the Narmada Canal notified area and escalate the speed of construction of the distributary canals in the villages. The canal water has been a long-term demand by the local farmers. The BBS made it a war cry 'SIR hatao, Narmada laao' (Remove SIR, bring Narmada) and has been lobbying for Narmada's canal water for decades. Suddenly, just before the provincial elections of 2017 as the BJP sensed the rural discontent, funds were allocated to start construction swiftly. The coming of Narmada water is contradictory because the SIR project is intended to move the 'farmers from agriculture to manufacturing since the area was infertile' as claimed by the CEO of DSIRDA. In that case, the construction of the canals would create further confusion, especially when it is also not aligned with the planning of the SIR by the consultants of INFINITY who arranged its own sources of water. However, the canal construction helped negotiate some of the demands of the anti-SIR farmers.

As the farmers' protests peaked in 2014–2015, authorities in Gandhinagar took steps to address the concerns of farmers. One such measure was to grant compensation to the farmers. In the SIR Act through the Dholara SIR (or smart city was being implemented), land is acquired using the Gujarat Town Planning and Urban Development Act 1976 (GTPUDA). Through the GTPUDA, the Town Planning Authority in any city declares a certain area to be under the municipal boundary of the city. This would mean that the notified area (usually farmland) would be taken over by the concerned authority. Land parcels of various sizes belonging to farmers are pooled together and the authority lays out infrastructure. A farmer who owns a parcel of land (referred to as original plot or OP) is then returned 50 per cent of the original size (referred to as final plot or FP) with basic infrastructure such as roads, electricity, sewerage put in place. As the prices of the serviced plots of land quickly increase, a farmer supposedly ends up profiting despite losing half of his original plot. There is no option for monetary compensation in the law. The process is referred to as land pooling or land readjustment instead of land acquisition that usually delivers monetary compensation.

Thus, when Dholera SIR was announced in 2009, there was no clause for monetary compensation. However, with the setback from Mandal Becharaji which had to be cancelled in 2015 following farmers' protests and a sustained campaign by the anti-SIR protestors in Dholera that culminated with the high court status-quo order, the state changed tactics. Farmers who were losing land to the Activation Area were to be paid compensation at the government-notified rate. The compensation diffused the possibility of court cases despite the high court ruling as none of the dispossessed farmers went to court after receiving compensation. In fact, the two villages that covered the Activation Area have the weakest representation in the BBS. In addition, compensation was swiftly paid which led to an overall positive perception. Farmers were also allowed to carry out farming indefinitely until the government began construction.

Such measures taken by the state in Dholera to diffuse farmers' protests are similar to what James Ferguson (2015) called 'redistributive neoliberalism' in South Africa where through cash transfers to the poor the state was somehow trying to mitigate the worsts of neoliberalism. He found that such economic support was key in a world of declining opportunities for agricultural livelihoods and formal wage labour. In similar ways, in a pan-Indian context of diminishing agricultural returns and farmers' suicide at a record high, some of these redistributions can be termed as a way to keep the neoliberal project going.

However, the Indian scenario is bleak. At the national level, Prime Minister Modi further dismantled state agricultural subsidies, moving to a model of crop insurance scheme. Although it was claimed to increase farmers' income, any addressal of their issues remains a distant dream while private corporations have cornered massive benefits (Agarwal and Mishra, 2018; Matthew, 2019). As Ferguson (2015) argued for cash transfers in South Africa, acts such as building canal infrastructure for agriculture, subsidising the building of the water reservoirs or even compensating the dispossessed farmers instead of leaving them to the market are particularly interesting because they break with the entrenched logics of neoliberalism. This underlines the disjuncture in the practices of neoliberalism in Dholera. While Ferguson (2015: 3) heralds the cash transfer as the coming of 'a new kind of welfare state', the measures adopted by the state in Dholera were probably targeted at diffusing the protests.

Murray and Overton (2011: 313) point out that the hardship and suffering which the neoliberal policies resulted across the world until the 1990s led to what Stiglitz (2008) termed as the 'post Washington Consensus consensus'. Others have referred this process of the 'more aggressive neoliberal doctrines, usually associated with Thatcher and Reagan' giving way to 'modified versions in the Clinton era and under Blair's Third Way' as Gooptu (2011: 36) has pointed out.[10] The central role of the state was emphasised again. States were encouraged 'to promote as well as regulate markets, and to provide various infrastructure and adopt frameworks of good governance ... to encourage transparency and accountability....' (Murray and Overton, 2011: 313).

On a separate issue although with a similar trajectory, with the extreme controversies due to land acquisition that was governed by a British-era law in India, there was an attempt to make land acquisition and subsequent transfer fairer by making the process more transparent and participatory. One step towards this was the Right to Fair Compensation and Transparency in Land Acquisition, Rehabilitation and Resettlement Act, 2013, that was cleared by cross-party consensus in the Indian Parliament in 2013.[11] Another key policy that was encouraged across the world was digitisation of land records aimed at making land transfer transparent (Nayak, 2013; 2020). This policy in India can be seen as a continuity to the economic reforms of the 1990s as it was targeted at creating an effective and smooth land market (Nayak, 2013: 72–74). Provinces such as Odisha and Gujarat were the earliest in the land records digitisation process (Nayak, 2013: 72–74). Gujarat eventually clubbed the digitisation of land records with the 'Ease of Doing Business' discourse, where it ranked amongst the top provinces in India during Modi's tenure as the chief minister. A senior GIDB bureaucrat argued that land records digitisation accelerated the speed as well as the number of land transactions in the province. 'With the availability of all these (land) records online and applications made through the

"Single Window", any investor could buy land [*pauses*], even sitting in London, New York....' He further argued that these measures helped improve Gujarat's 'Ease of Doing Business' index.

However, Schatz and Rogers (2016) have shown that despite the lofty talks of 'transparency' or 'public participation' in the 'post Washington Consensus consensus', actual practices stand in stark contrast. Scholars such as Cox (2004), Groves et al. (2013), Guarneros-Meza and Geddes (2010), McCarthy and Prudham (2004: 276) and Rodan (2006) have explored the apparent tension between transparency, public participation and neoliberalism in different contexts. Nayak (2013) has also argued that the reality of the process of land digitisation in India is far removed from what is argued by its proponents.

Taking a cue from such discourses, the Special Investment Region (SIR) Act of 2009 through which Dholera SIR came into existence made it compulsory to organise public hearings. The town planner or a designated official would take questions from the affected public and give them written responses within a specified time. This also included a compulsory Environmental Impact Assessment (EIA) public hearing. In 2013, during the EIA hearing for the Dholera SIR, a number of farmers raised important issues and many of those remained unanswered although the authorities went ahead with the project. An interesting incident on the complications of the land records digitisation process came to light during this EIA hearing. The computerised land records and the subsequent map that was used by the EIA consultants enlisted a village called Mandvipura that submerged in the Arabian Sea several decades ago. Even its former residents were rehabilitated in nearby villages by local administration. However, in the new plan of the Dholera SIR, farmers were allotted their 'Final Plot' in Mandvipura (*Counterview*, 2014). The petitioners against the SIR project highlighted these issues at the high court, and the authority's inability to answer those became a key argument against the project in the high court in 2015.

Learning from this experience, the authorities stopped the exercise of public hearings. When organised, it would be a low-key affair. The practice was to deliver the letter to the *sarpanch* through the village *talatis*. The *sarpanch* was supposed to inform the villagers. However, often, the letter did not arrive at the *sarpanch*'s office; or the *sarpanch* or the *talati* would forget about the letter altogether. On one occasion, when the public hearing for farmers losing land to the national highway project was ongoing, farmer leaders from the protesting group, BBS, attended it. However, they were not allowed to voice their concerns because they did not belong to the village where the public meeting was held.

The use of coercive measures on other occasions has also been frequent. Many BBS leaders have often been detained before the rallies. The Gujarat Khedut Samaj leaders who provide the leadership in Gandhinagar or Ahmedabad were taken into preventive custody when they planned a protest outside the Vibrant Gujarat venue (Chakravartty, 2015). Cases of surveillance of even the smallest of the BBS meetings are common. The use of these coercive measures has ensured that radical farmer organisations or progressive groups barely exist in Gujarat's rural politics.

To sum up, these strategies and policies of the AES demonstrate 'a dogged capacity to exploit these same crises in the course of its own adaptive reinvention' (Peck and Theodore, 2012). The process of implementing the neoliberal project displays a 'lurching dynamic, marked by serial policy failure and improvised adaptation and by combative encounters with obstacles and counter-movements' (Peck and Theodore, 2012: 178–179). What is idiosyncratic in Dholera is the use of caste, religion or ethnicity by Hindutva actors to keep the neoliberal project moving. In doing so, we witness the disjuncture that was a key theme of the book.

The chapter discerns the prevalence of Hindutva and how its actors have controlled the state and society. Hindutva's domination of state and society, through various processes of amelioration and brokerage, among others, has ensured that they come across as nothing extraordinary. Hence, Hindutva actors may simultaneously negotiate or help diffuse farmers' protests while also smoothening a business deal. Their practices may include contradictory steps ultimately to create acquiescence and further their dominance in the state and society. This is a 'disjuncture' in Hindutva through which its actors and practices depart from its foundational ideologies, ultimately to further entrench organisations and institutions of state and society. Even if Hindutva ideologies would argue for a unified Hindu society to bring back a caste order wherein upper castes are supposed to occupy higher positions, in practice, they may cede space to lower castes to gain a certain electoral advantage. This disjuncture represents a constellation of forces, practices not all of which are ideologically centred around Hindutva (Longkumer and Anderson, 2018; Reddy, 2011).

In similar tactics of disjuncture, through a host of economic measures that may signify a departure from the basic tenets of neoliberalism such as agricultural subsidies, the state negotiates the farmers' resistance. This brings to the fore the economic logic of the diffused protest. In his book *Give a Man a Fish*, Ferguson (2015) analyses redistributive neoliberalism in which the state has taken an active role in the process by handing out direct cash to citizens. While not argued by Ferguson, the strategies of the state actors in Dholera can be seen as an attempt to keep neoliberalism on track by negotiating some of the resistances, which may arise due to the extreme impact of neoliberal policies.

Notes

1. Bhal Bachao Samiti (BBS) is the banner under which a group of local farmers led the anti-SIR protest in Dholera. Gujarat Khedut Samaj is a provincial-level farmers' rights group.
2. While the bureaucrat claimed that farmers voluntarily accepted compensation, the process of land pooling that was practised did not have any chance for the farmers to decline the government offer.
3. A few of the scholarship include Borras and Franco (2012), Borras et al. (2011), Deininger (2011), Edelman (2013), Oya (2013), Scoones et al. (2013), Wolford (2004) and Zoomers (2010).
4. For this chapter and the book as a whole, I focus largely on the rural phenomenon. There is a wide scholarship that studies urban spaces through themes of neoliberalism, land acquisition, urban informality and resistance. On India particularly, see Benjamin (2000, 2008), Bhan (2014), Ghertner (2011), Gooptu (2011), Mahadevia (2006, 2014), Maringanti et al. (2015); Roy (2009a, 2009b, 2011b), Shatkin (2014) and Weinstein (2009) that represent a section of the wide scholarship.
5. The term appeared in Chapter 3 too. A *sarpanch* is the head of the village-level local self-government in India. S/he is the main point of contact between the village population and the government officials.
6. Bhupendrasinh's election win was challenged by the opposition Congress candidate in the courts. In May 2020, his election was declared void by the Gujarat High Court due to a host of irregularities in the voting process. This would have forced him to resign from the ministry. However, within days, the Supreme Court gave him a reprieve by putting the previous judgment on hold. See Vaidyanathan (2020) for details.
7. In fact, it was in 2013 when thirty-six out of forty-four villages under the Mandal-Becharaji SIR were cancelled after the 100-day long protests (Duncan and Agarwal, 2017).
8. Both Adaman et al. (2019) and Gürel et al. (2019) have developed similar arguments about neoliberal policies pursued by the Justice and Development Party while overlapping them with a call to go back to conservative Islam.
9. Simpson (2016: 117–119) has commented on this. Although Kim (2010) calls the movement apolitical, her work provides a great deal of detail on the movement.

10. Gooptu (2011) rightly clarified that exclusion or marginality has remained a consistent theme in the politics of urban spaces even in the pre-liberalisation era.
11. See Chakravorty (2016), Goswami (2016) and Nielsen and Nilsen (2015) for critical reviews of the 2013 law.

8

Conclusion

A Peek into the Gloomy Future

The book started with a quote by a local farmer, 'Development neither reaches us nor leaves us. It's an illusion', where he argued that the many versions of development which Dholera has been promised since the 1960s have been contradictory to the needs and wants of the local population. While some of the development projects such as the Narmada canal still remain the demand of the locals, not everyone celebrates the more recent avatars such as the smart city or the international airport. In fact, the farmer implied, various versions of development keep being imposed without consulting the locals or trying to understand their needs. More importantly, none of these versions has been delivered. This does not mean that Dholera is off the map of new development endeavours so much so that he terms them 'illusions', as the standard of living of the locals has not seen any major improvement through such projects. For him and many Dholera natives, instead of improving their living conditions or addressing inequalities, such development projects instead create scope for more politics and often threaten to dispossess them of whatever they have.

The preceding chapters discussed the implications of these endeavours through a close study of the role of the state in the development and delivery of Dholera smart city or the impact of such projects on the entity of the state. This was done after I laid out the case of Dholera and how the changing narratives of development in such a small place epitomise the journey of the Indian state when it comes to delivering development to its subjects. The choice of concepts, theories or analytical lens was, to a large extent, informed and guided by the field. The state was explored analytically while neoliberalism and Hindutva provided the context. In doing so, the book contributed to the scholarship on all three themes. The starting point of the book was the multifaceted nature and the contradictory practices of each of the themes.

At the same time, the book also involved the analysis of a set of processes and phenomena such as smart urbanism, real estate and farmers' resistance. I allowed the field to direct me towards the relevant theories instead of the other way around, ensuring a constant dialogue between my data and the theoretical concepts throughout the fieldwork. Hence, when I arrived at the site, I did not expect what the state looked like. I was guided to an understanding of the state through the practices of actors who play many roles within the state and its shadows. Hence, the site of research guided my proposal of the concept of the AES.

Development, State, Neoliberalism and Hindutva: Some Contributions

Overall, Dholera smart city project embodies most characteristics of neoliberalism: be it commodification of land, privatisation or financialisation (Harvey, 2005). A detailed picture of how Hindutva organisations and their actors or supporters have entrenched the state and the society in Dholera has been presented. As both neoliberalism and Hindutva intend to capture the state, the entity of the state became the main analytical lens while the two ideologies of neoliberalism and Hindutva provided the context for the study. Deriving from the existing scholarship on the state, especially from the likes of Philip Abrams (1988) and Timothy Mitchell (1991), the book argued that the state is an idea that comes into being through a set of practices as well as a lived material reality. To start with, I have taken a wider composition of the state by considering a host of actors and their practices who work in the shadow of the state. As illustrated in the preceding chapters, studying the everyday functioning of the state, at the ground level in Dholera or in Gandhinagar, brings dimensions that complicate a unified understanding of the state, impelling us to take on board the newer intermeshing of practices and actors that have now become part of the state. To do so, the concept of the AES was proposed. In framing the proposals around the AES, the influential scholarship by Mitchell (1991, 1999) and Abrams (1988), who widened our understanding of the state and its relation to society, were applied. However, when it comes to India and how the state functions in everyday lives, Harriss-White's (2003) proposed shadow state was used to better understand the Indian context. I put forth a set of four propositions on the AES to understand the phenomenon of Dholera. Each chapter (4, 5, 6, 7) then elaborated on one or more of these propositions through the field data.

The book contributed towards a more nuanced, situated understanding of how state policies emerge, how they take root in a particular place, their impact on the entity of the state and, most importantly, the role of the ideologies, actors and practices of Hindutva and neoliberalism in the everyday workings of the state. While existing scholarship disaggregates the state's interactions with society, it does not fully explain the newly emerging interactions between the state and businesses in infrastructure projects, lubricated by right-wing religious or cultural ideologies, within the backdrop of neoliberalism. These studies in India are usually at the macro level and fail to explain how these two projects interact in the everyday lives of the state and society. To provide a richer explanation of the processes and the shapes which both neoliberalism and Hindutva display in their endeavours, I focused on the political and social processes of capturing state institutions and organisations, rather than a specific set of policy templates. With respect to both the themes of Hindutva and neoliberalism, the book focused on the idiosyncratic expressions that operate outside their ideological framework and help them successfully become entrenched in a specific place. What was illustrated particularly was a disjuncture between the ideologies that supposedly guide them and the practices which they undertake that, on many occasions, depart from these ideologies. Hence, a set of contradictory strategies govern the implementation of neoliberalism or Hindutva in the real world, which ultimately mediate their existence.

As both ideologies undertake a host of contradictory measures, they depict the persistent capacity to generate their own adaptive reinvention (Brenner et al., 2010a). The book demonstrated how the process is 'non-linear and multi-dimensional' and marked by policy failures. This leads to adaptations or, on occasions, combative encounters with obstacles and counter-movements and hence, the path taken is shaped by 'opportunistic moments, workarounds and on-the-hoof recalibrations' (Brenner et al., 2010a). The farmers' resistance in Dholera discussed in Chapter 7 was a perfect example of this where the neoliberal proponents, or their facilitators in the state and Hindutva organisations, use all measures of manipulation to mitigate the protest and continue the SIR project. Whereas neoliberalism may profess the removal of subsidies in agriculture, when faced with farmers' protests, its proponents would simultaneously launch policies to deliver subsidies to farmers. The empirical chapters have shown similar instances of how neoliberal actors adopt various other contradictory strategies to keep the project alive.

Scholars such as Bhattacharjee (2019), Froerer (2007) and Thachil (2014) have shown how Hindutva organisations have become entrenched in various societies through local welfare services for education and health. In other cases, Longkumer (2020) has shown how similar organisations have entered newer and previously unexplored territories such as North-East India, developing a set of new discourses that at times move too far from the doctrinal Hindutva proposed by the likes of Savarkar or his disciples such as Gowalkar. These practices demonstrate the myriad ways in which Hindutva entrenches itself into the state and society. Within these debates, what I illustrated are the mundane practices that Hindutva organisations undertake to present Hindutva as banal and essentially a way of life. These practices make the everyday forms of Hindutva seem 'normal' or 'nothing special'. At the same time, these practices eventually help Hindutva to permeate different aspects of the state and society while also mitigating or negotiating issues such as farmers' protests against the Dholera SIR project. Overall, due to the lack of orthodoxies, such practices cannot be categorised under a strict framework.

Through these arguments, the idiosyncratic ways, which have helped Hindutva become mainstream and normalised even if in an obfuscated manner in recent years, were highlighted. As Anderson (2015) and Reddy (2011) have pointed out, such practices have a 'diffuse logic' that, even if nebulous, may become a mediating discourse in their own right (Reddy, 2011: 421). These hybrid forms 'negotiate local legal, social, moral, and political environments in ways that variously concentrate or dilute their ideological emphases' (Reddy, 2012, cited in Anderson and Longkumer, 2020: 3). However, these practices should not create an impression that Hindutva organisations are oblivious of foundational ideologies. As I have shown, the ultimate aim is to create the 'Hindu state' through whatever means possible and such departure at the level of practices depending on the context serves the larger goal. At the same time, as I have shown throughout the book, we also see a coming together of the actors and the practices of Hindutva and neoliberalism. This is not just at the level of practice. In fact, in the examples I show such as a bureaucrat justifying neoliberalism through ideologies of Hindutva, the coming together occurs at multiple levels and forms. Lastly, the strategies that may come across as a compromised Hindutva or as Ferguson's (2015) 'redistributive neoliberalism' should not lead us to believe that the Gujarat state does not resort to other means (such as violence) to intimidate its subjects into compliance. As mentioned, there are a few accounts of farmer leaders still behind bars, while protests are strictly banned prior to political rallies or business summits. Attacks on protestors by 'goons' are not uncommon. Hence, right-wing political leaders also resort to authoritarian tactics when confronted with challenges.

Several questions emerge from the book that may require further validation, opening up opportunities for future research. The first question that could be asked is about the changes that must have taken place over the last few years as BJP becomes a hegemonic power across the country, winning elections in province after province. Does this mean a replication of the pattern of Hindutva and neoliberalism capturing the state in other provinces? Or does this mean we will have similar disjuncture across different variables? How will development projects in the form of infrastructure building or smart cities bring out new modes of state practices amid disjuncture in neoliberalism or Hindutva? At the same time, as both Hindutva and neoliberalism become hegemonic and as the state and society are captured by these forces, do these ideologies go back to their orthodox foundations to usher in a 'purer' form when the compulsion to negotiate does not remain? How do these forces act in places (for example, in the province of Assam) where the arrival of Hindutva forces is much more recent, while political compulsions ensure the continuation of many provisions of the welfare state? The reach of Hindutva is becoming increasingly tangible as these newly conquered places too witness the leviathan that the state is, acquiring massive tracts of land for private corporations that have close associations with Hindutva forces. Answers to such questions will become increasingly important in what is probably going to be a gloomy future when these forces retain and strengthen their hold on power. However, the answers may possibly provide some ammunition to disparate groups to fight, resist or at least register their existence.

References

Abrams, P. (1988). 'Notes on the Difficulty of Studying the State'. *Journal of Historical Sociology* 1(1): 58–89.

Adaman, F., M. Arsel and B. Akbulut. (2019). 'Neoliberal Developmentalism, Authoritarian Populism, and Extractivism in the Countryside: The Soma Mining Disaster in Turkey'. *The Journal of Peasant Studies* 46(3): 514–536.

AECOM (2019). 'About AECOM: History'. Available at https://aecom.com/about-aecom/history/. Accessed 28 September 2019).

——— (2020). 'Dholera Special Investment Region India'. Available at https://aecom.com/projects/dholera-special-investment-region/. Accessed 8 October 2020.

AECOM Press Release (2013). 'AECOM Awarded US$30-Million Program Management Contract for Delhi Mumbai Industrial Corridor in Gujarat, India'. AECOM. Available at https://www.aecom.com/press-releases/aecom-announced-today-that-it-has-been-awarded-a-program-management-contract-for-the-dholera-special-investment-region-dsir-in-gujarat-india-for-the-delhi-mumbai-industrial-corridor-dmic/. Accessed 2 June 2019.

Agarwal, K. and D. Mishra (2018). 'Exclusive: Under Modi's Crop Insurance Scheme, Premiums up 350% but Farmers' Coverage Stagnant'. *The Wire*, 12 November. Available at https://thewire.in/agriculture/narendra-modi-farmers-crop-insurance-pmfby. Accessed 21 March 2020.

Ahmedabad Mirror (2018). 'Soon, A Japanese Town in Gujarat'. 26 July. Available at https://ahmedabadmirror.indiatimes.com/ahmedabad/others/soon-a-japanese-town-in-gujarat/articleshow/65140179.cms. Accessed 17 April 2019.

Akhtar, R. (2024). '"Development Has Gone Crazy": The Gujarat Model of "Unequal" Development through Neoliberalism and Hindutva'. *South Asia: Journal of South Asian Studies* 47(3): 576–595. https://doi.org/10.1080/00856401.2024.2350889.

Amit, V. (2000). *Constructing the Field: Ethnographic Fieldwork in the Contemporary World*. London: Routledge.

Anderson, E. (2015). '"Neo-Hindutva": The Asia House M.F. Husain Campaign and the Mainstreaming of Hindu Nationalist Rhetoric in Britain'. *Contemporary South Asia* 23(1): 45–66.

Anderson, E. and A. Longkumer, eds. (2020). Neo-Hindutva: Evolving Forms, Spaces, and Expressions of Hindu Nationalism. New York and Oxon: Routledge.

Anjaria, J. S. (2011). 'Ordinary States: Everyday Corruption and the Politics of Space in Mumbai'. *American Ethnologist* 38(1): 58–72.

Appadurai, A. (1990). 'Disjuncture and Difference in the Global Cultural Economy'. *Theory, Culture and Society* 7(2–3): 295–310.

———— (1997). 'Discussion: Fieldwork in the Era of Globalization'. *Anthropology and Humanism* 22(1): 115–118.

Arora, A. (2010). 'Federa, Father of All Airports'. *The Times of India*, 30 March. Available at Https://Timesofindia.Indiatimes.Com/City/Ahmedabad/Federa-Father-Of-All-Airports/Articleshow/5740836.Cms. Accessed 5 January 2019.

Bahree, M. (2014) 'Doing Big Business in Modi's Gujarat'. *Forbes Asia*, 12 March. Available at http://www.forbes.com/sites/meghabahree/2014/03/12/doing-big-business-in-modis-gujarat/. Accessed 15 February 2019.

Bailey, F. G. (1960). *Tribe, Caste and Nation*. Manchester: Manchester University Press.

———— (1963). 'Politics and Society in Contemporary Orissa'. In *Politics and Society in India*, edited by Philips C. H., 97–114. London: Allen and Unwin.

Baka, J. (2013). 'The Political Construction of Wasteland: Governmentality, Land Acquisition and Social Inequality in South India'. *Development and Change* 44(2): 409–428.

Balakrishnan, S. (2013). 'Land Conflicts and Cooperatives along Pune's Highways: Managing India's Agrarian to Urban Transition'. PhD dissertation, Harvard University, Cambridge, MA.

———— (2019). *Shareholder Cities: Land Transformations along Urban Corridors in India*. Philadelphia: University of Pennsylvania Press.

Ballaney, S. and B. Patel (2009). 'Using the "Development Plan—Town Planning Scheme" Mechanism to Appropriate Land and Build Urban Infrastructure'. In *India Infrastructure Report 2009:Land—A Critical Resource for Infrastructure*, edited by N. Mohanty, R. Sarkar and A. Pandey, 190–204. New Delhi: Oxford University Press.

Bandyopadhyay, S. (2016). 'Another History: Bhadralok Responses to Dalit Political Assertion in Colonial Bengal'. In *The Politics of Caste in West Bengal*, edited by U. Chandra, G. Heierstad and K. Nielsen, 35–59. Abingdon: Routledge.

Banerjee-Guha, S. (2008). 'Space Relations of Capital and Significance of New Economic Enclaves: SEZs in India'. *Economic and Political Weekly* 43(47): 51–59.

———, ed. (2010). *Accumulation by Dispossession: Transformative Cities in the New Global Order*. New Delhi: SAGE Publications India.

Bansal, S. (2019). 'How India Voted in 2019 Election? Here Is What India Today-Axis My India Post-poll Study Tells Us'. *India Today*, 4 June. Available at https://www.indiatoday.in/diu/story/how-india-voted-2019-lok-sabha-election-india-today-axis-my-india-poll-1539617-2019-05-31. Accessed 8 September 2019.

Bardhan, P. (1984). *The Political Economy of Development in India*. Oxford: Basil Blackwell.

———. (2000). 'The Political Economy of Reform in India'. In *Politics and the State in India*, edited by Z. Hassan, 158–174. New Delhi: SAGE Publications India.

Basu, A. (2000) The Transformation of Hindu Nationalism? In *Transforming India: Social and Political Dynamics of Democracy*, edited by F. R. Frankel, Z. Hasan, R. Bhagava and B. Arora, 378–404. New Delhi: Oxford University Press.

Basu, T., P. Datta, S. Sarkar, T. Sarkar and S. Sen (1993). *Khaki Shorts and Saffron Flags: A Critique of the Hindu Right*, Vol. 1. New Delhi: Orient Longman Limited.

Baviskar, A. (1995). *In the Belly of the River: Tribal Conflicts over Development in the Narmada Valley*. New Delhi: Oxford University Press.

Bedi, H. P. and L. Tillin (2015) 'Inter-state Competition, Land Conflicts and Resistance in India'. *Oxford Development Studies* 43(2): 194–211.

Bello, W. (2019) *Counterrevolution: The Global Rise of the Far Right*. Winnipeg: Fernwood Publishing.

Benjamin, S. (2000). 'Governance, Economic Settings and Poverty in Bangalore'. *Environment and Urbanization* 12(1): 35–56.

——— (2008). 'Occupancy Urbanism: Radicalizing Politics and Economy beyond Policy and Programs'. *International Journal of Urban and Regional Research* 32(3): 719–729.

Berenschot, W. (2010). 'Everyday Mediation: The Politics of Public Service Delivery in Gujarat, India'. *Development and Change* 41(5): 883–905.

———— (2011a). *Riot Politics: India's Communal Violence and the Everyday Meditation of the State*. London: Hurst & Company.

———— (2011b). 'Political Fixers and the Rise of Hindu Nationalism in Gujarat, India: Lubricating a Patronage Democracy'. *Journal of South Asian Studies* 34(3): 382–401.

Berkley Centre (2020). *Dharma (Hinduism)*. Berkley Center for Religion, Peace & World Affairs. Available at https://berkleycenter.georgetown.edu/essays/dharma-hinduism. Accessed 2 June 2020.

Bernstein, H. (2020). 'Unpacking "Authoritarian Populism" and Rural Politics: Some Comments on ERPI'. *The Journal of Peasant Studies* 47(7): 1526–1542.

Bhabha, H. (1984). 'Of Mimicry and Man: The Ambivalence of Colonial Discourse'. *October* 28(Spring): 125–133.

Bhagat-Ganguly, V. (2015). *Protest Movements and Citizens' Rights in Gujarat (1970–2010)*. Shimla: Indian Institute of Advanced Study.

Bhagwati, J. (1993). *India in Transition: Freeing the Economy*. Oxford: Clarendon Press.

Bhagwati, J. and A. Panagariya (2012a). *India's Tryst with Destiny: Debunking Myths that Undermine Progress and Addressing New Challenges*. Noida: Harper Collins Publishers.

———— (2012b). *India's Reforms: How They Produced Inclusive Growth*. New York, Oxford: Oxford University Press.

———— (2013). *Why Growth Matters*. New York: Public Affairs.

Bhan, G. (2014). 'The Real Lives of Urban Fantasies'. *Environment and Urbanization* 26(1): 232–235.

Bhandari, L. (2015). 'Defining Smart Cities: What and What Not'. *Laveesh Bhandari*, 17 March. Available at https://laveeshbhandari.wordpress.com/2015/03/17/defining-smart-cities-what-and-what-not/. Accessed 26 March 2017.

Bhatia, G. (2020). 'Beyond the Veils of Secrecy, the Central Vista Project Is Both the Cause and Effect of Its Own Multiple Failures'. *The Hindu*, 1 November. Available at https://www.thehindu.com/society/beyond-the-veils-of-secrecy-the-central-vista-project-is-both-the-cause-and-effect-of-its-own-multiple-failures/article32980560.ece. Accessed 26 October 2020.

Bhatt, C. (2001). *Hindu Nationalism: Origins, Ideologies and Modern Myths*. Oxford: Berg.

Bhattacharjee, M. (2019). *Disaster Relief and the RSS: Resurrecting 'Religion' through Humanitarianism*. New Delhi: SAGE Publications.

BJP (Bharatiya Janata Party) (2019a). 'Pandit Deendayal Upadhyaya'. Available at https://www.bjp.org/en/leaders/deendayalupadhyaya. Accessed 20 December 2019.

———— (2019b). 'Integral Humanism'. Available at https://www.bjp.org/en/ integralhumanism. Accessed 15 December 2019.

Bobbio, T. (2012). 'Making Gujarat Vibrant: Hindutva, Development and the Rise of Subnationalism in India'. *Third World Quarterly* 33(4): 657–672.

Borras, S. M. and J. Franco (2012). 'Global Land Grabbing and Trajectories of Agrarian Change: A Preliminary Analysis'. *Journal of Agrarian Change* 12(1): 34–59.

———— (2013). 'Global Land Grabbing and Political Reactions "From Below"'. *Third World Quarterly* 34(9): 1723–1747.

Borras, S. M., R. Hall, I. Scoones, B. White and W. Wolford (2011). 'Towards a Better Understanding of Global Land Grabbing: An Editorial Introduction'. *The Journal of Peasant Studies* 38(2): 209–216.

Bouchard, M. (2011). 'The State of the Study of the State in Anthropology'. *Reviews in Anthropology* 40(3): 183–209.

Bourdieu, P. (1998). *Practical Reason: On the Theory of Action*, 1st ed. Stanford: Stanford University Press.

Brass, P. R. (1994). *The Politics of India since Independence*. Cambridge: Cambridge University Press.

———— (1997). *Theft of an Idol: Text and Context in the Representation of Collective Violence*. Princeton, NJ: Princeton University Press.

Brass, T. (1994). 'Introduction: The New Farmers' Movements in India'. *The Journal of Peasant Studies* 21(3/4): 3–26.

Breman, J. (1974). *Patronage and Exploitation: Changing Agrarian Relations in Gujarat*. Berkeley: University of California Press.

———— (1985). *Of Peasants, Migrants and Paupers: Rural Labour Circulation and Capitalist Production in West India*. Oxford: Oxford University Press.

———— (1996). *Footloose Labor: Working in India's Informal Economy*. Cambridge: Cambridge University Press.

———— (2002). 'Communal Upheaval as Resurgence of Social Darwinism'. *Economic and Political Weekly* 37(16): 1485–1488.

———— (2004). *The Making and Unmaking of an Industrial Working Class: Sliding Down the Labour Hierarchy in Ahmedabad, India*. New Delhi: Oxford University Press and Amsterdam: Amsterdam University Press.

———— (2007). *The Poverty Regime in Village India: Half a Century of Work and Life at the Bottom of the Rural Economy in South Gujarat*. New Delhi and New York: Oxford University Press.

————— (2020). 'As the Gujarat Model Goes National, Hindutva Hunts for the "Enemy in Our Midst". *The Wire*. 5 March. Available at https://thewire.in/communalism/as-the-gujarat-model-goes-national-hindutva-hunts-for-the-enemy-in-our-midst. Accessed 8 April 2020.

Brenner, N. and N. Theodore (2002). 'Cities and the Geographies of "Actually Existing Neoliberalism"'. *Antipode* 34(3): 349–379.

Brenner, N., J. Peck and N. Theodore (2010a). 'Variegated Neoliberalization: Geographies, Modalities, Pathways'. *Global Networks* 10(2): 182–222.

————— (2010b). 'After Neoliberalization?' *Globalizations* 7(3): 327–345.

————— (2011). 'Neoliberal Urbanism: Cities and the Rule of Markets'. In *The New Blackwell Companion to the City*, edited by S. Watson and G. Bridge, 15–25. Oxford: Wiley Blackwell.

————— (2013). 'Neoliberal Urbanism Redux?' *International Journal of Urban and Regional Research* 37(3): 1091–1099.

————— (2018). 'Actually Existing Neoliberalism'. In *The Sage Handbook of Neoliberalism*, edited by D. Cahill, M. Konings, M. Cooper and D. Primrose, 3–15. London: Sage Publications.

Bunnell, T. (2015). 'Smart City Returns'. *Dialogues in Human Geography* 5(1): 45–48.

Burawoy, M. (1998). 'The Extended Case Method'. *Sociological Theory* 16(1): 4–33.

—————, ed. (2000). *Global Ethnography: Forces, Connections, and Imaginations in a Postmodern World*. London, Berkeley and Los Angeles: University of California Press.

Byres, T. J. (1991). 'The Agrarian Question and Differing Forms of Capitalist Agrarian Transition: An Essay with Reference to Asia'. In *Rural Transformation in Asia*, edited by J. Breman and S. Mundle, 3–76. New Delhi: Oxford University Press.

Casolari, M. (2000). 'Hindutva's Foreign Tie-Up in the 1930s: Archival Evidence'. *Economic and Political Weekly* 35(4): 218–228.

Castree, N. (2006). 'From Neoliberalism to Neoliberalisation: Consolations, Confusions, and Necessary Illusions'. *Environment and Planning A* 38(1): 1–6.

CCZMCSB (Centre for Coastal Zone Management and Coastal Shelter Belt) (2020). 'Database on Coastal States of India'. Anna University, Chennai. Available at http://iomenvis.nic.in/index2.aspx?slid=758&sublinkid=119&langid=1&mid=1. Accessed 15 February 2020.

Census India (2011). 'Gujarat Profile'. Available at https://censusindia.gov.in/2011census/censusinfodashboard/stock/profiles/en/IND024_Gujarat.pdf. Accessed 1 November 2019.

Chacko, P. (2018a). 'Marketizing Hindutva: The State, Society, and Markets in Hindu Nationalism'. *Modern Asian Studies* 53(2): 377–410.

——— (2018b). 'The Right Turn in India: Authoritarianism, Populism and Neoliberalisation'. *Journal of Contemporary Asia* 48(4): 541–565.

Chacko, P. and K. Jayasuriya (2017). 'Trump, the Authoritarian Populist Revolt and the Future of the Rules-Based Order in Asia'. *Australian Journal of International Affairs* 71(2): 121–127.

——— (2018). 'Asia's Conservative Moment: Understanding the Rise of the Right'. *Journal of Contemporary Asia* 48(4): 529–540.

Chakravartty, A. (2015). 'Farmers Detained for "Incident-Free" Vibrant Gujarat Summit'. *Down To Earth*, 13 January. Available at https://www.downtoearth. org.in/news/farmers-detained-for-incidentfree-vibrant-gujarat-summit-48187. Accessed 12 September 2019.

Chakravorty, S. (2016). 'Land Acquisition in India: The Political-Economy of Changing the Law'. *Area Development and Policy* 1(1): 48–62.

Chandhoke, N. (2003). 'Governance and the Pluralisation of the State: Implications for Democratic Citizenship'. *Economic and Political Weekly* 38(28): 2957–2968.

Chandra, K. (2004). *Why Ethnic Parties Succeed: Patronage and Ethnic Head Counts in India*. Cambridge: Cambridge University Press.

——— (2015). 'The New Indian State: The Relocation of Patronage in the Post-Liberalisation Economy'. *Economic and Political Weekly* 50(41): 46–58.

Chang, H. J. (2003). 'The Market, the State and Institutions in Economic Development'. In *Rethinking Development Economics*, edited by H. J. Chang, 41–60. London: Anthem Press.

Chatterjee, P. (1986). *Nationalist Thought and the Colonial World: A Derivative Discourse?* London: Zed Books.

——— (1998). 'Development Planning and the Indian State'. In *The State Development Planning and Liberalisation in India*, edited by T. J. Byres, 82–103. Delhi: Oxford University Press.

Chatterjee, P. (2001). 'Democracy and the Violence of the State: A Political Negotiation of Death'. *Inter-Asia Cultural Studies* 2(1): 7–21.

——— (2002). 'On Civil and Political Society in Post-Colonial Democracies'. In *Civil Society: History and Possibilities*, edited by S. Kaviraj and S. Khilnani, 165–178. Cambridge: Cambridge University Press.

——— (2004). *The Politics of the Governed: Reflections on Popular Politics in Most of the World*. New York: Columbia University Press.

——— (2008). 'Democracy and Economic Transformation in India'. *Economic and Political Weekly* 43(16): 53–62.

Chatterjee, E. and M. McCartney, eds. (2019). *Class and Conflict: Revisiting Pranab Bardhan's Political Economy of India*. New Delhi: Oxford University Press.

Chen, Y. (2013). 'Neoliberal-inspired Large-scale Urban Development Projects in Chinese Cities'. In *The Routledge Companion to Urban Regeneration*, edited by J. McCarthy and M. E. Leary, 77–87. Oxon and New York: Routledge.

Corbridge, S. (1999). '"The Militarization of All Hindudom"? The Bharatiya Janata Party, the Bomb, and the Political Spaces of Hindu Nationalism'. *Economy and Society* 28(2): 222–255.

Corbridge, S. and J. Harriss (2000). *Reinventing India: Liberalization, Hindu Nationalism, and Popular Democracy*. Cambridge: Polity Press.

Corbridge, S., G. Williams, M. Srivastava and R. Veron (2005). *Seeing the State: Governance and Governmentality in India*. Cambridge: Cambridge University Press.

Counterview (2014). 'No Land Acquisition in Dholera SIR, but Farmers Must Handover 50 Per Cent of Land for Infrastructure: Gujarat Govt at Public Hearing'. Available at https://counterview.org/2014/01/18/no-land-acquisition-in-dholera-sir-but-farmers-must-handover-50-per-cent-of-land-for-infrastructure-gujarat-govt-at-public-hearing/. Accessed 25 November 2017.

Cox, J. R. (2004). 'Free Trade and the Eclipse of Civil Society: Barriers to Transparency and Public Participation in NAFTA and the Free Trade of the Americas'. In *Communication and Public Participation in Environmental Decision Making*, edited by S. P. Depoe, J. W. Delicath and M. F. Elsenbeer, 201–219. New York: State University of New York Press.

Cross, J. (2010) 'Neoliberalism as Unexceptional: Economic Zones and the Everyday Precariousness of Working life in South India'. *Critique of Anthropology* 30(4): 355–373.

———— (2014). *Dream Zones: Anticipating Capitalism and Development in India*. London: Pluto Press.

———— (2015). 'The Economy Of Anticipation: Hope, Infrastructure, and Economic Zones in South India'. *Comparative Studies Of South Asia, Africa and the Middle East* 35 (3): 424–437.

Da Silva, S. (2014). 'Goa: The Dynamics of Reversal'. In *Power Politics and Protest: The Politics of India's Special Economic Zones*, edited by R. Jenkins, L. Kennedy and P. Mukhopadyay, 108–136. New Delhi: Oxford University Press.

Damle, S. and W. Anderson (1987). *Brotherhood in Saffron: The Rashtriya Sevak Sangh and Hindu Revivalism*. New Delhi: Vistaar Publications.

Das, D. (2015). 'Hyderabad: Visioning, Restructuring and Making of a High-Tech City'. *Cities* 43: 48–58.

———. (2020). 'In Pursuit of Being Smart? A Critical Analysis of India's Smart Cities Endeavor'. *Urban Geography* 41(1): 55–78.

Das, S. K. (2005). 'Reforms and the Indian Administrative Service'. In *The Politics of Economic Reforms in India*, edited by J. Mooij, 171–196. Delhi: Sage Publications.

Das, V. and D. Poole, eds. (2004). *Anthropology in the Margins of the State*. Santa Fe: School of American Research Press.

Datta, A. (2015). 'New Urban Utopias of Postcolonial India: "Entrepreneurial Urbanization" in Dholera Smart City, Gujarat'. *Dialogues in Human Geography* 5(1): 3–22.

Debroy, B. (2012). *Gujarat: Governance for Growth and Development*. Gurgaon: Academic Foundation.

Deininger, K. (2011). 'Challenges Posed by the New Wave of Farmland Investment'. *The Journal of Peasant Studies* 38(2): 217–247.

Desai, M. (2015). 'Rethinking hegemony: Caste, Class and Political Subjectivities among Informal Workers in Ahmedabad'. In *New Subaltern Politics: Reconceptualizing Hegemony and Resistance in Contemporary India*, edited by A. G. Nilsen and S. Roy, 54–74. New Delhi and Oxford: Oxford University Press.

Desai, Radhika (2006). 'Neoliberalism and Cultural Nationalism: A Danse Macabre'. In *Neoliberal Hegemony: A Global Critique*, edited by D. Plehwe, B. Walpen and G. Neunhöffer, 222–235. Oxon: Routledge.

——— (2011a). 'Gujarat's Hindutva of Capitalist Development'. *South Asia: Journal of South Asian Studies* 34, no. 3: 354–381.

——— (2011b). 'Hindutva's Ebbing Tide?' In *Understanding India's New Political Economy*, edited by S. Ruparelia, S. Reddy, J. Harriss and S. Corbridge, 188–201. London and New York: Routledge.

Desai, Renu (2008). 'The Globalising City in the Time of Hindutva: The Politics of Urban Development and Citizenship in Ahmedabad, India'. PhD thesis, University of California, Berkeley.

——— (2012). 'Entrepreneurial Urbanism in the Time of Hindutva: City Imagineering, Place Marketing and Citizenship in Ahmedabad'. In *Urbanizing Citizenship: Contested Spaces in Indian Cities*, edited by R. Desai and R. Sanyal, 31–57. New Delhi: Sage Publications.

Dholakia, A. and R. Dholakia (2015). 'Policy Reform in Economic Sectors'. In *The Making of Miracles in Indian States: Andhra Pradesh, Bihar and Gujarat*, edited by A. Panagariya and M. G. Rao, 246–264. New Delhi: Oxford University Press.

DIPP (2018). 'Delhi Mumbai Industrial Corridor (DMIC)'. Department for Promotion of Industry and Internal Trade, Government of India. Available at https://dipp.gov.in/japan-plus/delhi-mumbai-industrial-corridor-dmic. Accessed 19 January 2019.

Duncan, J. and M. Agarwal (2017). '"There Is Dignity Only with Livestock": Land Grabbing and the Changing Social Practices of Pastoralist Women in Gujarat, India'. In *Gender and Rural Globalization: International Perspectives on Gender and Rural Development*, edited by B. Bock and S. Shortall, 52–76. Boston: CABI.

Economic Times. (2019). 'Leaked Data Part II: Where India's Jobs Mess Is Most Acute'. 13 April. Available at https://economictimes.indiatimes.com/jobs/leaked-data-part-ii-where-indias-jobs-mess-is-most-acute/articleshow/68846924.cms. Accessed 23 January 2020.

Edelman, M. (2013). 'Messy Hectares: Questions about the Epistemology of Land Grabbing'. *The Journal of Peasant Studies* 40(3): 485–450.

Election Commission of India (2020). 'Gujarat'. Available at https://eci.gov.in/files/category/72-gujarat/. Accessed 14 February 2020.

Elections.in (2017). 'Dholka Election and Results 2017, Candidate list, Winner and Runner-up'. Available at http://www.elections.in/gujarat/assembly-constituencies/dholka.html. Accessed 29 March 2018.

Engineer, A. A. (1985). 'Ahmedabad: From Caste to Communal Violence'. *Economic and Political Weekly* 20(15): 628–630.

Express News Network (2015). 'Ahmedabad HC Orders Status Quo at Dholera SIR'. *The Indian Express*, 11 December. Available at https://indianexpress.com/article/cities/ahmedabad/ahemedabad-hc-orders-status-quo-at-dholera-sir/. Accessed 11 September 2019.

Express News Service (2017). 'Swaminarayan Temple in Vadtal Openly Backs BJP, Appeals to Devotees to Vote for "Modi"'. *The Indian Express*, 5 November. Available at https://indianexpress.com/elections/gujarat-assembly-elections-2017/swaminarayan-temple-in-vadtal-openly-backs-bjp-appeals-to-devotees-to-vote-for-narendra-modi-4922827/. Accessed 11 November 2018.

Evans, P. B., D. Rueschemeyer and T. Skocpol, eds. (1985). *Bringing the State Back In*. Cambridge: Cambridge University Press.

Ferguson, J. (1994). 'The Anti-Politics Machine: "Development," Depoliticization, and Bureaucratic Power in Lesotho'. *The Ecologist* 24(5): 176–181.

——— (2010). 'The Uses of Neoliberalism'. *Antipode* 41(S1): 166–184.

——— (2015). *Give a Man a Fish: Reflections on the New Politics of Distribution*. Durham, NC: Duke University Press.

Financial Express (2018). 'Gujarat Budget Highlights 2018–19: After Assembly Elections Scare, Here's What BJP Government Has Offered to Gujaratis'. 20 February. Available at https://www.financialexpress.com/economy/gujarat-budget-highlights-2018-19-after-assembly-elections-scare-heres-what-bjp-government-has-offered-to-gujaratis/1072878/. Accessed 8 June 2019.

Forbes (2019). 'Larsen & Toubro'. Available on https://www.forbes.com/companies/larsen-toubro/. Accessed 25 October 2019.

Froerer, P. (2007). *Religious Division and Social Conflict: The Emergence of Hindu Nationalism in Rural India*. New Delhi: Social Science Press.

Fuller, C. J. and J. Harriss (2001). 'For an Anthropology of the Modern Indian State'. In *The Everyday State and Society in Modern India*, edited by C. J. Fuller and V. Benei, 1–30. London: Hurst and Company.

Gaventa, J. (2019). 'Power and Powerlessness in an Appalachian Valley'. *The Journal of Peasant Studies* 46 (3–4): 440–456.

Geiger, R. K. and J. R. Wolch (1986). 'A Shadow State? Voluntarism in Metropolitan Los Angeles'. *Environment and Planning D: Society and Space* 4(3): 351–366.

Ghassem-Fachandi, P. (2012). *Pogrom in Gujarat: Hindu Nationalism and Anti-Muslim Violence in India*. Princeton, NJ: Princeton University Press.

Ghertner, D. A. (2011). 'Gentrifying the State, Gentrifying Participation: Elite Governance Programs in Delhi'. *International Journal of Urban and Regional Research* 35(3): 504–532.

GIDB (Gujarat Infrastructure Development Board) (1999). *Gujarat Infrastructure Agenda—Vision 2010*, Vols. I–III. Gandhinagar: GIDB.

Gidwani, V. K. (2008). *Capital, Interrupted: Agrarian Development and the Politics of Work in India*. Minneapolis: University of Minnesota Press.

Gier, N. F. (2014). *The Origins of Religious Violence: An Asian Perspective*. New York, London, Boulder and Lanham: Lexington Books.

GoG (Government of Gujarat) (2009). 'The Gujarat Special Investment Region Act, 2009'. *The Gujarat Government Gazette* L(3): 1–18. Available at https://prsindia.org/files/bills_acts/acts_states/gujarat/2009/2009Gujarat2.pdf and https://www.gidb.org/pdf/sirord.pdf. Accessed 17 April 2018.

——— (2016). 'Socio-Economic Review, Gujarat State, 2015–16'. Directorate of Economics and Statistics, February. Available at https://financedepartment.gujarat.gov.in/Documents/34 - Socio Economic Review (English).pdf. Accessed 18 April 2018.

Goldman, M. (2011). 'Speculative Urbanism and the Making of the Next World City'. *International Journal of Urban and Regional Research* 35(3): 555–581.

Gooptu, N. (1997). 'The Urban Poor and Militant Hinduism in Early Twentieth-Century Uttar Pradesh'. *Modern Asian Studies* 31(4): 879–918.

———— (2011). 'Economic Liberalization, Urban Politics and the Poor'. In *Understanding India's New Political Economy: A Great Transformation?* edited by S. Ruparelia, S. Reddy, J. Harriss and S. Corbridge, 35–48. London and New York: Routledge.

———— (2016). 'Divided We Stand: The Indian City after Economic Liberalization'. In *Routledge Handbook of Contemporary India*, edited by K. A. Jacobsen, 216–231. London: Routledge.

Gopalakrishnan, S. (2006). 'Defining, Constructing and Policing a "New India": Relationship between Neoliberalism and Hindutva'. *Economic and Political Weekly* 41(26): 2803–2813.

Goswami, A. (2016). 'Land Acquisition, Rehabilitation and Resettlement: Law, Politics and the Elusive Search for Balance'. *Journal of Land and Rural Studies* 4(1): 3–22.

Goswami, M. (1998). 'From Swadeshi to Swaraj: Nation, Economy, Territory in Colonial South Asia, 1870 to 1907'. *Comparative Studies in Society and History* 40(4): 609–636.

Gramsci, A. (1971). *Selections from the Prison Notebooks*. New York: International Publishers.

Greenfield, A. (2013). *Against the Smart City (The City Is Here for You to Use)*. New York: Do Projects.

Geiger, R. K. and J. R. Wolch (1986). 'A Shadow State? Voluntarism in Metropolitan Los Angeles'. *Environment and Planning D: Society and Space* 4(3): 351–366. https://doi.org/10.1068/d040351.

Groves, C., M. Munday and N. Yakovleva (2013). 'Fighting the Pipe: Neoliberal Governance and Barriers to Effective Community Participation in Energy Infrastructure Planning'. *Environment and Planning C* 31(2): 340–356.

Guarneros-Meza, V. and M. Geddes (2010). 'Local Governance and Participation under Neoliberalism: Comparative Perspectives'. *International Journal of Urban and Regional Research* 34(1): 115–129.

Guha, R. (2008). *India After Gandhi: The History of the World's Largest Democracy*. New York: Harper Perennial.

Guha, S. (2014). 'Patronage and State-Making in Early Modern Empires in India and Britain'. In *Patronage as Politics in South Asia*, edited by A. Piliavsky, 104–124. Cambridge: Cambridge University Press.

Guha Thakurta, P. (2009). 'Cheapest Car Rides on Govt Subsidies'. Inter Press Service, 5 June. Available at http://www.ipsnews.net/2009/06/corrected-repeat-india-cheapest-car-rides-on-govt-subsidies/. Accessed 19 January 2020.

———— (2015). 'The Incredible Rise and Rise of Gautam Adani: Part One'. *The Citizen*, 29 April. Available at https://www.thecitizen.in/index.php/en/

NewsDetail/index/1/3375/The-Incredible-Rise-and-Rise-of-Gautam-Adani-Part-One. Accessed 16 April 2020.

Gupta, A. (1995). 'Blurred Boundaries: The Discourse of Corruption, the Culture of Politics, and the Imagined State'. *American Ethnologist* 22(2): 375–402.

—— (2012). *Red Tape: Bureaucracy, Structural Violence, and Poverty in India*. Durham and London: Duke University Press.

Gupta, A. and J. Ferguson (1997). *Anthropological Locations: Boundaries and Grounds of a Field Science*. Berkeley: University of California Press.

—— (2002). 'Spatialising States: Towards an Ethnography of Neoliberal Governmentality'. *American Ethnologist* 29 (4): 981–1002.

Gupta, A. and A. Sharma, eds. (2006). *The Anthropology of the State: A Reader*. Oxford: Blackwell Publishing.

Gupta, A. and K. Sivaramakrishnan. (2011). 'Introduction: The State in India after Liberalization'. In *The State in India after Liberalization: Interdisciplinary Perspectives*, edited by A. Gupta and K. Sivaramakrishnan, 1–28. Abingdon: Routledge.

Gürel, B., B. Küçük and S. Taş (2019). 'Rural Roots of the Rise of the Justice and Development Party in Turkey'. *The Journal of Peasant Studies* 46(3): 457–479.

Hall, R., M. Edelman, S. M. Borras Jr, L. Scoones, B. White and W. Wolford (2015). 'Resistance, Acquiescence or Incorporation? An Introduction to Land Grabbing and Political Reactions "From Below"'. *The Journal of Peasant Studies* 42(3–4): 467–488.

Hansen, T. B. (1999). *The Saffron Wave: Democracy and Hindu Nationalism in Modern India*. Princeton, NJ: Princeton University Press.

Hansen, T. B. and C. Jaffrelot (1998) *The BJP and the Compulsions of Politics in India*. New Delhi: Oxford University Press.

Hansen, T. B. and F. Stepputat (2001). *States of Imagination: Ethnographic Explorations of the Postcolonial State*. Durham, NC: Duke University Press.

Harriss-White, B. (1997). 'Informal Economic Order: Shadow States, Private Status States, States of Last Resort and Spinning States a Speculative Discussion on S Asian Case Material'. QEH Working Paper Series 6. Oxford: University of Oxford, Queen Elizabeth House.

—— (2003). *India Working: Essays on Society and Economy*. Cambridge: Cambridge University Press.

Hart, H. C., ed. (1976). *Indira Gandhi's India: A Political System Reappraised*. Boulder, CO: Westview Press.

Harvey, D. (1989). 'From Managerialism to Entrepreneurialism: The Transformation in Urban Governance in Late Capitalism'. *Geografiska Annaler* 71(1): 3–17.

———. (2005). *A Brief History of Neoliberalism*. Oxford: Oxford University Press.

Herring, R. J. (1999). 'Embedded Particularism: India's Failed Developmental State'. In *The Developmental State*, edited by WooCumings, 304–334. Ithaca, NY: Cornell University Press.

Hirway, I. (1995). 'Selective Development and Widening Disparities in Gujarat'. *Economic and Political Weekly* 30(41 and 42): 2603–2618.

——— (2000). 'Dynamics of Development in Gujarat: Some Issues'. *Economic and Political Weekly* 35(35/36): 3106–3120.

——— (2002). 'Employment and Unemployment Situation in 1990s: How Good Are NSS Data?' *Economic and Political Weekly* 37(21): 2027–2036.

——— (2003). 'Identification of BPL Households for Poverty Alleviation Programmes'. *Economic and Political Weekly* 38(45): 4803–4808.

——— (2014). 'Assessing the Inclusiveness of Growth in Gujarat'. In *Growth or Development: Which Way Is Gujarat Going*, edited by I. Hirway, A. Shah and G. Shah, 83–138. New Delhi: Oxford University Press.

——— (2015). 'Unpaid Work and the Economy: Linkages and Their Implications'. *Indian Journal of Labour Economics* 58(1): 1–21.

——— (2016). 'Rethinking Reservations and "Development"'. *The Hindu* (online). Available at https://www.thehindu.com/opinion/op-ed/hardik-patels-call-for-reservations/article7596766.ece (Accessed 24th December 2019).

——— (2017). 'The Truth Behind the Gujarat Growth Model'. *The Wire*, 8 December. Available at https://thewire.in/economy/the-truth-behind-the-gujarat-growth-model. Accessed 22 December 2019.

Hirway, I. and D. Mahadevia (2005). *Gujarat Human Development Report, 2004*. Ahmedabad: Mahatma Gandhi Labour Institute.

Hirway, I. and N. Shah (2011). 'Labour and Employment under Globalisation: The Case of Gujarat'. *Economic and Political Weekly* 46(22): 57–65.

Hirway, I., S. P. Kashyap and A. Shah, eds. (2002) *Dynamics of Development in Gujarat*. New Delhi: Concept Publishing Company.

Hirway, I., A. Shah and G. Shah, ed. (2014). *Growth or Development: Which Way Is Gujarat Going*. New Delhi: Oxford University Press.

HT Correspondent (2017). 'Vijay Rupani Reacts to "Vikas Has Gone Crazy" Social Media Campaign Mocking BJP's Development Plank'. *Hindustan Times*, 7 September. Available at https://www.hindustantimes.com/india-news/vijay-rupani-reacts-to-vikas-gando-thayo-che-social-media-campaign-mocking-bjp-s-development-plank/story-zf75bYvzvIvcbXYqqKqnsL.html. Accessed 19 February 2019.

Human Rights Watch (2002). 'We Have No Orders to Save You'. April. http://www.hrw.org/reports/2002/India /. Accessed 10 December 2019.

Hurl, C. and A. Vogelpohl (2021). *Professional Service Firms and Politics in a Global Era. Public Policy, Private Expertise.* Cham: Palgrave Macmillan.

Idiculla, M. (2016). 'New Regimes of Private Governance: The Case of Electronic City in Peri-Urban Bangalore'. *Economic and Political Weekly* 51(17): 102–109.

India Today (2019). 'Gujarat FM Nitin Patel Presents Highest-ever Rs 2 Lakh Crore-plus Budget, Calls It Historic Moment'. 3 July. Available at https://www.indiatoday.in/india/story/gujarat-finance-minister-nitin-patel-presents-highest-ever-rs-2-lakh-crore-plus-budget-1560867-2019-07-03. Accessed 12 August 2019.

International Initiative for Justice (2003). 'Threatened Existence: A Feminist Analysis of the Genocide in Gujarat'. December. Available at http://www.onlinevolunteers.org/gujarat/reports/iijg/2003/fullreport.pdf. Accessed 31 March 2020.

Jaffrelot, C. (1996). *The Hindu Nationalist Movement and Indian Politics: 1925 to the 1990s.* London: Hurst & Company.

———, ed. (2005). *The Sangh Parivar: A Reader.* New Delhi: Oxford University Press.

———, ed. (2007). *Hindu Nationalism: A Reader.* Princeton, NJ: Princeton University Press.

——— (2009). 'The Hindu Nationalist Reinterpretation of Pilgrimage in India: The Limits of Yatra Politics'. *Nations and Nationalism* 15(1): 1–19.

——— (2012). 'Gujarat 2002: What Justice for the Victims? The Supreme Court, the SIT, the Police and the State Judiciary'. *Economic and Political Weekly* 47(8): 77–89.

——— (2015a). 'What "Gujarat Model"?—Growth without Development—And with Socio-Political Polarisation'. *South Asia: Journal of South Asian Studies* 38(4): 820–838.

——— (2015b). 'The Modi-centric BJP 2014 Election Campaign: New Techniques and Old Tactics'. *Contemporary South Asia* 23(2): 151–166.

——— (2016). 'Narendra Modi between Hindutva and Subnationalism: The Gujarati Asmita of a Hindu Hriday Samrat'. *India Review* 15(2): 196–217.

——— (2017). 'Gujarat Model?'. *The Indian Express.* 20 November. Available at https://indianexpress.com/article/opinion/columns/gujarat-assembly-elections-2017-bjp-demonetisation-gst-industrialists-businessmen-4945328/. Accessed 22 March 2019.

——— (2019). 'Business-Friendly Gujarat under Narendra Modi: The Implications of a New Political Economy'. In *Business and Politics in India,* edited by C. Jaffrelot, A. Kohli and K. Murali, 211–233. New York and Oxford: Oxford University Press.

Jaffrelot, C. and L. Gayer (2012). *Muslims in Indian Cities: Trajectories of Marginalisation*. London: Hurst & Company.

Jaffrelot, C., A. Kohli and K. Murali, eds. (2019). *Business and Politics in India*. New York and Oxford: Oxford University Press.

Jain, V. (2019). 'Examining the Town Planning Scheme of India and Lessons from Land Readjustment in Japan'. ADBI Working Paper Series. Available at https://www.adb.org/sites/default/files/publication/539736/adbi-wp1037.pdf. Accessed 19 February 2019.

Jeffrey, C. and J. Lerche (2000). 'Stating the Difference: State, Discourse and Class Reproduction in Uttar Pradesh, India'. *Development and Change* 31(4): 857–878.

Jeffrey C., J. C. Harriss and S. Corbridge. (2017). 'Is India Becoming the "Hindu Rashtra" Sought by Hindu Nationalists?' Simons Papers in Security and Development No. 60. School for International Studies, Simon Fraser University, Vancouver.

Jenkins, R. (1999). *Democratic Politics and Economic Reform in India*. Cambridge: Cambridge University Press.

————. (2006). 'Political Economy of Liberalisation'. In *Encyclopaedia of India*, edited by S. Wolpert, 61-63. New York: Thomson Gale. Available at http://www.hunter.cuny.edu/polsci/faculty/Jenkins/repository/files/2006-%20Encyclopedia%20of%20India-%20Pol%20Econ%20of%20Liberalization.pdf. Accessed 22 March 2019.

Jenkins, R. and J. Manor (2017). *Politics and the Right to Work: India's National Rural Employment Guarantee Act*. London: Hurst & Company.

Jenkins, R., L. Kennedy and P. Mukhopadhyay (2014). *Power, Policy, and Protest: The Politics of India's Special Economic Zones*. New Delhi: Oxford University Press.

Jenkins, R., L. Kennedy, P. Mukhopadhyay and K. C. Pradhan (2015). 'Special Economic Zones in India: Interrogating the Nexus of Land, Development and Urbanization'. *Environment and Urbanization ASIA* 6(1): 1–17.

Jessop, B. (1977). 'Recent Theories of the Capitalist State'. *Cambridge Journal of Economics* 1(4): 353–373.

———— (1985). *Nicos Poulantzas: Marxist Theory and Political Strategy*. New York: Macmillan.

———— (1990). *State Theory: Putting Capitalist States in Their Place*. Cambridge: Polity.

———— (1999). 'The Strategic Selectivity of the State: Reflections on a Theme of Poulantzas'. *Journal of the Hellenic Diaspora* 25(1–2): 41–77.

———— (2015). 'Crises, Crisis-Management and State Restructuring: What Future for the State?' *Policy and Politics* 43(4): 475–492.

Jones, D. E. and R. W. Jones (1976). 'Urban Upheaval in India: The 1974 Nav Nirman Riots in Gujarat'. *Asian Survey* 16(11): 1012–1033.

Joseph G. and D. Nugent, eds. (1994). *Everyday Forms of State Formation: Revolution and the Negotiation of Rule in Modern Mexico*. Durham, NC, and London: Duke University Press.

Juneja, S. (2015). 'Nirma Plant in Trouble Again'. *Down To Earth*, 30 May. Available at https://www.downtoearth.org.in/news/nirma-plant-in-trouble-again-33554. Accessed 24 March 2020.

Kalia, R. (2004). *Gandhinagar: Building National Identity in Postcolonial India*. Columbia, SC: University of South Carolina Press.

———— (2006). 'Modernism, Modernization and Post-Colonial India: A Reflective Essay'. *Planning Perspectives* 21(2): 133–156.

Kapoor, A. (2020). 'Modi the Fanatic Is Using the Coronavirus Crisis to Destroy India's Heritage'. *The Guardian*. Available at https://www.theguardian.com/culture/2020/may/21/modi-the-fanatic-is-using-the-coronavirus-crisis-to-destroy-indias-heritage. Accessed 24 September 2020.

Kapur, D., C. Prasad, L. Pritchett and D. Babu (2010). 'Rethinking Inequality: Dalits in Uttar Pradesh in the Market Reform Era'. *Economic and Political Weekly* 45(35): 39–49.

Kashwan, P. (2014). 'Botched-Up Development and Electoral Politics in India'. *Economic and Political Weekly* 49(34): 48–55.

Katakam, A. (2014). 'Cement for Grain?' *Frontline*, 19 March. Available at https://frontline.thehindu.com/cover-story/cement-for-grain/article5787665.ece. Accessed 11 September 2018.

Kaur, P. (2007). 'Growth Acceleration in India'. *Economic and Political Weekly* 42(15): 1380–1386.

Kaviraj, S. (1984). 'On the Crisis of Political Institutions in India'. *Contributions to Indian Sociology* 18(2): 223–243.

———— (1988). 'A Critique of the Passive Revolution'. *Economic and Political Weekly* 23(45/47): 2429–2444.

Kaya, A. (2015). 'Islamisation of Turkey under the AKP Rule: Empowering Family, Faith and Charity'. *South European Society and Politics* 20(1): 47–69.

Kennedy, L. (2013). *The Politics of Economic Restructuring in India: Economic Governance and State Spatial Rescaling*. Abingdon: Routledge.

Kennedy, L. and A. Sood (2019). 'Outsourced Urban Governance as a State Rescaling Strategy in Hyderabad, India'. *Cities* 85: 130–139.

Kennedy, L. and M. H. Zérah (2008). 'The Shift to City-Centric Growth Strategies: Perspectives from Hyderabad and Mumbai'. *Economic and Political Weekly* 43(39): 110–117.

Kim, H. (2010). 'The Swaminarayan Movement and Religious Subjectivity'. In *The Idea of Gujarat: History, Ethnography, and Text*, edited by E. Simpson and A. Kapadia, 207–228. New Delhi: Orient Blackswan.

Kitchin, R. (2014). 'The Real-Time City? Big Data and Smart Urbanism'. *GeoJournal* 79(1): 1–14.

——— (2015). 'Making Sense of Smart Cities: Addressing Present Shortcomings'. *Cambridge Journal of Regions, Economy and Society* 8(1): 131–136.

Kohli, A. (1990). *Democracy and Discontent: India's Growing Crisis of Governability*. Cambridge: Cambridge University Press.

——— (2006a). 'Politics of Economic Growth in India, 1980–2005: Part I: The 1980s'. *Economic and Political Weekly* 41(13): 1251–1259.

——— (2006b). 'Politics of Economic Growth in India, 1980–2005: Part II: The 1990s and Beyond'. *Economic and Political Weekly* 41(14): 1361–1370.

——— (2009). *Democracy and Development in India: From Socialism to Pro-Business*. New Delhi: Oxford University Press.

Kothari, R. (1964). 'The Congress "System" in India'. *Asian Survey* 4(12): 1161–1173.

——— (1970). *Politics in India*. Delhi: Orient Longman.

Kothari, R. (2016). 'The Patel Agitation and the "Paradox" of Demanding OBC Status'. *Kafila*, 17 September. Available at https://kafila.online/2015/09/17/the-patel-agitation-and-the-paradox-of-demanding-obc-status-rita-kothari/. Accessed 29 January 2020.

Krishna, A. (2003). *Active Social Capital: Tracing the Roots of Development and Democracy*. New York: Columbia University Press.

Kumar, A. (1999). *The Black Economy in India*. New Delhi: Orient Longman.

Kumar, D. (2017). 'Opinion: Deeper Analysis of Gujarat Verdict Will Disappoint Congress Cheerleaders'. News18, 27 December. Available athttps://www.news18.com/news/opinion/opinion-deeper-analysis-of-gujarat-verdict-will-disappoint-congress-cheerleaders-1611695.html. Accessed 12 May 2019.

Kundra, A. (2000). *The Performance of India's Export Zones: A Comparison with the Chinese Approach*. New Delhi: Sage Publications.

Langa, M. (2017). '"Crazy Vikas" Drives BJP Bonkers in Gujarat'. *The Hindu*, 19 September. Available at https://www.thehindu.com/news/national/other-states/crazy-vikas-drives-bjp-bonkers-in-gujarat/article19715781.ece. Accessed 24 July 2019.

Lefebvre, H. (1976). *The Survival of Capitalism*. London: Allison & Busby.

Levien, M. (2011). 'Special Economic Zones and Accumulation by Dispossession in India'. *Journal of Agrarian Change* 11(4): 454–483.

——— (2012). 'The Land Question: Special Economic Zones and the Political Economy of Dispossession in India'. *Journal of Peasant Studies* 39(3–4): 933–969.

——— (2013a). 'Regimes of Dispossession: From Steel Towns to Special Economic Zones'. *Development and Change* 44(2): 381–407.

——— (2013b). 'Regimes of Dispossession: Special Economic Zones and the Political Economy of Land in India'. PhD dissertation, University of California, Berkeley.

——— (2018). *Dispossession without Development: Land Grabs in Neoliberal India.* New York: Oxford University Press.

Levien, M. and S. Agarwal (2020). 'Dalits and Dispossession: A Comparison'. *Journal of Contemporary Asia* 50(5): 696–722.

Lewis, D. and D. Mosse (2006). 'Encountering Order and Disjuncture: Contemporary Anthropological Perspectives on the Organization of Development'. *Oxford Development Studies* 34(1): 1–13.

Li, T. M. (2014). *Land's End: Capitalist Relations on an Indigenous Frontier.* Durham, NC: Duke University Press.

Lobo, L. and S. Kumar (2009). *Land Acquisition, Displacement and Resettlement in Gujarat: 1947–2004.* New Delhi: Sage Publications India.

Longkumer, A. (2020). *The Greater India Experiment: Hindutva and the Northeast.* Stanford, CA: Stanford University Press.

Longkumer, A. and E. Anderson (2018). 'Special Issue: Neo-Hindutva: Evolving Forms, Spaces, and Expressions of Hindu Nationalism'. *Contemporary South Asia* 46(2): 371–490.

Ludden, D., ed. (1996). *Contesting the Nation: Religion, Community, and the Politics of Democracy in India.* Philadelphia: University of Pennsylvania Press.

Mahadevia, D. (1997). *Economic Growth and Land and Water Resources in Gujarat.* Ahmedabad: School of Planning, Centre for Environmental Planning and Technology.

——— (1998). *Development Dichotomy in Gujarat.* New Delhi: Research Foundation for Science Technology and Ecology.

——— (2003). *Globalisation, Urban Reforms and Metropolitan Response: India.* New Delhi: Concept Publishing Pvt Ltd.

——— (2005). 'From Stealth to Aggression: Economic Reforms and Communal Politics in Gujarat'. In *The Politics of Economic Reforms in India,* edited by J. Mooij, 291–321. New Delhi and London: Sage Publication.

———— (2006). 'NURM and the Poor in Globalising Mega Cities'. *Economic and Political Weekly* 41(31): 3399–3401, 3403.

———— (2014). 'Dynamics of Urbanization in Gujarat'. In *Growth or Development: Which Way Is Gujarat Going*, edited by I. Hirway, A. Shah and G. Shah, 340–379. New Delhi: Oxford University Press.

Mahadevia, D., M. Pai and A. Mahendra (2018). 'Ahmedabad: Town Planning Schemes for Equitable Development—Glass Half Full or Half Empty'. World Resources Report Case Study. Available at https://wriorg.s3.amazonaws.com/s3fs-public/wrr-case-study-ahmedabad.pdf. Accessed 5 January 2019.

Mahaprashasta, A. A. (2017). 'In Gujarat Mandate, Urban–Rural Divide Writ Large'. *The Wire*, 18 December. Available at https://thewire.in/politics/gujarat-assembly-elections-results-2017. Accessed 25 June 2019.

Mamonova, N., J. Franquesa and S. Brooks (2020). '"Actually Existing" Right-Wing Populism in Rural Europe: Insights from Eastern Germany, Spain, the United Kingdom and Ukraine'. *The Journal of Peasant Studies* 47(7): 1497–1525.

Manoj, P. (2007). 'Mundra SEZ to Take Over Dholera Port Development from JK Group'. *Livemint*, 14 September. Available at https://www.livemint.com/Companies/iobnx199CWX5p0bhxuPIAO/Mundra-SEZ-to-take-over-Dholera-port-development-from-JK-Gro.html. Accessed 8 August 2019.

Manor, J. (1995). 'The Political Sustainability of Economic Liberalisation in India'. In *India: The Future of Economic Reform*, edited by R. Cassen and V. Joshi, 341–363. New Delhi: Oxford University Press.

———— (2000). 'Small-Time Political Fixers in India's States: "Towel over Armpit"'. *Asian Survey* 40(5): 816–835.

Maringanti A., E. Sheppard, A. Roy, V. Gidwani, M. Goldman and H. Leitner (2015). 'Introduction: Urban Revolutions in the Age of Global Urbanism'. *Urban Studies* 52 (11): 1947–1961.

Mathur, N. (2015). *Paper Tiger: Law, Bureaucracy and the Developmental State in Himalayan India*. Cambridge: Cambridge University Press.

Matthew, G. (2019). 'Private Insurers Set to Make Rs 3000 Crore Profit from Crop Cover, PSUs in Loss'. *The Indian Express*, 17 January. Available at https://indianexpress.com/article/business/private-insurers-set-to-make-rs-3000-crore-profit-from-crop-cover-psus-in-loss-5542095/. Accessed 11 January 2020.

McCarthy, J. and S. Prudham (2004). 'Neoliberal Nature and the Nature of Neoliberalism'. *Geoforum* 35(3): 275–283.

McKinsey Global Institute (2010). *India's Urban Awakening: Building Inclusive Cities, Sustaining Economic Growth*. New Delhi: McKinsey Global Instiute.

———— (2011). *Big Data: The Next Frontier for Innovation, Competition, and Productivity*. New Delhi: McKinsey Global Instiute.

Mehta, M. (1982). *The Ahmedabad Cotton Textile Industry: Genesis and Growth*. Ahmedabad: New Order Book Company.

Mehta, M. G. (2010). 'A River of No Dissent: Narmada Movement and Coercive Gujarati Nativism'. *South Asian History and Culture* 1(4): 509–528.

———— (2015). 'How Gujarat's Lopsided Growth Model Is Being Unraveled by the Dominant Patel Group'. *Scroll.in*, 27 August. Available at https://scroll.in/article/751485/how-gujarats-lopsided-growth-model-is-being-unravelled-by-the-dominant-patel-group. Accessed 10 October 2018.

———— (2016). 'Ahmedabad: The Middleclass Megacity'. *South Asian History and Culture* 7(2): 191–207.

Mehta, M. G. and D. Banerjee (2017). 'Caste and Capital in the Remaking of Ahmedabad'. *Contemporary South Asia* 25(2): 182–195.

Migdal, J. S. (2001). *State in Society: Studying How States and Societies Transform and Constitute One Another*. Cambridge: Cambridge University Press.

Miliband, R. (1969). *The State in Capitalist Society*. New York: Basic Books.

Mitchell, K. (2001). 'Transnationalism, Neo-Liberalism, and the Rise of the Shadow State'. *Economy and Society* 30(2): 165–189.

Mitchell, T. (1991). 'The Limits of the State: Beyond Statist Approaches and their Critics'. *The American Political Science Review* 85(1): 77–96.

———— (1999). 'Society, Economy, and the State Effect'. In *State/Culture: State Formation After the Cultural Turn*, edited by G. Steinmetz, 76–97. Ithaca and London: Cornell University Press.

———— (2002). 'Can the Mosquito Speak?' In *Rule of Experts: Egypt, Techno-Politics, and Modernity*, edited by T. Mitchell, 19–53. Berkeley, Los Angeles and London: University of California Press.

Mooij, J. E. (1996). *Food Policy and Politics. The Public Distribution System in Karnataka and Kerala, South India*. Wageningen: Faculty of Politics and Social-Cultural Sciences.

———— (1999). *Food Policy and the Indian State: The Public Distribution System in South India*. New Delhi and Oxford: Oxford University Press.

————, ed. (2005). *The Politics of Economic Reforms in India*. New Delhi and London: Sage Publication.

Mosse, D. (2001). 'Irrigation and Statecraft in Zamindari South India'. In *The Everyday State and Society in Modern India*, edited by C. J. Fuller and V. Benei, 163–190. London: Hurst and Company.

———— (2020). 'The Modernity of Caste and the Market Economy'. *Modern Asian Studies* 54(4): 1225–1271.

Murray, W. E. and J. D. Overton (2011). 'Neoliberalism Is Dead, Long Live Neoliberalism? Neostructuralism and the International Aid Regime of the 2000s'. *Progress in Development Studies* 11(4): 307–319.

Nagaraj, R. (1991). 'Discussion—Increase in India's Growth Rate'. *Economic and Political Weekly* 26(15): 1002–1004.

Nanda, M. (2009). *The God Market: How Globalisation is Making India More Hindu*. New Delhi: Random House.

Naqvi, S. (2017). 'Why Modi Is Resorting to Claims of Pak Fixing Gujarat Result'. NDTV Opinion, 11 December. Available at https://www.ndtv.com/opinion/why-modi-is-resorting-to-claims-of-pak-fixing-gujarat-result-1786275. Accessed 14 April 2018.

Nayak, P. (2013). 'Policy Shifts in Land Records Management'. *Economic and Political Weekly* 48(24): 71–75.

Nayar, B. R. (2006). 'When Did the "Hindu" Rate of Growth End? *Economic and Political Weekly* 41(19): 1885–1890.

Newsd (2020). 'Why Is #Dholerasmartcity Trending on Twitter? Netizens Slams Modi Government for His Promises, Check Tweets'. 15 May. Available at https://newsd.in/why-is-dholerasmartcity-trending-on-twitter-netizens-slams-modi-government-for-his-promises-check-tweets/. Accessed 6 September 2020. Full lecture by Narendra Modi is available at https://www.youtube.com/watch?v=_tWv10aRW9w. Accessed 24 September 2018.

Nielsen, K. B. (2018). *Land Dispossession and Everyday Politics in Rural Eastern India*. London and New York: Anthem Press.

——— (2020). 'Orchestrating Anti-Dispossession Politics: Caste and Movement Leadership in Rural West Bengal'. *Journal of Contemporary Asia* 50(5): 761–784.

Nielsen, K. B. and A. G. Nilsen (2015). 'Law Struggles and Hegemonic Processes in Neoliberal India: Gramscian Reflections on Land Acquisition Legislation'. *Globalizations* 12(2): 203–216.

———, eds. (2016*). Social Movements and the State in India: Deepening Democracy?* London: Palgrave.

Nielsen, K. B., S. Sareen and P. Oskarsson (2020). 'The Politics of Caste in India's New Land Wars'. *Journal of Contemporary Asia* 50(5): 684–695.

Nilsen, A. G. (2019). 'From Inclusive Neoliberalism to Authoritarian Populism: Trajectories of Change in the World's Largest Democracy'. In *State of Democracy: Essays on the Life and Politics of Contemporary India*, edited by M. Ray. Delhi: Primus Books.

Nugent, D. (1994). 'Building the State, Making the Nation: The Bases and Limits of State Centralization in "modern" Peru'. *American Anthropologist* 96(2): 333–369.

Oldenburg, P. (1987). 'Middlemen in Third-World Corruption: Implications of an Indian Case'. *World Politics* 39(4): 508–535.

Ong, A. (2006). *Neoliberalism as Exception*. Durham, NC, and London: Duke University Press.

Outlook (2017). 'Rs 33,000 Crore Given for Nano but I Haven't Seen a Single Car in Past 10–15 Days: Rahul Gandhi'. 3 November. Available at https://www.outlookindia.com/website/story/rs-33000-crore-given-for-nano-but-i-havent-seen-a-single-car-in-past-10-15-days-/303869. Accessed 24 July 2019.

Oya, C. (2013). 'Methodological Reflections on "Land Grab" Databases and the "Land Grab" Literature "Rush"'. *The Journal of Peasant Studies* 40(3): 503–520.

Panagariya, A. (2008). *India: The Emerging Giant*. New York: Oxford University Press.

Pandey, G. (1992). *The Construction of Communalism in Colonial North India*. New York: Oxford University Press.

Panikkar, K. N. (1993). 'Religious Symbols and Political Mobilization: The Agitation for a Mandir at Ayodhya'. *Social Scientist* 21(7/8): 63–78.

Patel, S. (1991). 'Growing Regional Inequalities in Gujarat'. *Economic and Political Weekly* 26(26): 1618–1623.

———— (2002). 'Narendra Modi's One-Day Cricket: What and Why?' *Economic and Political Weekly* 37(48): 4826–4837.

Pathak, M. (2012). 'Will GIFT End Up as Another Real Estate Project?' *Livemint*, 31 October. Available at https://www.livemint.com/Politics/B97c8M0agIjMLsIJ2nR1tK/Will-GIFT-end-up-as-another-real-estate-project.html. Accessed 29 November 2019.

Pattenden, J. (2005). 'Trickle-Down Solidarity, Globalisation and Dynamics of Social Transformation in a South Indian Village'. *Economic and Political Weekly* 40(19): 1975–1985.

Peck, J. (2013). 'Explaining (with) Neoliberalism'. *Territory, Politics, Governance* 1(2): 132–157.

Peck, J. and N. Theodore (2012). 'Reanimating Neoliberalism: Process Geographies of Neoliberalisation'. *Social Anthropology* 20(2): 177–185.

Pedersen, J. D. (2000). 'Explaining Economic Liberalisation in India: State and Society Perspectives'. *World Development* 28(2): 265–282.

Polanyi, K. (2001 [1944]). *The Great Transformation: The Political and Economic Origins of Our Time*. Boston: Beacon Press.

Poulantzas, N. (1978). *State, Power, Socialism*. London: Verso.

Pow, C. (2002). 'Urban Entrepreneurialism, Global Business Elite and Urban Mega Development: A Case Study of Suntec City'. *Asian Journal of Social Science* 30(1): 53–72.

Prabhune, T. (2006). 'Adani Group Set to Hike Dholera Port Stake to 74%'. *The Economic Times*, 28 August. Available at https://economictimes.indiatimes.com/industry/transportation/shipping-/-transport/adani-group-set-to-hike-dholera-port-stake-to-74/articleshow/1931002.cms?from=mdr. Accessed 14 March 2018.

Praharaj, S., J. H. Han and S. Hawken (2018). 'Urban Innovation through Policy Integration: Critical Perspectives from 100 Smart Cities Mission in India'. *City, Culture and Society* 12: 35–43.

Prakash, A. (2003). 'Re-imagination of the State and Gujarat's Electoral Verdict'. *Economic and Political Weekly* 38(16): 1601–1610.

Projects Today (2006). 'GMB Approves Dholera Port Project'. 11 January. [online] Available at https://www.projectstoday.com/News/GMB-approves-Dholera-port-project. Accessed 16 February 2019.

PTI (Press Trust of India) (2011). 'Bhalia Wheat Gets GI Tag'. *Business Line*, 12 March. Available at https://www.thehindubusinessline.com/economy/agri-business/bhalia-wheat-gets-gi-tag/article20322702.ece1#. Accessed 26 December 2018.

Qureshi, A. (2015). 'The Marketization of HIV/AIDS Governance: Public–Private Partnerships and Bureaucratic Culture in Pakistan'. *The Cambridge Journal of Anthropology* 33(1): 35–48.

Ramakumar, R. (2017). 'Jats, Khaps and Riots: Communal Politics and the Bharatiya Kisan Union in Northern India'. *Journal of Agrarian Change* 17(1): 22–42.

Raza, G. and S. Hashmi (2002). *State of Ruins: The Dispossessed at the Vortex of Communal Whirlpool in Gujarat*. Report prepared for Prashant (Ahmedabad) and Sahmat (New Delhi).

Reddy, D. S. (2011). 'Hindutva as Praxis'. *Religion Compass* 5(8): 412–426.

——— (2012). 'Hindu Transnationalisms: Organisations, Ideologies, Network'. In *Public Hinduisms*, edited by J. Zavos, P. Kanungo, D. Reddy, M. Warrier and R. B. Williams, 309–323. New Delhi: Sage Publications.

——— (2018). 'What Is Neo about Neo-Hindutva?' *Contemporary South Asia* 26(4): 483–490.

Reddy, R. G. and G. Haragopal (1985). 'The Pyraveekar: The Fixer in Rural India'. *Asian Survey* 25(11): 1148–1162.

Reno, W. (1995). *Corruption and State Politics in Sierra Leone.* Cambridge: Cambridge University Press.

Reserve Bank of India (2006). *State Finances: A Study of Budgets of 2006–07.* Mumbai: Reserve Bank of India.

——— (2016). *State Finances: A Study of Budgets of 2015–16.* Mumbai: Reserve Bank of India.

——— (2020). *State Finances: A Study of Budgets of 2020–21.* Mumbai: Reserve Bank of India.

Rodan, G. (2006). 'Neo-liberalism and Transparency: Political versus Economic Liberalism'. In *The Neoliberal Revolution: Forging the Market State,* edited by R. Robison, 197–215. New York: Palgrave Macmillan.

Rodrik, D. and A. Subramanian (2004). 'From "Hindu Growth" to Productivity Surge: The Mystery of the Indian Growth Transition'. IMF Working Paper, WP/04/07.

Rossi, B. (2004). 'Order and Disjuncture: Theoretical Shifts in the Anthropology of Aid and Development'. *Current Anthropology* 45(4): 556–560.

Roy, A. (2009a). 'Why India Cannot Plan Its Cities: Informality, Insurgence and the Idiom of Urbanization'. *Planning Theory* 8(1): 76 –87.

——— (2009b). 'The 21st Century Metropolis: The New Geographies of Theory'. *Regional Studies* 43(6): 819–830.

——— (2011a). 'The Blockade of the World-Class City: Dialectical Images of Indian Urbanism'. In *Worlding Cities: Asian Experiments and the Art of Being Global,* edited by A. Roy and A. Ong, 259–278. Sussex: Wiley-Blackwell.

——— (2011b). 'Slumdog Cities: Rethinking Subaltern Urbanism'. *International Journal of Urban and Regional Research* 35(2): 223–238.

Rudolph, L. I. and S. H. Rudolph (1987). *In Pursuit of Lakshmi: The Political Economy of the Indian State.* Chicago: University of Chicago Press.

Rutten, M. F. (1986). 'Social Profile of Agricultural Entrepreneurs: Economic Behaviour and Life-Style of Middle-Large Farmers in Central Gujarat'. *Economic and Political Weekly* 21(13): A15–A23.

——— (1995). *Farms and Factories: Social Profile of Large Farmers and Rural Industrialists in West India.* New Delhi: Oxford University Press.

Saad Filho, A. and D. Johnston (2004). *Neoliberalism: A Critical Reader.* London: Pluto Press.

Saikia, S. (2020). 'Saffronizing the Periphery: Explaining the Rise of the Bharatiya Janata Party in Contemporary Assam'. *Studies in Indian Politics* 8(1): 69–84.

Sami, N. (2012). 'Building Alliance: Power and Politics in Urban India.' PhD dissertation, University of Michigan.

Sami, N. and S. Anand (2021). 'Expert Advice? Assessing the Role of the State in Promoting Privatized Planning'. In *Professional Service Firms and Politics in a Global Era*, edited by C. Hurland Vogelpohl, 273–292. Cham: Palgrave Macmillan.

Sampat, P. (2008). 'Special Economic Zones in India'. *Economic and Political Weekly* 43(28): 25–29.

———— (2010). 'Special Economic Zones in India: Reconfiguring Displacement in a Neoliberal Order?' *City and Society* 22(2): 166–182.

———— (2015a). 'Right to Land and the Rule of Law: Infrastructure, Urbanization and Resistance in India'. PhD dissertation, City University of New York.

———— (2015b). 'The "Goan Impasse": Land Rights and Resistance to SEZs in Goa, India'. *The Journal of Peasant Studies* 42(3–4): 765–790.

———— (2015c). 'Why Dholera's Farmers Are Resisting Giving Up Their Land for a Shining, Smart City'. *The Wire*, 18 December. Available at https://thewire.in/agriculture/why-dholeras-farmers-are-resisting-giving-up-their-land-for-a-shining-smart-city. Accessed 2 June 2019.

———— (2016). 'Dholera: The Emperor's New City'. *Economic and Political Weekly* 51(17): 59–67.

Sanghavi, N. (2010). 'From Navnirman to the Anti-Mandal Riots: the Political Trajectory of Gujarat (1974–1985)'. *South Asian History and Culture* 1(4): 480–493.

Sassen, S. (1991). *The Global City*. Princeton, NJ: Princeton University Press

Savarkar, V. D. (1969 [1923]). *Hindutva: Who Is a Hindu?* Bombay: Veer Savarkar Prakashan.

————. (1971 [1924]). *Six Glorious Epochs of Indian History*. Prabhat Prakashan.

Schatz, L. and D. Rogers (2016). 'Participatory, Technocratic and Neoliberal Planning: An Untenable Planning Governance Ménage À Trois'. *Australian Planner* 53(1): 37–45.

Scoones, I., R. Hall, S. M. Borras Jr, B. White and W. Wolford (2013). 'The Politics of Evidence: Methodologies for Understanding the Global Land Rush'. *The Journal of Peasant Studies* 40(3): 469–483.

Scoones, I., M. Edelman, S. M. Borras Jr, R. Hall, W. Wolford and B. White (2018). 'Emancipatory Rural Politics: Confronting Authoritarian Populism'. *The Journal of Peasant Studies* 45(1): 1–20.

Scott J. C. (1985). *Weapons of the Weak: Everyday Forms of Peasant Resistance*. New Haven, CT: Yale University Press.

———— (1990). *Domination and the Arts of Resistance: Hidden Transcripts*. New Haven, CT: Yale University Press.

——— (1998). *Seeing Like a State: How Certain Schemes to Improve the Human Condition Have Failed*. New Haven, CT: Yale University Press.

Searle, L. G. (2010). 'Making Space for Capital: The Production of Global Landscapes in Contemporary India'. PhD dissertation, University of Pennsylvania, Philadelphia.

Sen, A. and J. Drèze (2013). *An Uncertain Glory: India and Its Contradictions*. Princeton, NJ: Princeton University Press.

Senes Consultants (2013). 'DRAFT EIA of Dholera Special Investment Region (DSIR) in Gujarat'. Available at http://www.gpcb.gov.in/pdf/DMICDC_DHOLERA_SPECIAL_INVEST_DSIR_EIA.PDF. Accessed 14 December 2016.

Shah, G. (1970). 'Communal Riots in Gujarat: Report of a Preliminary Investigation'. *Economic and Political Weekly* 5(3/5): 187–200.

——— (1974a). 'Anatomy of Urban Riots: Ahmedabad 1973'. *Economic and Political Weekly* 9(6/8): 233–240.

——— (1974b). 'Upsurge in Gujarat'. *Economic and Political Weekly* 9(32–34): 1429–1454.

——— (1975). *Caste Association and Political Process in Gujarat: A Study of Gujarat Kshatriya Sabha*. Bombay: Popular Prakashan.

——— (1976). 'The 1975 Gujarat Assembly Election in India'. *Asian Survey* 16(3): 270–282.

——— (1996). 'BJP's Rise to Power'. *Economic and Political Weekly* 31(2/3): 165–170.

——— (1987). 'Middle Class Politics: Case of Anti-reservation Agitations in Gujarat'. *Economic and Political Weekly* 22(19): AN155–AN172.

——— (1998a). 'Polarised Communities'. *Seminar* 470: 30–36.

——— (1998b). 'The BJP's Riddle in Gujarat: Caste, Factionalism and Hindutva'. In *The BJP and the Compulsions of Politics in India*, edited by T. B. Hansen and C. Jaffrelot, 243–266. New Delhi: Oxford University Press.

——— (2002a). 'Caste, Hindutva and Hideousness'. *Economic and Political Weekly* 37(15): 1391–1393.

——— (2002b). 'Contestation and Negotiations: Hindutva Sentiments and Temporal Interests in Gujarat Elections'. *Economic and Political Weekly* 37(48): 4838–4843.

——— (2011). 'Goebbel Type Propaganda and Governance: The 2009 Lok Sabha Elections in Gujarat'. In *India's 2009 Elections: Coalition Politics, Party Competition and Congress Continuity*, edited by P. Wallace and R. Roy, 167–191. New Delhi: Sage Publications.

Shah, G. and D. C. Sah, eds. (2002). *Land Reforms in India: Performance and Challenges in Gujarat and Maharashtra*, Vol. 8. New Delhi: Sage Publications.

Shah, J. (2018). 'Gujarat Government Unclear on Kalpasar Dam Project after Spending Crores'. *India Today*, 22 February. Available at https://www. indiatoday.in/india/story/despite-spending-rs-30-71-cr-gujarat-govt-unclear-on-viability-of-kalpasar-dam-project-1174787-2018-02-21. Accessed 1 December 2019.

Shah, R. (2008). 'Mini-Japan between Fedara, Dholera'. *The Times of India*, 15 October. Available at https://timesofindia.indiatimes.com/city/ahmedabad/Mini-Japan-between-Federa-Dholera/articleshow/3596980.cms?. Accessed 14 December 2018.

——— (2009). 'GMR, GVK, Changi in Race to Pilot Fedara Airport'. *The Times of India*, 18 January. Available at https://timesofindia.indiatimes. com/city/ahmedabad/GMR-GVK-Changi-in-race-to-pilot-Fedara-airport/articleshow/3996083.cms. Accessed 10 December 2018.

———. (2016). 'Model Gujarat Fails to Spend "Enough" on Social Sector, Especially Education, Reveals RBI's State Budgets Study'. *Counterview*, 20 April. Available at https://www.counterview.net/2016/04/model-gujarat-fails-to-spend-enough-on.html. Accessed 11 November 2017.

Shani, O. (2005). 'The Rise of Hindu Nationalism in India: The Case Study of Ahmedabad in the 1980s'. *Modern Asian Studies* 39(4): 861–896.

——— (2007). *Communalism, Caste and Hindu Nationalism: The Violence in Gujarat*. Cambridge: Cambridge University Press.

——— (2010a). 'Conceptions of Citizenship in India and the "Muslim Question"'. *Modern Asian Studies* 44(1): 145–173.

——— (2010b). 'Bootlegging, Politics and Corruption: State Violence and the Routine Practices of Public Power in Gujarat (1985–2002)'. *South Asian History and Culture* 1(4): 494–508.

Shatkin, G., ed. (2014). *Contesting the Indian City: Global Visions and the Politics of the Local*. Malden and Oxford: Wiley-Blackwell.

Shekhar, K. S. (2017). '7 Challenges BJP Faces in Gujarat Assembly Elections'. *DailyO*, 22 September. Available at https://www.dailyo.in/politics/gujarat-polls-vijay-rupani-anandiben-patel-narendra-modi/story/1/19661.html. Accessed 5 January 2019.

Shinoda, T., ed. (2002). *The Other Gujarat: Social Transformations among Weaker Sections*. Mumbai: Popular Prakashan.

Simon, G. L. (2009). 'Geographies of Mediation: Market Development and the Rural Broker in Maharashtra, India'. *Political Geography* 28(3): 197–207.

Simpson, E. (2004). '"Hindutva" as a Rural Planning Paradigm in Post-earthquake Gujarat'. In *The Politics of Cultural Mobilisation in India*, edited by J. Zavos, A. Wyatt and V. Hewitt, 136–165. New Delhi: Oxford University Press.

——— (2006). 'The State of Gujarat and the Men without Souls'. *Critique of Anthropology* 26(3): 331–348.

——— (2013). *The Political Biography of an Earthquake: Aftermath and Amnesia in Gujarat, India*. London: Hurst.

——— (2016). 'Is Anthropology Legal—Earthquakes, Blitzkrieg, and Ethical Futures'. *Focaal—Journal of Global and Historical Anthropology* 74(1): 113–128.

Sinha, A. (2005). *The Regional Roots of Developmental Politics in India: A Divided Leviathan*. Bloomington: Indiana University Press.

——— (2011). 'An Institutional Perspective on the Post-Liberalization State in India'. In *The State in India after Liberalization: Interdisciplinary Perspectives*, edited by A. Gupta and K. Sivaramakrishnan, 49–68. New York: Routledge.

——— (2019). 'India's Porous State'. In *Business and Politics in India*, edited by C. Jaffrelot, A. Kohli and K. Murali, 50–87. New York and Oxford: Oxford University Press.

Sinha, A. and A. Wyatt (2019). 'The Spectral Presence of Business in India's 2019 Election'. *Studies in Indian Politics* 7(2): 247–261.

Sinha, B. K. and Pushpendra, eds. (2000). *Land Reforms in India: An Unfinished Agenda*. New Delhi and London: Sage Publications.

Sood, A. and L. Kennedy (2020). 'Neoliberal Exception to Liberal Democracy? Entrepreneurial Territorial Governance in India'. *Territory, Politics, Governance* 8(1): 23–42.

Spodek, H. (1972). '"Injustice to Saurashtra": A Case Study of Regional Tensions and Harmonies in India'. *Asian Survey* 12(5): 416–428.

——— (1976). 'Urban–Rural Integration in Regional Development: A Case Study of Saurashtra, India—1800–1960'. Research paper, University of Chicago, Dept of Geography, No. 171.

——— (1989). 'From Gandhi to Violence: Ahmedabad's 1985 Riots in Historical Perspective'. *Modern Asian Studies* 23(4): 765–795.

——— (2002). 'In the Hindutva Laboratory: Pogroms and Politics in Gujarat'. *Modern Asian Studies* 44(2): 349–399.

———. (2011). *Ahmedabad: Shock City of Twentieth-Century India*. Bloomington and Indianapolis: Indiana University Press.

Srinivas, M. N. (1991). 'On Living in a Revolution'. *Economic and Political Weekly* 26(13): 833–835.

Streefkert, H. (1997). 'Gujarati Entrepreneurship: Historical Continuity against Changing Perspectives'. *Economic and Political Weekly* 32(8): M2–M10.

Streefkert, H., G. Shah and M. Rutten, eds. (2002). *Development and Deprivation in Gujarat*. New Delhi: Sage Publications.

Steur, L. (2015). 'Theorizing Thervoy: Subaltern Studies and Dalit Praxis in India's Land Wars'. In *New Subaltern Politics: Reconceptualizing Hegemony and Resistance in Contemporary India*, edited by A. Nilsen and S. Roy, 177–201. New Delhi: Oxford University Press.

Stiglitz, J. (2008). 'Is There a Post-Washington Consensus Consensus?' In *The Washington Consensus Reconsidered: Towards a New Global Governance*, edited by N. Serra and J. Stiglitz, 41–56. Oxford: Oxford University Press.

Sud, N. (2007). 'From Land to the Tiller to Land Liberalisation: The Political Economy of Gujarat's Shifting Land Policy'. *Modern Asian Studies* 41(3): 603–637.

——— (2009). 'The Indian State in a Liberalizing Landscape'. *Development and Change* 40(4): 645–665.

——— (2012). *Liberalization, Hindu Nationalism and the State*. New Delhi: Oxford University Press.

——— (2014a). 'The Men in the Middle: A Missing Dimension in Global Land Deals'. *Journal of Peasant Studies* 41(4): 593–612.

——— (2014b). 'Governing India's Land'. *World Development* 60: 43–56.

——— (2017). 'Rising Discontent among Dalit–OBC–Patidar Combine Poses a Serious Challenge for BJP in Gujarat'. *The Wire*, 28 October. Available at https://thewire.in/politics/bjp-gujarat-congress-dalit-patidar-obc. Accessed 15 February 2020.

——— (2020a). 'Making the Political, and Doing Politics: Unfixed Land in an Amoebal Zone in India'. *The Journal of Peasant Studies* 47(6): 1–23.

——— (2020b). 'The Actual Gujarat Model: Authoritarianism, Capitalism, Hindu Nationalism and Populism in the Time of Modi'. *Journal of Contemporary Asia* 52(1): 1–25.

Suhrud, T. (2008). 'Modi and Gujarati "Asmita"'. *Economic and Political Weekly* 43(1): 11–13.

Sundar, N. (2014). 'Mimetic Sovereignties, Precarious Citizenship: State Effects in a Looking-Glass World'. *The Journal of Peasant Studies* 41(4): 469–490.

Tambs-Lyche, H. (2004). *The Good Country: Individual, Situation, and Society in Saurashtra*. New Delhi: Manohar Publishers.

——— (2012). 'A Comparison of Traditional Centre–Periphery Relations: Saurashtra and South Kanara'. In *Voices from the Periphery. Subalternity and Empowerment in India*, edited by M. Carrin and L. Guzy, 225–249. Delhi: Routledge.

Tambs-Lyche, H. and N. Sud (2016). 'Gujarat and the Contradictory Co-Existence of Economic Enterprise and Political Illiberalism'. In *Routledge Handbook of Contemporary India*, edited by K. A. Jacobsen, 271–282. London: Routledge.

Thachil, T. (2014). *Elite Parties, Poor Voters: How Social Services Win Votes in India.* Cambridge: Cambridge University Press.

Thapar, R. (2000). *Narratives and the Making of History: Two Lectures.* New Delhi: Oxford University Press.

———— (2005). *Somanatha: The Many Voices of a History.* London and New York: Verso.

Tiwari, R. and L. Verma (2017). 'Gujarat Elections Result: BJP Deepens Urban Support, Congress Widens Rural Reach'. *The Indian Express*, 19 December. Available at https://indianexpress.com/elections/gujarat-assembly-elections-2017/bjp-deepens-urban-support-congress-widens-rural-reach 4989021/. Accessed 11 March 2018.

TNN (2008). 'Fedara Airport Gets Praful's Nod'. *The Times of India*, 23 February. Available at https://timesofindia.indiatimes.com/Cities/Fedara_airport_gets_Prafuls_nod/rssarticleshow/2806355.cms. Accessed 1 January 2020.

———— (2009). 'Fedara Airport Gets Airspace Clearance'. *TheTimes of India*, 8 February. Available at https://timesofindia.indiatimes.com/city/ahmedabad/Fedara-airport-gets-airspace-clearance/articleshow/4093977.cms?. Accessed 19 December 2018.

Tolan, C. (2014). 'Cities of the Future? Indian PM Pushes Plan for 100 "Smart Cities"'. CNN, 18 July. Available at http://edition.cnn.com/2014/07/18/world/asia/india-modi-smart-cities/index.html. Accessed 1 October 2018.

Townsend A. (2013). *Smart Cities: Big Data, Civic Hackers, and the Quest for a New Utopia.* New York: W.W. Norton & Co.

Trivedy, S. (2019). 'Parliament to Kashi Vishwanath: Why Modi Always Hires Architect Bimal Patel for Pet Projects'. *The Print*, 4 December. Available at https://theprint.in/features/parliament-to-kashi-vishwanath-why-modi-always-hires-architect-bimal-patel-for-pet-projects/329968/. Accessed 30 December 2019.

Trudeau, D. (2008). 'Towards a Relational View of the Shadow State'. *Political Geography* 27(6): 669–690.

UNPD (United Nations Population Division) (2018). 'World Urbanization Prospects: the 2018 Revision'. Available at https://esa.un.org/unpd/wup/. Accessed 11 June 2020.

Vaidyanathan, A. (2020). 'Supreme Court Reprieve for Gujarat Minister Whose Election Was Cancelled'. NDTV, 15 May. Available at https://www.ndtv.com/india-news/relief-for-gujarat-minister-bhupendrasinh-chudasama-supreme-court-puts-on-hold-high-court-order-cancelling-his-election-2229255. Accessed 11 June 2020.

Vanaik, A. (1990). *The Painful Transition: Bourgeois Democracy in India*. London: Verso Books.

———— (2001). 'The New Indian Right'. *New Left Review* 9(2): 43–67.

Van der Veer, P. (1994). *Religious Nationalism: Hindus and Muslims in India*. New Delhi: Oxford University Press.

Varadarajan, S. (2002). *Gujarat, the Making of a Tragedy*. New Delhi: Penguin Books India.

Varshney, A. (1995). *Democracy, Development and the Countryside: Urban–Rural Struggles in India*. New York: Cambridge University Press.

———— (1999). 'Mass Politics or Elite Politics? India's Economic Reforms in Comparative Perspective'. In *India in the Era of Economic Reforms*, edited by J. D. Sachs, A. Varshney and N. Bajpai, 222–260. New Delhi: Oxford University Press.

———— (2002). *Ethnic Conflict and Civic Life: Hindus and Muslims in India*. New Haven: Yale University Press.

Venugopal, R. (2015). 'Neoliberalism as Concept'. *Economy and Society* 44(2): 165–187.

Vijayabaskar, M. (2010). 'Saving Agricultural Labour from Agriculture: SEZs and Politics of Silence in Tamil Nadu'. *Economic and Political Weekly* 45(6): 36–43.

Vijayabaskar, M. and A. Menon (2018). 'Dispossession by Neglect: Agricultural Land Sales in Southern India'. *Journal of Agrarian Change* 18(3): 571–587.

Wacquant, L. (2009). *Punishing the Poor: The Neoliberal Government of Social Insecurity*. Durham and London: Duke University Press.

———— (2012). 'Three Steps to a Historical Anthropology of Actually Existing Neoliberalism'. *Social Anthropology* 20(1): 66–79.

Weber, M. (1964). *Theory of Social and Economic Organization*. New York: Free Press.

———— (1967). *Party Building in a New Nation: The Indian National Congress*. Chicago: University of Chicago Press.

Weiner, M. (1967). *Party Building in a New Nation: The Indian National Congress*. Chicago: Chicago University Press.

Weinstein, L. (2009). 'Redeveloping Dharavi: Toward a Political Economy of Slums and Slum Redevelopment in Globalizing Mumbai'. PhD dissertation, University of Chicago.

Williamson, J. (1990). 'What Washington Means by Policy Reform'. In *Latin American Adjustment: How Much Has Happened*, edited by J. Williamson, 5–38. Washington: Institute for International Economics.

Witsoe, J. (2012). 'Everyday Corruption and the Political Mediation of the Indian State: An Ethnographic Exploration of Brokers in Bihar'. *Economic and Political Weekly* 47(6): 47–54.

Wolch, J. R. (1990). *The Shadow State: Government and Voluntary Sector in Transition*. New York: The Foundation Center.

Wolford, W. (2004). 'This Land Is Ours Now: A New Perspective on Social Movement Formation'. *Annals of the Association of American Geographers* 94(2): 409–424.

World Bank (1997). 'The State in a Changing World'. In *World Development Report*. Washington: IBRD.

———— (2019). 'Master Planning'. Available at https://urban-regeneration.worldbank.org/node/51. Accessed 11 February 2019.

Wu, F. (2018). 'Planning Centrality, Market Instruments: Governing Chinese Urban Transformation under State Entrepreneurialism'. *Urban Studies* 55(7): 1383–1399.

Yadav, Y. (2017). 'What Is to Be Done'. India-seminar.com. Available at https://www.india-seminar.com/2017/699/699_yogendra_yadav.htm. Accessed 19 January 2019.

Yagnik, A. and A. Bhatt (1984). 'The Anti-Dalit Agitation in Gujarat'. *South Asia Bulletin* 4(1): 49.

Yagnik, A. and S. Sheth (2005). *The Shaping of Modern Gujarat: Plurality, Hindutva and Beyond*. New Delhi: Penguin Books.

———— (2011). *Ahmedabad: From Royal City to Megacity*. New Delhi: Penguin.

Zoomers, A. (2010). 'Globalisation and the Foreignisation of Space: Seven Processes Driving the Current Global Land Grab'. *The Journal of Peasant Studies* 37(2): 429–447.

Index